The Healthy Weigh

Learn How to Eat, Not How to Diet

by

Claire Friefeld, B.Sc., P.Dt.

and

Franceen Friefeld, R.P.Dt., P.H.Ec.

The Healthy Weigh to fill up, not out

The Healthy Weigh to lean down

The Healthy Weigh to lose fat

Published by
Creative Bound Inc.
P.O. Box 424
Carp, Ontario K0A 1L0

ISBN 0-921165-28-5
Printed and bound in Canada

Editing by Janet Shorten
Book design by Wendelina O'Keefe
Cover photo by David Andrews
Illustrations by Dennis Proulx, Momentum Brothers

Canadian Cataloguing in Publication Data

Friefeld, Claire
The healthy weigh

Includes bibliographical references and index.
ISBN 0-921165-28-5

1. Diet therapy. 2. Nutrition. I. Friefeld, Franceen II. Title.

RA784.F74 1993 613.2 C93-090122-3

The Healthy Weigh

Learn How to Eat, Not How to Diet

To
Milton
husband and father
for your
love
encouragement
and support.

Introduction

If you have tried dieting to lose weight and you have not been able to keep the weight off, it is time for you to read this book.

We are two dietitians, a mother and daughter team, and we have helped many clients, both men and women, achieve permanent weight loss. We have taught them the Healthy Weigh to lose weight by showing them how to eat, not how to diet.

Diets don't work. If dieting really worked, you wouldn't have to keep doing it. How many times have you embarked on a new low-calorie diet plan with great gusto, and later found yourself with more body baggage than you started with? Your body defends itself from starving when it is not given enough food, and this makes dieting self-defeating. Your body slows down while dieting to avoid starvation and converts food more readily to fat. It conserves every morsel of food you eat and stores the calories easier than ever before. The problem with this is that your body stays this way after dieting and cannot metabolize larger amounts of food as it did before.

The reason you can lose weight so quickly on some fad diets is that you lose muscle and water, not fat, and you always gain this type of weight back. Not only that, but each time you regain your weight, you replace the muscle you lost with fat, and that creates a fattier body in the end. To make matters even worse, the higher the proportion of fat in your body, the slower your metabolism, so the slower you burn calories. That's why quick weight-loss diets are self-defeating. They end up making you fatter and they turn your body into a slower calorie burner.

Just as a car needs gasoline to get it going, we as humans need calories to get us going: to pump our heart, circulate our blood, give us energy to walk and talk and live. We get calories from food. When we eat food, it is broken down by our body, and the calories from the food are used to help us function. Each person burns their calories at different rates depending on their metabolism. A person with a fast metabolism will burn calories quickly, and a person with a slow metabolism will burn calories slowly. When a person takes in more calories than they burn, they store their excess calories as fat. To lose body fat, your goal is to burn calories quicker than they are taken in. You want to turn your body into a FAT-BURNING MACHINE. The only way to lose fat and to successfully keep it off for a lifetime is to feed yourself in a way that will increase your metabolic rate. **Learn how to eat . . . not how to diet!!** Dieting slows your metabolism. That's why diets don't work.

The first stages of a regimented diet may bring you a sense of euphoria; a feeling that you are in control; and a vision of a future thin you. However, since strict diets are monotonous, they cannot be adapted to your lifestyle. Most diets can cause a great deal of anxiety since they do not allow for dining out, parties, vacations and social events.

The intention before dieting is to "be good," to follow the diet without cheating and without including any "illegal foods," but an inevitable cheat or binge soon puts an end to this false hope. Episodes of overeating often begin due to your body's hunger resulting from consuming too few calories while dieting.

You may argue that if you don't eat, you don't feel hungry, but as soon as you begin to eat, you can't stop! This is the result of low calorie dieting. When you go long hours without food, certain products called "ketones" are released in your body. They temporarily depress your appetite and allow you to continue starving without feeling hungry for many hours. But beware, because you are setting yourself up for an overindulgence of food. As soon as you begin to eat, or taste something you have been depriving yourself of, the effect of the waste products disappears, and your appetite is really "turned on." Not only will you overeat because you lack nourishing food, your body cannot burn the extra calories well because of your slowed down metabolic rate. That binge after dieting is like dumping a load of firewood on a dead fire. The food just sits there instead of being burned. As a result, you easily gain back weight.

Another common problem is that **we eat far too much, much too late!** When trying to lose weight, many people starve through the day to save their calories for later.

Most of us take in 75-80% of our calories for the whole day crammed into three concentrated hours in the evening. It is so much, so late, that the body does not have the chance to burn it up the way that it should.

When we starve through the day, no matter how much willpower or discipline we think we have had, it often all goes down the drain at 3:00 p.m. This is the time of day we call "the danger hour," when we will eat anything and everything that is available.

Those people who happen to be home at this danger hour are in trouble, as they have been known to eat right through the afternoon until suppertime. They may eat in front of the television, or standing in front of the refrigerator and eating right out of the containers. A chunk of cheese here, a leftover chicken leg there, a hunk of bread and on it goes. If their work day ends later, they may be able to postpone this danger hour. But when they do arrive at home, they will go straight to the refrigerator and can eat an entire meal's worth of calories while deciding "what, oh what" to have for supper.

It is interesting to note how well we justify this type of eating. So many of us forget about the food we eat when we are not sitting at a table and eating from a plate.

The following are some of the most common justifications:

> *"If I don't put the food on a plate, but eat straight out of the containers, the calories don't count."*

> *"If I eat standing over the sink, the calories don't count."*

> *"If I don't take a second helping at dinner but I pick the leftovers to death, it doesn't count."*

> *"If I don't cut myself a full piece of cake but even off the ends, and eat the uneven parts, again I'm home free."*

The Right Way to Lose Weight

The right way to lose weight and keep it off begins by choosing our Healthy Weigh plan of eating and living. It is a plan that can last a lifetime, *not* a quick-fix diet.

Your goal for lifelong weight control must be to avoid very low-calorie dieting. This means avoiding extreme drops in your metabolic rate and episodes of binge-eating. *Your success* in weight management will be achieved by following the guidelines set out in this book. Our plan provides you with plenty of delicious satisfying foods during the day, balanced in a way that will keep your metabolism burning at a high rate and your appetite in control.

The Healthy Weigh plan will cause your body to lose fat and losing this *right* kind of weight, *fat weight*, will keep your metabolism in high gear. It will make you look and feel great.

Be patient with yourself. Habits don't change overnight. Many of us are "all or nothing" people, and we want instant results. We set high expectations for ourselves, but we must realize that life is not always going to be perfect, nor does it have to be.

Try not to think in terms of "good" or "bad," "on it" or "off it." If you overeat at a meal, instead of thinking "I've blown it," get right back on track at the next meal. Don't look back at what you have done, just look to the future. That one meal, or that one party where you overeat, is not going to make the difference. It is what you do day by day that counts with the Healthy Weigh plan. Eat the best you can when you can, so that when you *can't* it won't matter as much.

With this in mind, if you overeat at one meal, thinking that you might as well eat ad lib for the rest of the day because "you've blown it" and then starve the next day to make up for it, you will only set yourself up for disaster. The following day, you will gorge again, and fall right back into that vicious cycle, where the more you eat and the more out of control you feel, the heavier you get and the more depressed you feel, and the more depressed you feel, the more you eat, and on and on it goes.

This book will help you break that vicious cycle. Instead, you will turn it into a more positive one, which is: "The better you eat, the better you feel about yourself and the better you will want to feed yourself, so the leaner you will get, thereby the better you will want to eat and the better you will feel."

The Healthy Weigh plan will teach you how to eat to lose fat and attain a lifestyle that will allow your body to look and feel so good. When you start looking great and feeling great, you will want to hold on to the habits that are allowing this to happen and never let them go.

You ***can*** achieve weight control! We will help you convert your body from a fat-storing to a fat-burning machine.

Part I of this book will teach you how to break the dieting mentality, eat to lose fat, gain energy and free yourself from every diet that comes along.

In Part II, you'll discover how you can eat delicious volumes of food that will fill you up . . . not out. Eating to lose weight will be enjoyable enough that you can stay with it for life. You will find it easy to keep the weight off because you will have no reason to go back to your old way of eating.

Whether you want to lose weight, or maintain weight, in Part III we will provide you with food plans that can be applied anywhere, at home, on vacation, at work or in restaurants. We will also teach you how to create your own personalized food plans so that you can incorporate your favourite foods.

In Part IV, we will show you how and what to order—in every restaurant. From fast food to the finest cuisine. It will help you make healthful eating decisions, whether you are eating Chinese, Mexican, Indian or sitting down to an elegant French dinner. In our hidden fat food list, you'll discover where fat is most commonly hidden in restaurant food.

Our grocery guide will provide you with the healthiest products in your supermarket. It will certainly help combat the confusion in the grocery store aisles.

In Part IV, you will also learn all the tricks necessary to make healthy, tasty and easy to prepare meals. By cooking the Healthy Weigh, you will be using much less fat, sugar and salt without anyone knowing the difference.

Learn How to Eat, Not How to Diet

Part I
No More Diets

Learn How to Eat, Not How to Diet

One of the most common things people say when they are trying to lose weight is "I can't eat that, I'm on a diet."

Dieting causes us to focus on all the foods that we must avoid, instead of concentrating on all the foods we can eat. There are so many great-tasting healthy foods today. Eating to lose weight must be enjoyable enough that you can stay with it. You want a plan that will result in weight loss as a bonus or net result of eating better, and then it will be easy to keep the weight off because you have no reason to go back to your old way of eating.

Eating right to lose weight is much more than following a regimented diet and cutting out foods. Eating right means looking forward to having all the right foods. Keeping your energy levels as high as they can be. Being in control of eating rather than letting food control you. Feeling great instead of dragging through the day.

Here are the stories of two of our clients whom we will name Judy and Jackie. If you can relate to even part of their diet dilemmas, our program is for you.

Judy

When Judy came to see us, she was at her highest weight ever. She had a long history of crash dieting and gorging—the yo-yo syndrome of losing and regaining weight.

Judy's last diet was an 800-calorie plan that she was able to follow for only 2 weeks. She lost 4 1/2 kilograms (10 pounds) and felt very good about her results, but the next week she began to experience episodes of overeating. They began one evening on her way home from work, when she decided to buy a cheesecake "for her family." Even though this was her favourite dessert, she was certain that she would be able to control herself and not give in to having a slice.

That evening, Judy ate a diet supper consisting of baked fish and vegetables. While her family was enjoying their cheesecake, she was so tempted to have some that she quickly got up from the table and began to clear the dishes. When alone, cleaning up the kitchen, she noticed the cheesecake on the counter, and began to feel a little out of control. The temptation became too great. She convinced herself that a "nibble" wouldn't hurt, and scooped up some crumbs from the cheesecake tray. It tasted so good that she decided to even off each end, and she cut herself a couple of thin slices. (This way her family wouldn't notice any missing, and she felt the calories wouldn't count if she just ate the crumbs and uneven parts.) However, unable to resist, she cut herself a thicker slice. Now, feeling that she had "blown her diet" and that she might as well "go for it," she soon found herself into the fresh bread, chips, ice cream and cookies. Stricken with shame and guilt, she left the kitchen and promised herself that she would not eat at all the next day.

Judy awoke the next morning feeling depressed, and reluctantly stepped onto the scale—a 1-1/2 kilogram (3 pound) gain! She felt bloated and puffy, and couldn't understand why she was hungrier than usual. She struggled through the morning with black coffee and diet drinks. On her lunch break, she went shopping to try to get her mind off eating, but since she had no energy, she decided to stop for a frozen yogurt. Then, she picked up a couple of large muffins "for her children," but gave into temptation, and ate them herself that afternoon. When she arrived home after work, another binge set in. She soon regained all her lost weight and more.

This episode of dieting and regaining weight was typical for Judy. She continuously lacked energy, thought about food and dieting all the time, and felt very out of control. She often dieted during the day, overate at night and felt very guilty about it.

Our Healthy Weigh plan taught Judy how to eat, not how to diet. She learned how to stop crash-dieting and be in better control of her food intake. She has successfully maintained her weight loss ever since.

Jackie

The following is a sample record of a typical day's intake of one of our clients whom we will call "Jackie."

This is one of Jackie's typical days:

Time	Place	Food Intake	Feelings	Calories and Fat
8:00 a.m.	Home	Black coffee with artificial sweetener	Happy that will start new day in control of diet.	2 calories
9:00 a.m.	Office	Black coffee with artificial sweetener	A little hungry, but feels coffee will do the trick.	2 calories
10:00 a.m.	Office	Diet drink	Quite hungry, but feels can hold off until lunch if fills stomach with liquid.	2 calories
10:00 a.m–12:00 p.m.	Office	3 sticks of sugarless gum	Hungry and looking forward to lunch	12 calories
12:00 p.m.	Cafeteria, office building	"Diet platter" of 168 grams (6 ounces) chopped steak with a scoop of cottage cheese, tomato slices and dressing. Diet drink, coffee with artificial sweetener.	Ravenous—but feels OK to eat because missed breakfast. Chooses a "diet platter". Feels this is a "legal" choice.	800 calories 51% fat
3:00 p.m.–5:00 p.m.	Office	Diet drink	Tired and hungry. Vending service comes by. Tempted by the fresh muffins but feels must have control and save calories for supper.	2 calories
3:00 p.m.	Office	Black coffee	Has a headache. Thinking about supper. Cancelled gym class because no energy.	0 calories
6:00 p.m.	Home, kitchen	1 "chunk" of cheese 85 grams (3 ounces)	Very hungry. Impatient to prepare her meal. Grabs what is easily available.	320 calories 85% fat

6:10 p.m.	Home, kitchen	2 pieces leftover cold BBQ chicken	Still hungry. Looking in fridge and eating standing up with fridge open.	450 calories 38% fat
6:15 p.m.	Home, kitchen	1 large bran muffin	Feels is eating healthy foods but does not realize the number of calories in this large muffin.	440 calories 57% fat
6:30 p.m.	Home, dinner table	Salad with dressing, leftovers (1/2 hamburger patty, roast potato)	Does not want to eat supper so brings a salad to place setting. Eats some leftovers while clearing the dishes.	500 calories 54% fat
9:00 p.m.	Home, watching TV	2 diet fudgesicles 20 jujubes 1 bowl of cheese popcorn 1 diet coke	Craving for snacks and sweets.	600 calories 11% fat
			TOTAL	**3130 calories 40% calories from fat**

We have shown Jackie's typical day's intake along with the times food was consumed and her feelings before eating. From the type of foods, portion sizes and preparation methods, we were able to determine the number of calories and the percentage of fat that was consumed.

Carbohydrates	**Protein**	**Fat**
4 calories per gram	4 calories per gram	9 calories per gram

Fat supplies the body with more than twice the number of calories of lean protein and carbohydrate. One of the reasons Jackies's total calories (3130) were so high was because of the high fat intake of 40%. (Our clients consume 30% fat intake or less to reduce calories.)

Jackie's first meal at 12:00 noon consisted of a typical "diet" platter, available in many "family" restaurants, but 800 calories for a diet meal is excessive, and 51% fat content is far too high. There were also other foods eaten during the day that contained hidden fat, such as the hamburger meat, chicken with skin and creamed cottage cheese. At 6 p.m., the large chunk of high-fat cheese, 85 grams (approximately 3 ounces), contained 320 calories with 85% of its calories from fat. Two pieces of chicken eaten at 6:10 p.m. were too large a portion for a snack. The large bran muffin contained far more calories than Jackie thought (440), and 57% of them were fat.

To reduce the number of calories, Jackie should have eaten foods that were lower in fat, because **it is truly fat that makes us fat**. Fifteen millilitres (1 tablespoon) of salad dressing covers only a fraction of a salad but adds 100 calories. The typical ladle at most salad bars holds 40 millilitres (2-3 tablespoons), thereby adding 200-300 calories. Margarine or butter on bread contains more calories than the bread itself. One hundred twenty-five millilitres (1/2 cup) of oil added to a recipe contributes 960 calories.

Jackie felt hungry too soon after eating such high-calorie food choices, because the foods were high in fats and sugar, which lower the body's blood sugar level and cause hungry feelings! To keep Jackie less hungry, more satiated and full of energy, more complex carbohydrate foods should have been consumed, such as whole grain breads, cereals, fruits and vegetables. These foods are naturally low in fat, and they contain fibre, which adds bulk and satisfies the appetite. Jackie should have chosen leaner and smaller portions of the protein and dairy foods, since meat, cheese and chicken contain a lot of hidden fat. The other high-fat foods eaten were the bran muffin, the salad dressing and the cheese popcorn. The cravings for sweets and snacks in the evening could have been reduced if Jackie had begun the day with breakfast and distributed the food intake more evenly throughout the day.

Complex Carbohydrates
(Low-fat, low-calorie filling foods)

The following schedule illustrates an improved eating day for Jackie. The total calories are cut to 1350, and the percentage of total calories from fat is less than 22%, far healthier than the previous intake of 40%.

The day now begins with breakfast, and regular meals and snacks are eaten to control the appetite all day long. As a result, temptations to eat at night are reduced, and Jackie now has the energy to participate in physical activity.

Because of the Healthy Weigh plan, Jackie lost weight and has kept it off ever since.

Improvements to Jackie's day:

Time	Place	Food Intake	Feelings	Calories and Fat
8:00 a.m.	Home	125 ml (1/2 cup) orange juice 1/2 banana 125 ml (1/2 cup) whole grain cereal 250 ml (1 cup) lowfat milk 1 glass of water	Eats a balanced breakfast to keep hunger levels low, metabolic rate in full gear, and to avoid "gorging" later on.	250 calories 21% fat
10:00 a.m.	Office	1 orange 1 glass of water	Not hungry. Joining co-workers for coffee break.	60 calories

12:00 p.m.	Cafeteria, office building	Turkey sandwich on whole wheat bread with mustard, lettuce and tomato side salad with low-fat dressing 1 glass of water	Hungry for lunch. Feels satisfied from lunch. Ready to work.	110 calories 12% fat
3:00 p.m.	Office	15 g (1/2 oz) reduced calories cheese 4 melba toasts	Feels like having a snack, but not very hungry. Wants energy because going to a fitness class after work.	300 calories 25% fat
5:30 p.m.	Fitness centre	250 ml (1 cup) low-fat milk	Ready to take class. Now has the energy.	125 calories 29% fat
7:00 p.m.	Fitness centre	2 glasses of water	Thirsty from class. Replacing water loss from gym class. Feels very much in control of food intake. Not ravenous but looking forward to supper with family.	
8:00 p.m.	Home, dinner table	85 grams (3 oz) lean hamburger patty 1 baked potato with 30 ml (2 tablespoons) low-fat yogurt & chive topping 125 ml (1/2 cup) mixed vegetables salad with 30 ml (2 tablespoons) low-fat dressing 125 ml (1/2 cup) cut-up fresh fruit decaffeinated coffee 1 glass of water		425 calories 28% fat
9:30 p.m.	Home	125 ml (1/2 cup) frozen raspberries blended with 125 ml (1/2 cup) low-fat milk	Wants a snack before bed. Not tempted to gorge.	80 calories
			TOTAL	**1350 calories 22% calories from fat**

Boost Your Metabolism with Breakfast

"I don't have time for breakfast."

"I can't face food in the morning."

"I'm not hungry for breakfast."

"If I don't eat breakfast I'm not hungry all day long. I have better control over food if I don't eat breakfast."

If you can identify with any of the above comments, or if you skip breakfast for some other reason, read on!

Breakfast truly is the most important meal of the day. You require food first thing in the morning to give you energy, raise your metabolic rate and get your body burning calories and fat.

To understand this, think of your metabolism as a campfire. While you sleep at night, the campfire dies down. In the morning there are a few sparks, but the fire is no longer burning as it was the night before. In a similar way, the metabolism slows itself down during the night to conserve energy. In the morning it is important to get fuel in the form of food to gear up the metabolic rate, just as a log added to the fire will get it burning more efficiently. So, in order to properly stoke up your metabolic fire, the goal is to have breakfast within the first hour of arising.

If you skip breakfast, not only is your metabolic rate in a low gear, but your body throws itself into such a state of imbalance that it begins to produce certain substances known as "ketones" which may depress your appetite. The longer you go without food, the less hungry you will be. If you skip breakfast, you may be able to last until 2:00 or 3:00 in the afternoon, or maybe even until dinner. However, once you finally begin to eat, the effect of the ketones disappears, your appetite "turns on" and all of a sudden you feel ravenous. When this happens, it is hard to stop eating. You can end up eating more at night than you would have eaten during a whole day of balanced intake.

Starving all day, and then piling in all that food at one time, creates another problem. When you skip breakfast in the morning, your body stays in such a low gear that your metabolism slows down. When you do eat, it will be like dumping logs on a dead fire. The logs will just sit there, instead of being burned.

Taking in food in the morning is like adding logs to a fire; it stokes up your metabolic fire and gets it burning optimally.

So if you want to get your day started off with energy, your metabolism in high gear and your body working for you, you should *never* skip breakfast.

Some Healthy Breakfast Suggestions

- Low-fat yogurt mixed with all-fruit jam and whole grain cereal
- Mock Milkshake*
- Light Grilled Cheese Sandwich* with tomato
- Orange Cinnamon French Toast* topped with all-fruit jam and fresh fruit salad
- Healthy Breakfast Danish*
- Healthy Topped Baked Potato*
- Whole wheat english muffin and cheese and fruit spread
- Buckwheat Pancakes* topped with Creamy Maple Topping * and fresh fruit
- Turkey sandwich with a glass of low-fat milk
- Cinnamon raisin bagel and low-fat cheese and fruit
- Oatbran Raisin Muffins* and skim milk and a fruit
- Cinnamon Whole Grain Pancakes* and Strawberry Sauce*
- Healthy Vegetable Omelette* and toast
- Healthy Scramble in a Pita*

More healthy breakfast suggestions can be found in Part III of this book.
* See "Recipes."

Eat Regular Meals and Snacks

In the last section, your metabolism was compared to a campfire. During the night, the fire dies down, and eating breakfast gets it burning again. You need to keep throwing logs on that fire at regular intervals throughout the day. In our practice we have found that meals should not be further apart than 4 to 5 hours unless you have a snack in between to keep your metabolism working for you in a higher gear.

If you give someone the same number of calories on 3 different days but distribute the calories differently during each of the days, that person's metabolism will burn the food at different rates. Even though 1200 calories is a low total calorie intake for the day, when the person eats it all at one meal and starves the rest of the day, he or she can gain weight on 1200 calories. When the person divides that 1200 calories into 3 meals and 2 snacks, he or she can lose weight.

Eating regular meals and snacks also keeps your appetite in control. Your appetite is influenced by the level of blood sugar in your body. If your eating patterns are erratic, your blood sugar level will have roller coaster highs and lows. Every time your blood sugar level drops, it sends a signal to your brain that says "feed me; I need food coming in to bring the level up." The problem is that when your blood sugar level drops, you will be tempted to eat anything and everything in sight. It is hard to control your appetite when this happens because your mind is saying "I want it," and your body is saying "I need it." If you meet your physical needs by eating the right thing at the right time your appetite will be well-controlled.

Breakfast should be eaten within an hour of arising, and from that point on, we suggest that you eat every 4 to 5 hours.

If you are trying to lose weight and are not used to eating frequently, you may be wondering how you can lose weight by eating so often. Those extra snacks will be burned. It is just like throwing a log on the campfire. Eating regular meals and snacks keeps your blood sugar levels even and your metabolism geared up. As a result, not only will you take in less food in the evening, but what you eat will be burned and burned well.

- **Spread calories throughout the day.**
- **3 meals and 2 snacks**
  for
- **Appetite control.**
- **Higher metabolic rate.**

Keep a Healthy Snack Available

If you don't have the right healthy snack on hand, you're probably going to reach for the wrong thing; or just as poor a choice, you may not eat at all!

It's easy to be fooled by manufacturers who try to make their products look healthy. For example, think about those wheat and cheese crackers from the vending machine. They sound healthy, but did you know that one little package of those crackers has 360 calories? How about those giant bran muffins from some of the popular muffin chains? Most of them are made with white four, and molasses is added to give the brown colour. A little bran is added, but certainly not enough to call them a good source of fibre. What they do add is a lot of is excess fat, and one of those muffins can contain approximately 450-500 calories!

Try to keep the right snacks with you, wherever you go and change the variety of your snacks often. You want your eating plan to be exciting enough to keep your interest alive. If you eat the same foods every day, you will become more and more tempted to eat the foods you are missing. We find that clients who do this tend to go off their plan at restaurants because all of those previously avoided foods become so appealing.

Some Healthy Snack Ideas

- 250 millilitres (1 cup) Mock Milkshake*
- 250 millilitres (1 cup) vegetable soup topped with 15 millilitres (1 tablespoon) parmesan cheese
- All-vegetable salad sprinkled with 15 millilitres (1 tablespoon) Parmesan and no-oil Italian dressing
- 1/2 whole wheat pita stuffed with lettuce, tomato, cucumber, alfalfa sprouts and mustard
- 1/2 baked potato topped with cooked broccoli and sprinkled with 15-30 millilitres (1-2 tablespoons) Parmesan cheese
- 1 potato sliced and baked (without oil) until crisp
- Marinated Vegetables*
- 250 millilitres (1 cup) non-cream soup and 2 crackers
- A corn or flour tortilla sliced and baked until crisp
- 1 pita bread sliced and toasted until crisp
- 350 millilitres (1-2 cups) cooked vegetables topped with 60 millilitres (1/4 cup) tomato sauce, herbs and spices
- 850 millilitres (3-4 cups) Healthy Popcorn*
- One wedge calorie-reduced cheese and 2-4 crackers and raw vegetable sticks
- 125 millilitres (1/2 cup) plain low-fat yogurt (1% fat or less) mixed with 15 millilitres (1 tablespoon) all-fruit jam or 125 millilitres (1/2 cup) chopped fruit
- 125 millilitres (1/2 cup) cereal with low-fat milk

More healthy snack ideas can be found in Part III of this book.
* See "Recipes"

If a Food Tempts You, Don't Keep it Around

One of the easiest ways to fall off a healthy eating plan is to keep foods around that you have difficulty controlling. That can mean in your home or at the office or in your car—any place that is easily accessible to you. Even a low-fat food can interfere with your healthy eating efforts if you have a tendency to overeat it.

We have clients who have trouble controlling portion sizes of cereals. They pour too much of it into their bowls or grab handfuls of it throughout the day. We recommend for these clients that they do not buy the cereals in bulk, but instead purchase the small portion packs, which makes portion control much easier to apply.

We have other clients who have trouble controlling their intake of ice cream or frozen yogurt, even the very low-fat varieties. Our advice is to not bring these foods into the home, but instead, purchase a single serving when they go out. The same thing applies to other commonly hard-to-control foods such as muffins, cookies, cakes, crackers, nuts, chips, pretzels, popcorn, candy, etc.

It is especially important to keep tempting foods away when you first start to change your eating habits. Ask your family members or roommates to support you. Encourage them to purchase single servings of desserts and snacks so that uneaten portions are not left around.

Listen to Your Body

Many of us eat for reasons that have nothing to do with what our bodies need. By doing that, we can lose touch with our inner signals. The signals are there, but they can become deranged if we don't pay attention to them. Many of our clients don't even know what physical hunger means, because they eat so often during the day. Even if they have been eating throughout the afternoon, when 6:00 p.m. comes, they may eat again just because it is suppertime, not because they're hungry. This reason for eating has nothing to do with their body's signals; it's all external.

Our suggested Healthy Weigh of eating is to eat three to five intakes daily, at regular times each day. Eating should be regulated so that your body will eventually give you the right signals. You should eat because you are physically hungry and stop eating when you feel comfortable.

You may have lost touch with your inner signals of hunger and fullness through habits you have acquired or because of the diets you have followed in the past. The starvation/binge pattern caused by dieting might have prevented you from trusting your body's signals to tell you when to eat and when to stop eating.

You should eat the amount it takes to fill you until you feel comfortable. If you have a capacity for a large amount of food, but you do not want to be overweight, follow our suggested Healthy Weigh Low-Fat Food Mix. This mix encourages regular intakes of healthy food—a way of eating that will decrease your desires for high-fat foods. If you like to eat, you will feel satisfied with the mix because it allows certain foods (e.g., vegetables) to be eaten in unlimited quantities. With this way of eating, you will fill up, be satisfied and have the energy to do your work. The bonus or net result of this will be weight control.

Healthy eating will give you healthy signals. If your body is healthy and your signals are working well, you will have no need to follow diets. You will be able to rely on your body's signals to tell you when to eat and how much to eat.

It does take time to change, so be patient with yourself. Eventually you will realize that you never really needed those large portions of protein and fat that you ate in the past. You will find that you actually have **more energy** with **smaller portions** of these foods. You won't feel as sluggish. You will be able to work more efficiently. You will look better and feel better. All of this will assure you that this is the right way of eating. **This is not a diet! This is a way of life!**

The readiness for meals and snacks will be a new thing; a new enjoyment; a sense of knowing that your body needs food. Hunger is going to be your new signal that you are ready for a meal. Doesn't it make sense to control your snacks so that they don't interfere with that nice feeling you want to have that tells you it is time to eat?

How Hungry Should You Be Before You Eat?

Don't wait until you are ravenous to eat, because you will eat more quickly. It takes 15-20 minutes after you start a meal for your brain to receive a signal of satiety. So if you eat quickly, you will take in a lot more food than you need before you actually feel full. If you eat quickly for 15-20 minutes, you will feel stuffed and uncomfortable.

There are certain foods that will enable you to slow your eating down, such as soups, vegetables and other high-fibre foods that require more chewing. If it takes longer to eat, you can recognize a satiated feeling while you are still eating your meal. Your fullness, rather than a clean plate, should signify the end of the meal.

Listening to your body's signals for satiety will also enable you to know if you need a little more food. If you have taken at least 15 or 20 minutes to finish your meal, and you do not feel that comfortable sense of fullness, you may need to eat a little more. Be sure that the foods you take seconds of are those that will fill you up, not out. They will preferably be vegetables, vegetable soups or fruits. If you leave the table without the feeling of satiety, you may find it hard to control your snacks a few hours later. If you are the type of person who finds it hard to stop eating, then satiating yourself at each meal is important. You do not want to deal with controlling your intake too many times during the day.

Plan Ahead

Planning ahead—purchasing the foods you need to make sure you have them on hand, and preparing as much as you can in advance—will make it easier for you to reach for the right things at the right time. This is especially important for vegetables that take some time to prepare. Part of the reason why people eat proteins and other foods rather than vegetables is because these other foods are more convenient to eat. The real high-fibre, low-calorie vegetables, the nourishing ones that you really need, should be cut up in advance so that they are easier to have as snacks or as part of your meal.

Vegetables alone may not satisfy you unless they are eaten 30 minutes or so before your meal. But if it's 3:00 or 4:00 in the afternoon, and you really feel hungry, a low-fat dip or low-calorie salad dressing is good to have on hand to eat with the vegetables.

Planning to overeat works much better than *unplanned overeating.* Let's say you have a social function and you know you are going to have something special there, or that the food may be prepared with a bit more fat than you want to have. Wise planning would mean that you still have your meals and light snacks during the day. If you starve during the day and are too hungry when you arrive, you will have difficulty controlling the amount you eat. The best thing you can do to plan for the event is to have your meals, but perhaps cut back during the day and not add the additional fat, or save a fruit or grain or protein for later.

If you go out to eat at the last minute, you will not have had the opportunity to cut back during the day. In this case, if you would like some wine or a favourite dessert, you should cut back on your portion of the main meal. A good way to do this is to order an appetizer portion or share a main meal with someone else and accompany it with a salad or light soup.

Keep Yourself Physically Active

It's no longer IN just to be THIN, it's IN to be FIT.

You will not be permanently successful with weight control unless you learn to be physically active. Your goal is to boost your metabolic rate as much as you can. You cannot control all of the factors that affect this rate, but you can control one very important factor: EXERCISE.

Your metabolic rate declines by as much as 20% within 14 days of dieting. If you wanted to lose weight without exercising, you would have to cut back daily on food intake to such an extent that it would be difficult to stay on your "diet." This low-calorie intake would also decrease your body's metabolic rate, which in turn would make weight loss really difficult.

Exercise increases your metabolic rate, which means that you burn more calories. This increase in metabolism stays elevated even hours after you stop exercising.

Exercise changes the body's composition to contain more muscle and less fat. This makes you look more trim, since muscle tissue is more compact and takes up less room than fat. The result is a leaner body that can burn calories faster than a fatty body.

Which exercises are the best to burn body fat?

Aerobic exercise (such as swimming, walking, jogging, cycling, aerobic dance, etc.) for at least 30 minutes 4-5 times per week *at a moderate intensity*, that is, at 75% of your maximum heart rate, is the best way to burn fat. With your heart rate in this range, fat is burned for energy. Your body has the ability to store a lot of fat, and you can exercise for a long time without depleting your stores. An added benefit is that when fat is burned, it breaks down, releasing products into your blood that decrease your appetite.

The net result of a moderate intensity aerobic workout for 30 minutes:

- **Your body fat is burned**
- **Your appetite decreases**
- **Your energy is high**

On the other hand, if you exercise aerobically at a higher intensity, at your maximum heart rate, your body burns carbohydrate stores for energy. Your body has a limited amount of carbohydrate stores, and once they are used up (which can happen after 30 minutes of intense aerobic exercise), you "konk out," and your appetite increases!

The net result of a high intensity aerobic workout for 30 minutes:

- **You have burned carbohydrate instead of fat stores**
- **Your appetite increases**
- **Your energy is zapped!**

Some people can actually **gain** weight from running at too an high intensity for too long. We have had clients who would run for several hours almost daily, and still would not lose fat. The only thing that happened to them after they ran was that their appetites soared and they tended to eat more all through the day.

For these clients, we slowed down the intensity of their workouts and had them walk on a treadmill with an incline or outside carrying weights. The result was appetite control, fat loss and energy gain.

What are Aerobic and Anaerobic exercises?

Aerobic exercise is any exercise that keeps you in motion and elevates your heart rate. Examples of aerobic exercises are brisk walking, jogging, running, swimming, bicycling, aerobic dancing and cross-country skiing. These types of exercises are excellent for burning fat and decreasing your risk of heart disease.

Anaerobic exercises are ones that help you build and firm your muscles, such as weight lifting and floor exercise to tone and build body muscle. Since a higher proportion of muscle will increase your metabolic rate, both types of exercise, aerobic and anaerobic, are good for you to do if you want to burn fat.

How do I get rid of cellulite?

Cellulite is the puckering of fat under the skin. The best ways to remove cellulite are aerobic exercise at a moderate pace and a lowfat diet.

How can I slim flabby thighs?

If you are attempting to reduce flabby thighs by swinging heavy weights with legs, you will actually increase the size of the muscle, making the thigh even bigger. This form of exercise is too anaerobic (short duration) to burn significant amounts of fat. You must do aerobic exercise for at least 30 minutes each time for the best results.

I am working so hard at physical activity; are there other benefits for me besides keeping trim and losing fat?

Yes, moderate exercise also reduces the appetite, helps you to cope better with the moods and stresses of the day and can help to reduce blood pressure. It has also been shown to increase the good "HDL" cholesterol in your blood which helps to prevent heart disease.

How do those slim people who seem to eat everything stay slim?

A lean person may eat like a horse and stay slim because of a high metabolic rate. A fat body lowers the metabolism, so a fat person may "eat like a bird" and still get fatter.

How much water should I drink when I exercise?

One of the most common problems associated with exercise is not drinking enough water.

When you exercise, fluids are lost from your body through perspiration. You must replace that lost fluid so that you do not become dehydrated. If you dehydrate, your blood volume decreases, which puts extra stress on your heart. In addition, if your muscles dehydrate, it is harder for them to move and this can affect performance.

Do not count on thirst as an indication of your need for water. If you wait until you are thirsty, you are already dehydrated.

Water also cools your body down and keeps your body temperature in the safe range.

We stress the importance of drinking 1-1/2 to 2 litres (6-8 cups) of water daily. When you exercise, you require even more. In addition to your daily requirement, drink at least 1 litre (4 cups) 2 to 3 hours before exercising, and at least 1/2 litre (2 cups) for every hour of exercise.

Can exercise help to reduce stress?

Absolutely! Exercise relieves stress by releasing chemicals called "endorphins." Endorphins are substances produced by the body that alleviate pain. They are released after exercise and are thought to cause the "high" or good feeling that occurs after exercising.

Exercise is usually the first thing we ignore when we are busy and stressed! We don't make the time to fit it into our busy schedules. However, stressful times are the most important times to exercise because exercise can be our way of *taking control of stress* rather than *letting it control us.*

Another way to improve how our bodies respond to stress is to eat well. Following the Healthy Weigh plan will show you how to gear up your metabolism and keep your blood sugar level more stable. Eating in this way will help you to have balanced moods, better concentration and greater stamina.

We live in very stressful times, and a lot of demands are placed on our bodies. If we tend to eat most of our food in the latter part of the day, then the supply to meet the demands comes in too late.

The body's response to stress is a survival response; that is, it tries to protect itself against that stress. In order to survive, it goes into a conservation mode. The metabolism slows down so that every calorie can be conserved. Calories are stored away instead of burned.

When stress comes in, the metabolism begins to slow down, and if we don't relieve ourselves of that stress, we stay in this slowed-down state. Another thing that slows down under stress is the gastrointestinal tract, resulting in constipation.

Stress also causes the blood sugar level to take more dips and dives than normal, because the body's reaction to stress is to eat and conserve more food. The appetite is controlled by the blood sugar level, and when it drops we feel physical hunger, especially for sweets. That is why we crave sweets when we are stressed, not just because of an emotional need, but because of a true physical need as well. When the blood sugar level falls, energy falls as well. We are not as productive, we cannot concentrate as well and we're subject to more mood swings.

Take time each day to treat yourself to good-tasting healthy food and to exercise that you enjoy. The better you feel from within, the easier it will be for you to make the necessary changes to succeed and reach your realistic goal!

Myths

Grapefruit burns fat! Protein supplements build muscle! Bread is fattening! Lose 4-1/2 kilograms (10 pounds) in a week!

With false claims such as these, promoted by the media and unqualified "nutritionists," it is no wonder there is confusion about nutrition.

How many of these nutrition myths are you familiar with?

All calories are created equal; FALSE

TRUTH: Fat calories are the most fattening. Studies show that your body stores calories from fat more easily than calories from carbohydrate or protein foods. Therefore, if you are trying to lose weight, the first thing you should limit in your diet is fat.

Salt makes you fat; FALSE

TRUTH: Salt contains sodium which is needed by the body in small amounts and it is found in many foods. However, when too much is consumed it causes you to retain water. Note that this is not fat weight but water weight which can easily drop off. The solution is to use sodium in moderation and to increase your consumption of water. Drinking water actually causes you to retain less of it in the body, so drink! drink! drink! You need at least six to eight glasses every day.

Margarine has fewer calories than butter; FALSE

TRUTH: They have the same number of calories—120 per 15 millilitres (1 tablespoon). They are just different types of fat.

Potatoes, bread and other starchy foods are fattening; FALSE

TRUTH: By themselves, these foods are not fattening. A medium-sized baked potato contains fewer calories than a large apple. These foods are naturally low in fat, but their caloric value can easily be tripled by adding high-fat spreads such as sour cream, butter and margarine.

Milk should be omitted from a weight-reducing diet; FALSE

TRUTH: Never omit milk, which contains healthy essential nutrients. Decrease foods like fats, sugars and alcohol to reduce calories.

You don't harm your body by losing weight and gaining it back again; FALSE

TRUTH: When weight is regained, your body's metabolism slows down. With each loss and gain cycle, your ability to burn calories decreases. As a result, it becomes more and more difficult to lose weight with each successive weight-loss program.

That is why it is important to choose a weight-control program such as the Healthy Weigh plan which you will want to follow for life. Eating the Healthy Weigh lets you break out of the loss and gain cycle. You will enjoy it so much, there will be no reason to go back to your old way of eating.

You should lose weight every week while following a lower-calorie food plan; FALSE

TRUTH: If you were to follow a lower-calorie food plan for more than a few weeks you would probably reach a plateau (weight stabilization). A number of factors, including water retention, can halt weight loss temporarily. You may also plateau if you lose more than 4 1/2 kilograms (10 pounds). At a lower weight, you require fewer calories to maintain your weight. To institute further loss, increase your physical activity. Remember that the danger lies not in reaching the plateau but in your attitude. If you become discouraged and your old eating patterns return, you will gain all your weight back. So keep going! If you continue your program, the plateau will break and you will continue to lose weight.

Walking one mile does not burn as many calories as running one mile; FALSE

TRUTH: Walking and running burn the same number of calories provided the distance covered is the same.

Bran is the only high-fibre food; FALSE

TRUTH: Many foods are high in fibre, including fruits, vegetables, whole grain breads, cereals and legumes.

Oat bran is the only food that can lower blood cholesterol; FALSE

TRUTH: It is the soluble fibres in oat bran that lower blood cholesterol levels. You can get soluble fibres from other foods that are just as effective at lowering blood cholesterol, for example, barley, kidney beans, rice bran and some fruits and vegetables.

All high-fibre foods can help you lose weight; FALSE

TRUTH: Fibre has many nutritional benefits. Fibre is an undigested part of some foods that fills you up and helps prevent constipation. However, some foods can contain fibre along with a lot of fat and/or sugar, such as large bran muffins, granola cereals, oat-bran pretzels and trail mix.

Grapefruits burn fat, and celery has less than zero calories; FALSE

TRUTH: There is no magical food that burns fat or causes weight loss. Grapefruit and celery, like all other foods, have calories. One half grapefruit has 40-60 calories, and a stalk of celery has 8 calories.

Tonic water has no calories; FALSE

TRUTH: Don't be fooled by this beverage's name. Tonic water has approximately 100 calories per 250 millilitre (1 cup) glass.

Inexpensive cuts of meat are not as nutritious as the expensive cuts; FALSE

TRUTH: Sometimes it's the other way around. Inexpensive cuts can actually be more nutritious if they are leaner.

If you don't eat meat your cholesterol will drop and you will lose weight; FALSE

TRUTH: Even if you don't eat meat, you can still be consuming cholesterol, fat and calories from other foods. Lean meat is recommended occasionally, in moderate amounts, because of its essential nutritional benefits.

Toasting bread lowers calories; FALSE

TRUTH: Water is the only thing that is lowered when bread is toasted. The calories are the same.

All salads are low in calories; FALSE

TRUTH: Salads made with fresh vegetables and small amounts of low-fat dressing can be low in calories. However, salad mixtures containing larger amounts of dressing, mayonnaise, sour cream, meats or cheeses can be packed with fat and calories.

The "diet menus" and "diet plates" offered in restaurants are always low in calories; FALSE

TRUTH: Many that we have evaluated are not low in calories. For example, the "dieters' plate" containing 165 grams (6 ounces) of hamburger, cottage cheese, lettuce and tomato can add up to 800 calories.

"Light", "lite" and "diet" foods are all low in calories; FALSE

TRUTH: "Light" or "lite" can mean a number of things, including light in colour, texture or taste. There are some diet or light foods that are advertised as being low in calories, but many are not. For example, some products cut the sugar content but add more fat, and the net result is a product with the same or even a greater number of calories.

Frozen yogurt and Tofutti are low in calories; FALSE

TRUTH: Some frozen yogurts and frozen Toffutti are actually higher in calories than some ice creams. Check the nutritional information and labels. The ones to choose are those with less than 3 grams of fat per 100 gram serving.

Sugar foods give you energy; FALSE

TRUTH: Actually, sugar has the opposite effect. Sugar supplies a boost of quick energy, but this is followed by an even greater drop in energy soon after. This tends to make you tired, hungry and craving more sweets. Better sources of energy are complex carbohydrate foods with fibre, such as fruits, vegetables, whole grain breads and cereals. They do not cause the peaks and valleys of energy levels, as sugary foods do.

Fructose is a healthy sugar; FALSE

TRUTH: Fructose, sometimes referred to as "natural sugar," is digested differently than table sugar. However, this difference has little effect on the body. Fructose is found in fruit, and it is healthier if you ingest it by eating the whole fruit. This is because of the other healthy ingredients found in fruit such as fibre, vitamins and minerals.

Artificial sweeteners will help you lose weight; FALSE

TRUTH: They are not a solution to a weight problem. The use of artificial sweeteners has actually been shown to increase appetite and the desire for sweet foods. Real sugar has only 16 calories per 5 millilitres (1 teaspoon); why not use a little?

Any food that is "enriched" or "fortified" is healthy; FALSE

TRUTH: Enriched or fortified foods do not necessarily have large amounts of nutrients added to them. For example, an orange drink may be fortified with vitamin C, but this may be the only nutrient added. The drink contains mainly sugar and water and it lacks the other important nutrients found in orange juice. For breads and cereal products, choose the whole grain ones instead of refined, enriched ones. Don't be misled by the word "fortified" or "enriched." Read the label to get the whole picture.

Natural foods are low in calories; FALSE

TRUTH: Some natural foods are actually very high in calories, for example, granola, carob chips, nuts, seeds, natural potato chips and cheese.

Foods that are natural or organic are healthier; FALSE

TRUTH: The words "natural" and "organic" can have many meanings. Natural doesn't necessarily mean foods without any additives, even though labels can lead you to believe that these products are healthier. For example, a dessert product can be called natural if made with natural flavour, but it can be filled with other additives. Honey is advertised as being natural, but it has no more health benefits than ordinary white table sugar. Organic means food from plants that have been grown with natural rather than chemical fertilizers. However, plants cannot recognize the difference between the two types; they grow identically and the food ends up being the same nutritionally.

One thing these two names on a product do guarantee is a high cost, so don't be fooled.

Chemicals added to food makes it less nutritious; FALSE

TRUTH: Of the 1300 food additives approved for use in our food, many serve a wide variety of purposes. Actually, processing of foods often removes toxic substances. Some additives prevent the growth of dangerous microorganisms, making the food safe and attractive. However, there are some additives that have been proven to be harmful, such as sulfites and nitrites. They are found in cured products, such as some luncheon meats, hot dogs and sausages. Moderate use of all processed foods is recommended.

Vitamins give you energy; FALSE

TRUTH: Vitamins do not produce energy themselves. They help to break down food into a type of energy that your body can use.

Vitamin pills ensure a healthy diet; FALSE

TRUTH: Vitamins and mineral supplements do not undo bad food choices, and they can be toxic to your body if taken in large doses. You can learn to adjust your daily food intake to meet your nutrient needs much better from foods than from pills. If you take a supplement, remember that it should contain no more than 100% of the recommended nutrient intake (RNI).

Large doses of vitamin C are healthy and prevent the common cold; FALSE

TRUTH: It has not been proven that vitamin C prevents viruses such as the ones that cause colds. Too much vitamin C can be dangerous. Your body tissues can absorb only a certain amount of vitamin C, and then they become saturated and excrete it from the body via the kidneys. This can lead to kidney damage. By megadosing on this vitamin, your body becomes used to taking in larger amounts, and if less is taken a deficiency can result. Your daily requirement is 30 mg for women and 40 mg for men, which can be obtained by eating 2-3 servings of fruits or vegetables.

Gelatin tablets keep your nails healthy; FALSE

TRUTH: Gelatin is not a complete protein, and it is of poor quality. It does not contain all the essential amino acids needed to promote growth and repair of protein tissue such as hair and nails. A good quality protein such as animal protein, dairy foods or proper vegetarian protein combinations would correct brittle nails if this condition was due to protein deficiency.

A strict vegetarian does not require supplements; FALSE

TRUTH: If you are a strict vegetarian and do not eat eggs, milk or animal products, you have a requirement for B12, since it is found only in these foods. You are at risk for deficiency unless you drink B12 fortified soy milk or take B12 supplements.

Calcium supplements are just as healthy as calcium-rich foods; FALSE

TRUTH: We suggest the use of calcium supplements for those who cannot tolerate milk products; however, your body absorbs calcium much better from calcium-rich foods than from supplements. This is because there are other important vitamins and minerals in these foods that help increase calcium absorption.

Protein supplements are necessary if you want to build muscle; FALSE

TRUTH: Contrary to what many people believe, protein supplements are not needed for muscle building. They do not increase muscle mass, exercise does! As a matter of fact, when too much protein is eaten it is converted to fat. Muscle builders need a little more protein for tissue repair, but this requirement is minimal. What they really need is a wide variety of healthy foods, not just protein.

Pills and "Diet Aids" such as thyroxin, amphetamines and diuretics are safe and effective ways to help you lose weight; FALSE

TRUTH: Many diet aids have dangerous side effects. You cannot use them for a long period of time, certainly not long enough to learn new habits and incorporate a new healthy style of eating. After you stop taking the pills, the weight is often regained. Thyroxin increases the metabolic rate but has the negative side effects of hyperactivity and heart palpitations.

Amphetamines and other pills that decrease appetite are not useful for weight reduction. These pills may become addictive and their side effects include nervousness and irritability. Most overweight people do not rely on hunger to signal eating and fullness to stop eating. Some people even feel like snacking more after a meal when they are full.

Diuretics can dehydrate you, and the weight that is lost is not permanent. It comes back as soon as you drink water. The goal to successful permanent weight management is the loss of fat, not water.

Laxatives may be downright dangerous. Overuse can cause weakness, thirst, abdominal pain, nausea and water retention. As well, both laxatives and diuretics cause your body to lose important minerals.

Fad diets are healthy and good diets to follow; FALSE

TRUTH: Fad diets are just that. They are in fashion from time to time but rarely promote long lasting food and behavioural change. Some are potentially harmful.

Part II
An Easy Guide to Nutrition

The Healthy Weigh Low-Fat Food Mix

The key to lifelong weight control is to take in the proper food mix. This food mix does not mean deprivation. It does not mean portions of food that are too small to satisfy a canary! It does not mean boring food with no taste! The Healthy Weigh Low-Fat Food Mix is balanced in such a way that will give you volumes of food to satisfy your appetite. We will teach you how to flavour your foods so that you will truly enjoy the taste. This will make weight control a pleasure and you will have no reason to go back to your old way of eating.

The goal of the Healthy Weigh Low-Fat Food Mix is to give you the greatest volume of food for your required number of calories.

This is achieved by (1) Cutting down the fat and (2) Filling your plate with foods according to the proportion on the diagram shown below.

Healthy Weigh Low-Fat Food Mix

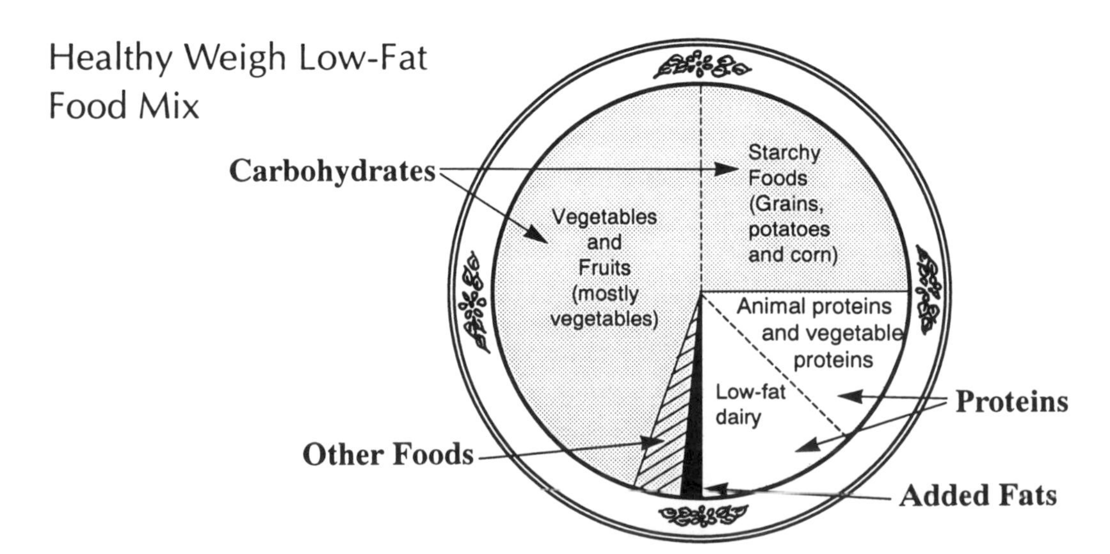

Cutting Down the Fat

Fat is the most concentrated source of calories. A very small volume of it, a mere 15 millilitres (1 tablespoon) provides us with a whopping 120 calories. That's the same number of calories that we find in 250 millilitres (1 cup) of rice or 750 millilitres (3 cups) of cooked vegetables. It takes a lot of fat to fill us up but very little fat to fill us out.

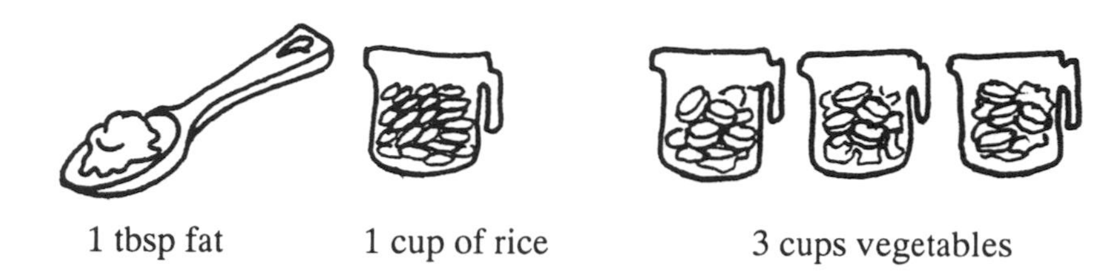

1 tbsp fat 1 cup of rice 3 cups vegetables

Even though all fats have the same number of calories, some are healthier for the body than others. The healthiest fats are the unsaturated ones, which come from plant oils such as olive, canola, peanut, corn, sunflower and safflower, as well as margarine, nuts and seeds.

The unhealthiest type of fat is the saturated type, which comes from animal products such as meats, poultry skin, butter, cream, whole dairy products and hydrogenated fats. Saturated fat is also found in 2 plant oils: coconut and palm oil.

SATURATED FAT = 120 CALORIES / TBSP UNSATURATED FAT = 120 CALORIES / TBSP

Keep in mind that no matter what type of fat, saturated or unsaturated, it contains the same number of calories. Therefore, the key to successful weight management is to keep all fat intake to a minimum.

Not only is fat high in calories, but excessive intake has been related to almost every disease known to man. It contributes to plaque formation in your arteries and blood vessels and increases your blood cholesterol levels, which can lead to heart disease and stroke. Excess fat increases the risk of cancer, diabetes and gall bladder disease as well.

So, even for those people who do not need to reduce calories, a low-fat diet is recommended to maintain general health. Your extra calories should come from healthy sources like carbohydrates and lean protein, not fat.

It's easy to be confused about all the different fats. Some common questions we hear are "What's the best margarine?" "What's the best oil?" "What food should I cut down on, to decrease my cholesterol level?" "My triglycerides are high! What should I do?"

The following simple explanation will make it easier to understand.

1) Cholesterol

Cholesterol has important roles to play in the body, such as forming hormones and cell walls. Your body has the ability to manufacture its own cholesterol; however, when cholesterol levels become too high, it accumulates in your blood, leading to blood vessel disease. Cholesterol levels can become too high from a number of factors, such as cigarette smoking, alcohol consumption, stress, lack of exercise, genetic tendency due to a family history of high cholesterol levels, and eating too much saturated fat.

It's not only the cholesterol in the blood that determines your risk of heart disease, it is also **where that cholesterol goes**—out of your body or into your arteries. Cholesterol does not travel in the body on its own, since it is a fatty substance and cannot mix well with the blood. It is carried by products called "cholesterol carriers," and there are two types. There are the "bad" ones called LDLs (low-density lipoproteins) and the "good" ones called HDLs (high-density lipoproteins). LDL's are bad because they carry cholesterol from your blood to your arteries, which can lead to heart and artery disease. Saturated fat is the culprit that has been shown to increase your bad LDL levels; therefore it is not just the cholesterol you should moderate in your diet, it is the saturated fat as well.

LDLs carry cholesterol from your blood into your arteries where it forms plaque.

HDLs are good because they carry cholesterol from the blood to the liver, where it is excreted from the body. Naturally, the aim is to have a high level of HDLs because it will help remove cholesterol from the body and protect against heart disease.

HDLs carry cholesterol from your blood to your liver where it is excreted out of your body

Read your labels!

Cholesterol only comes from animal products. No vegetable products contain cholesterol. However, food manufacturers take advantage of this point. As you just learned, saturated fat is just as bad as cholesterol, and there are some vegetable products that contain saturated fat, such as palm oil, coconut oil and hydrogenated oil. Therefore, even if the food contains "no cholesterol" and "100% vegetable oil," it can still contain palm oil or coconut oil, which are saturated.

2) Triglycerides

Triglycerides are fats that can accumulate in the blood vessels, just like cholesterol. When they do, they lead to increased risk for heart disease.

Triglycerides can become elevated from eating too much sugar, drinking excess alcohol, not exercising enough and, more commonly, from taking in most of the calories for the day at one time. This is one of the reasons not to overload at one time.

3) Hydrogenated fats

When manufacturers convert vegetable oils, which are liquid in nature, into a more solid substance, they process it by "hydrogenation." This is how some margarines are made. During this process, the oils become more saturated. There are varying degrees of hydrogenation depending on the product, so read the labels.

How Different Fats Affect Your Blood Cholesterol Levels

1) Saturated fat comes from animal products and includes butter, cream, whole milk, high-fat yogurt, bacon, sausage, hot dogs, marbling in meats, poultry skin and coconut and palm oil. Saturated fat from food contributes to your total blood cholesterol level.

2) Polyunsaturated fat is found in vegetable oils such as corn, sesame, sunflower, safflower and cottonseed. It is also found in walnuts, pecans, almonds and avocados. Polyunsaturated fat decreases your total cholesterol, and may decrease your good "HDL cholesterol."

3) Monounsaturated fat is found in vegetable oils such as olive oil, peanut oil and canola oil. Monounsaturated fat increases your good "HDL cholesterol", decreases your bad "LDL cholesterol." It can also decrease your triglyceride levels.

4) Omega 3 fatty acids are oils found in fatty cold-water fish like salmon and mackerel. Omega 3 fatty acids increase your good "HDL cholesterol" and decrease your bad "LDL cholesterol." They also decrease your triglyceride levels and reduce the tendency to form clots in blood vessels.

Sources of Fat

We get fat in our diet in 2 ways: the fat we add to foods and the fat hidden in foods.

1) The fat we add to foods

butter/margarine
oils
salad dressings
cream
mayonnaise, tartar sauce
sauces made with cream or cheese
high-fat cheeses
bacon bits
nuts and seeds
peanut butter
dips made with mayonnaise or cream

It is easier to cut back on the fats that we add to foods in cooking or at the table because we are in control; we can simply choose not to add them. The chapter "Cooking the Healthy Weigh" will teach you how to flavour and cook foods with little or no fat.

When it comes to controlling fat, a much bigger problem is the foods that are loaded with hidden fat.

2) The fat hidden in foods

Fat hides in the animal protein foods and dairy products such as:
marbled meat
poultry skin
egg yolk
whole milk
cheese
yogurt

Many people have the incorrect idea that cutting down on the carbohydrates—breads, cereals, pastas, rice and potatoes—and eating mostly protein foods like fish, poultry, meat and cheese is the best way to cut calories.

They could not be further from the truth. Proteins are important for your body, but a large proportion of protein foods is fat, not protein. Since fat has twice as many calories as protein, people who are loading up on protein and dairy foods are loading up on calories. It's not the protein in the steak that is fattening, it's the fat. Did you know that some popular cheeses, such as cheddar and brie, contain over 75% of the calories as fat?

Choose lean meats whenever possible. Sometimes the less expensive the cut of meat, the leaner it is! That's good news for your budget. Also, cut away as much visible fat as possible from meat prior to cooking. Take the skin off poultry before you season it. That will allow the wonderful flavour of the sauce or spices you use to be right on the chicken meat.

Try to use the egg white without the yolk because the whites are fat-free and cholesterol-free and are an excellent source of protein. If you want to replace whole eggs in cooking, remember that one egg is equal to 2 whites.

There are certain dairy products that are low in fat, such as low-fat yogurt. Most cheeses can be very high in fat, so be sure to choose those with less than 20% M.F. (milk fat) whenever possible.

Most vegetable sources of protein, such as legumes (dried beans and peas), are 100% fat-free. They are a good replacement for the animal sources of protein and can also be used to extend a meal. However, remember that vegetable proteins do not contain all the component parts our bodies need to be able to use them efficiently. They must be mixed with a grain, seed, lean animal protein or low-fat dairy product to make them a complete protein source for our body to use.

A wide variety of beans are now available on the market. Pre-cooked beans are available in cans and require much less cooking time than uncooked beans.

The fat hidden in processed carbohydrate foods

The carbohydrate foods (pasta, bread, cereal, rice, oatmeal, barley, fruits and vegetables) do not contain any hidden fat. However, a low-fat carbohydrate can quickly be turned into a high-fat one.

For example, all these carbohydrate foods are loaded with fat:

• muffins
• sweetbreads, cheesebreads, croissants
• granola cereals
• cookies, cakes, etc.
• potato chips, french fries
• fried apple chips
• fried banana chips
• other salty snacks

The fat hidden in restaurant meals

If it's shiny, beware! Chefs make their food glisten with fat!

There is hidden fat in prepared dishes like white creamy salad mixtures, cheese and cream sauces, cream soups, fried foods, even stir-fries.

Consider this typical roast beef dinner:

1/3 kilogram (12 ounce) piece of roast beef
salad with blue cheese dressing
1 slice bread with margarine
baked potato with margarine
1 slice cheesecake

This meal contains almost 250 millilitres (1 cup) of fat in just one meal!

2 SOURCES OF FAT

THE FAT WE ADD TO FOOD	THE FAT HIDDEN IN FOOD				
	Protein foods	*Processed carbohydrated foods*	*Restaurant food*	*Salad Bar mixtures*	*Convenience Products*
butter/margarine salad dressings, oil, cream, mayonnaise, sauces, peanut butter, dips	proteins	muffins cheesebreads croissants cookies, cakes salt snacks	fast foods rest. meals	mixtures made with oil and mayonnaise	baked goods canned frozen in sauces

As you can see, fat is everywhere!

In many restaurants, meals contain about 13 to 14 pats of fat. That does not include the butter you put on your rolls, the salad dressing you add to your salad and the sour cream you put on your potato. Tell your waiter to have the chef prepare your food with little or no fat, and learn to use the words "on the side" (see "Dining Out" section for more information).

The following words all signal "high fat" on the restaurant menu:

- alfredo
- au gratin
- au fromage
- béchamel
- breaded
- bisque
- casserole
- creamy
- hash
- parmigiana
- pan-fried
- stir-fried* (can be prepared with less fat)
- a la mode
- au lait
- béarnaise
- battered
- basted
- buttered
- crispy
- escalloped
- hollandaise
- puffed
- sautéed
- tempura

The fat hidden in salad mixtures

Many people think that the word "salad" automatically means "light" and "low in calories." However, salads can be a very high source of calories. Any salad made with mayonnaise, oil or regular salad dressing, and any salad topping with cheese, bacon bits or meats, can contain more fat and calories than a banana split. One scoop of marinated vegetables in an oil-based dressing has over 150 calories, and one scoop of tuna, egg, chicken or turkey salad made with mayonnaise has over 250 calories. So watch the choices you make at the salad bar.

Avoid these high-fat, high-calorie salad choices:
- white mixtures made with mayonnaise
- shiny mixtures made with oil
- regular salad dressing
- high-fat toppings such as cheese, croutons, bacon bits, fried banana chips

The fat hidden in processed convenience products

Read those labels! Fat can appear in some unexpected places, such as:
- frozen foods (in cheese or cream sauces)
- canned fish (in oil)
- salty snacks (fried in fat)
- fancy crackers
- baked goods

Don't be fooled by the words:
- "no cholesterol" or "100% pure vegetable oil"
- or "sugar-free"
- or "light"
- or "diet"

Even these products can have a lot of fat and calories. "No cholesterol" and "100% pure vegetable oil" products can still be loaded with fat, even saturated fat, like palm oil, coconut oil and hydrogenated vegetable oil. Also, remember that no matter what oil it is, saturated or unsaturated, it still has a whopping 120 calories for every 10 millilitres (1 tablespoon).

Fill 1/4 of Your Plate with Lean Protein and Low-Fat Dairy Foods

Protein is the nutrient from which our bodies grow and regenerate. It is needed to form the building blocks for muscles, nails, hair and skin. Protein also regulates your body's functions such as boosting your metabolism to burn food quickly and efficiently.

Proteins are what your body uses to keep your fluid in proper balance. It is not unusual for some people who do not eat protein in the proper way to bloat, and hold 1-1/2 kilograms (3 to 4 pounds) of extra water on their bodies.

Proteins are also important for building your body muscle while you lose body fat.

So, as you can see, protein is very important for your body. You could not be healthy and attractive without it.

There are 2 types of protein foods, which differ in composition. The first type of protein foods are called *complete proteins*, because they contain all the protein building blocks the body needs. They are referred to as excellent sources of dietary protein. These "complete" proteins are found in animal foods such as milk, yogurt, eggs, cheese, poultry, seafood, fish, beef, lamb and pork.

The second type of protein foods are called *incomplete protein* because they lack one or more of the building blocks the body needs to use them properly.

Incomplete protein is found in plant foods such as legumes (lentils, soybeans, pinto beans, kidney beans, navy beans, black beans, red beans and peanuts) tofu and seeds. Incomplete protein is also found in grains (wheat, oats, rye, barley, rice, and products made from them, such as breads, rice, pasta, etc.)

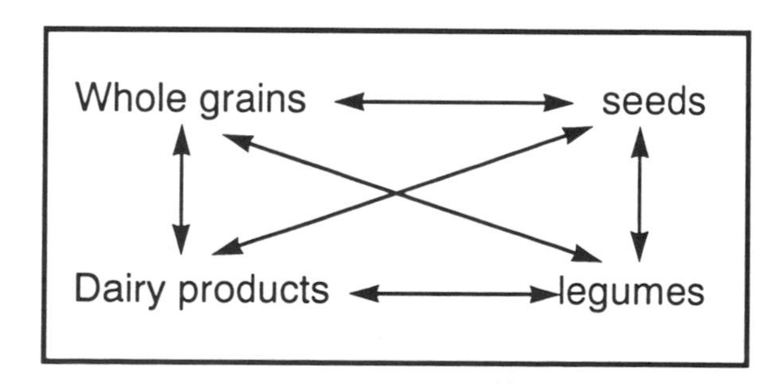

You can make *incomplete proteins* into *complete proteins* by combining them properly. Some examples of proper combinations are:

- legumes and seeds, e.g., chick-peas and sunflower seeds
- legumes and grains, e.g., lentils and rice, peanut butter on toast
- dairy products and grains, e.g., pancakes made with milk; breads and muffins made with milk; macaroni and low-fat cheese; egg sandwich

Complete Proteins **Animal Protein**	**Incomplete Proteins** **Plant Proteins**
Animal foods Milk, Yogurt, Eggs, Cheese Poultry, Fish, Meat	Legumes, Tofu, Grains

Pure protein provides 4 calories for every gram, which is less than half the calories of fat. However, most foods that give us protein (the animal protein foods) have a lot of hidden fat marbled throughout them. You can cut away any fat you see, take the skin off chicken, purchase only lean meats and low-fat dairy products. However, that does not necessarily mean that all the fat is gone. Skinless poultry, lean meats and part skim dairy products still do have some fat. The problem with this is that you cannot get this fat out. The good news is that protein is so powerful your body does not require more than 200 grams (6-8 ounces) spread evenly throughout the day. That means a 70 gram (2-3 ounce) portion at every meal.

There are very few people in this country who do not eat enough protein. In fact most people consume more than they need. However, the problem most people have is that they do not spread their intake evenly though throughout the day. **Your body cannot store protein in the form you eat it, and it must be eaten in small amounts several times a day for your body to use it efficiently.**

Whereas before you may have thought in terms of "what shall I serve or order with my chicken, instead now think "what will I serve or order with my vegetables and rice," Make protein *the side dish* instead of the main part of your meal.

Proteins

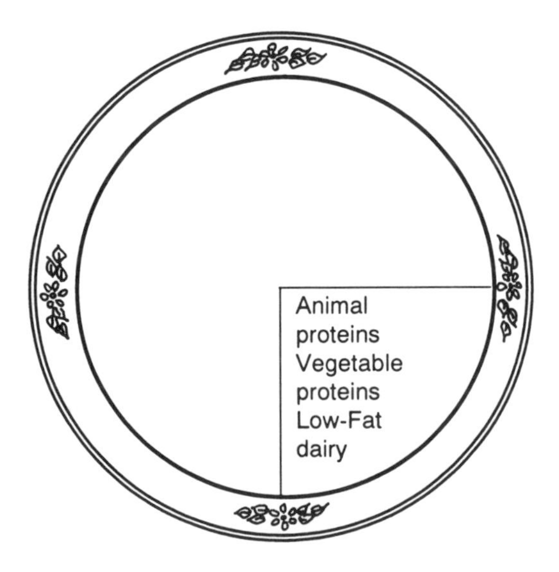

Dairy products (milk, yogurt and cheese) are not only sources of protein, but are also the best sources of calcium, which is essential for healthy bones and teeth. Therefore, make at least 2-3 of your protein choices daily from low-fat milk, low-fat cheese, low-fat yogurt, canned salmon with bones, tofu or legumes, as these foods contain calcium, which your body needs for strong bones and teeth. We may think of our bones as fixed objects, but actually, minerals and nutrients are constantly moving in and out of them. The blood level requires a certain amount of calcium, and if we don't get enough from the foods we eat, the blood draws it from bones and teeth. This causes weak bones, osteoporosis and dental problems. These diseases are not reversible. Weakening of bones and teeth can start at a very early age, so make sure you get enough calcium at *every* stage of your life.

Even though we don't recommend depending on vitamin pills for your nutrients, calcium supplements are an exception to this. It is sometimes difficult to get all the calcium you need from food. The recommendation for teenage years to age 30 is to have at least 3 servings daily of high-calcium foods. After age 30 increase your servings to 4-5 daily. One serving is equal to 250 millilitres (1 cup) milk or yogurt, 40 grams (1-1/2 ounces) cheese, 85 grams (3 ounces) canned salmon with bones, or 250 millilitres (1 cup) tofu or legumes. The recommendation, if you cannot get all your calcium from food, is to take a calcium supplement with your evening meal, or before bedtime.

Fill Most of Your Plate with Carbohydrate Foods

The carbohydrate foods are those that come from plants (i.e., grain, potato, corn, other vegetables and fruits) and they provide energy for your body. The plants absorb energy from the sun, and when you eat them, their carbohydrates give your body the energy it needs to function.

Carbohydrates

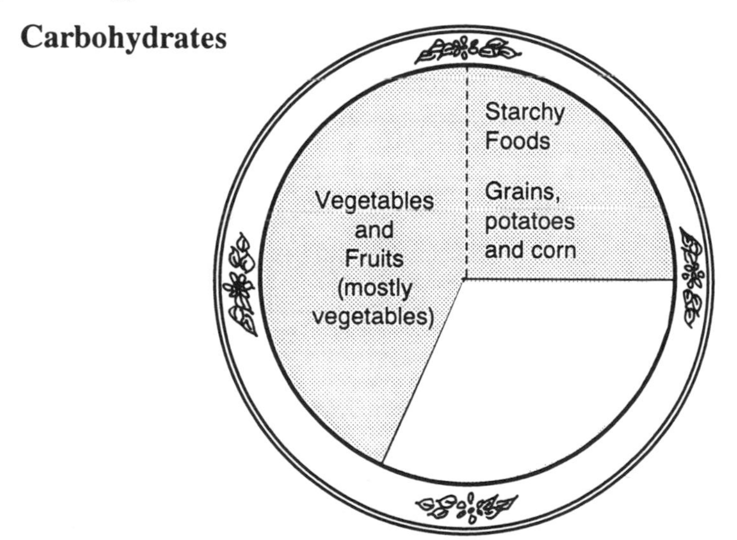

Fruits and vegetables enter your system faster than grain products because your body digests them more quickly. When you are hungry, your blood sugar level is low, and fruits and vegetables raise the level and reduce your hunger quickly. By eating them at the beginning of the meal, you feel fuller faster. Therefore, a good way to control your intake is to start your meal with a fruit or vegetable as an appetizer.

Grain products (breads, crackers, cereals, pasta, rice, barley, couscous, etc.) take longer to digest and absorb. Therefore, they stay in your body longer and keep your hunger levels stable over a longer period of time.

The goal is to eat these grains in the most whole grain form possible. "Whole grain" means that it contains fibre and more nutrients. Choose products that list "whole" as the description of the first ingredient ("whole wheat," "whole grain," "whole rye," etc.).

Too many people have the wrong idea that cutting out the carbohydrate foods is the best way to lose weight. This could not be farther from the truth. Carbohydrates contain the same number of calories as protein—4 calories for every gram—which is less than half the calories of fat.

Whereas protein foods have hidden fat, which increases the calories, most carbohydrate foods are fat-free.

As you can see on the plate, vegetables and fruits should take up the largest section. This is because these foods are filled with calorie-free water. These foods will increase the volume of your food mix without significantly increasing the calories; they will fill you up instead of filling you out. If you are the type of person who likes to eat a large amount of food, this is especially important.

Vegetables and Fruits are loaded with Nutrition!

Not only do vegetables and fruits provide the greatest volume for the least number of calories, they are also powerhouses of vitamins and minerals.

When it comes to good nutrition, these foods play a very important role in providing substances not found in any other foods. Vegetables belonging to the cabbage family ("cruciferous vegetables": cabbage, cauliflower, broccoli, brussels sprouts, kohlrabi) are power packed with compounds called "indoles", which have a protective effect against cancer.

Another protective substance found in some vegetables and fruits is called "beta carotene," It is found in all vegetables and fruits that have a strong, bright colour (asparagus, carrots, squash, sweet potatoes, pumpkin, peaches, apricots, spinach, tomatoes, peppers, romaine lettuce, brussels sprouts, broccoli). The general rule of thumb is: the deeper the colour of the vegetables and fruits, the more nutritious they are.

Another important thing to remember about fruits and vegetables is to eat a *variety* of them daily. There is more to fruit than apples, oranges and bananas. There is more to vegetables than lettuce, peas and carrots. Be sure to bring home different fruits and vegetables from the store to keep your food exciting.

Fibre

Fibre is needed by the body for proper bowel function. It absorbs moisture and speeds the transit time of food through the bowel. Fibrous foods also take longer to eat. They require more chewing (e.g., an apple) than food with less fibre (e.g., apple juice or applesauce).

They take longer to eat, and keep you full for longer periods of time. This is good news for those interested in weight loss without hunger.

When you can, eat the fruits and vegetables instead of just drinking the juice. This is because of the wonderful fibre you get in the fresh fruit or vegetable. If you have a juicer, the juice extracted from it is more nutritious than juice from a bottle, but it is still not as good as eating the fresh fruit or vegetable. Fruits and vegetables that have been canned or crushed (like applesauce) have less fibre than the fresh product. Frozen fruits and vegetables are as good as fresh, providing they are frozen without any sauces.

Do not be fooled by brown colours added to products. Manufacturers sometimes add molasses or brown dye to make products look healthful. Some breads and muffins are not brown because they are whole wheat, they are mainly white flour, with molasses added for colour.

The best sources of fibre are fruits, vegetables and whole grains, such as whole grain breads, whole grain cereals, legumes, and brown rice.

Fibre needs water to work! Some people complain of still being constipated after eating a lot of fibre. That is because they are not drinking enough water. The requirement—every day—is for 1-1/2 to 2 litres (6-8 cups) of water.

Combine Carbohydrates and Proteins at Every Meal

The main function of carbohydrates is to provide our bodies with energy in the form of calories. Protein also contains calories and can supply our body with energy, but it has other more important roles to play, such as building beautiful hair, skin and nails, repairing and building body muscles, boosting the metabolism and releasing excess fluid from the body.

Protein must always be eaten with a carbohydrate, so that the body uses the carbohydrate instead of the protein for energy. This will leave the protein available to do all the wonderful things it is supposed to do for our bodies.

If you are not eating protein in the proper way, your body cannot use it properly, and as a result you will either dehydrate or hold excessive amounts of body fluid. If you fight fluid retention all the time, you need to examine your protein intake. You may take enough in, but if it is not coming in evenly enough throughout the day, or if it is not being protected by carbohydrate, your body is not using it properly. As a result, your fluids can be out of balance.

The all-protein, low-carbohydrate diets put your body into a state of imbalance resulting in dehydration of body tissues. You can lose great amounts of weight on these diets—usually a 10% loss of body weight in the first 10 days. However, what you are losing is water, not fat. You always gain water weight back since your body has been so carbohydrate deprived; as soon as you eat even 1 slice of bread, your body rehydrates, and the water weight comes back. It is not uncommon to gain back 2 kilograms (3-5 pounds) in a day, just from a bowl of cereal or a few crackers.

On these low-carbohydrate diets, you lose water and muscle and you gain back water and *fat*. With each loss and regain of weight, your body loses more muscle, and regains more fat. Therefore, you end up with a higher proportion of fat mass; and the higher your percentage of body fat, the slower your metabolism, and the slower you burn the calories you eat. That is why this kind of dieting is self-defeating; it makes you fat!

Vitamins and Minerals

Get Your Vitamins and Minerals from Foods—Not Pills

Contrary to what you may think, vitamins do not give you energy. It is food that does. Vitamins are what the body uses to convert food into a form of energy it can use.

If you follow the basic principles of the Healthy Weigh plan, you will have an adequate intake of the essential vitamins and minerals. However, this may not apply to people who are at high risk of inadequacies, such as chronic dieters, heavy smokers or drinkers, strict vegetarians, pregnant or nursing mothers, those with specific food allergies or those who limit their intake of food choices. For these people we suggest vitamin and mineral supplements.

Remember that supplements do not undo bad food choices, and that when megadoses are taken, toxicity can develop.

There are two types of vitamins, water soluble (B complex and C) and fat soluble (A, D, E, K). The water soluble ones cannot be stored in the body, and are released in the urine. However, large doses can still be dangerous. For example, the daily requirement for vitamin C can be obtained by drinking 125 millilitres (1/2 cup) of orange juice or by eating 1 orange or 1/2 grapefruit. Many people are misled by the notion that the more Vitamin C they take, the better. The body's tissues can absorb only a certain amount, and the excess has been shown to cause kidney damage, diarrhea, abdominal cramps and damage to tooth enamel. Fat-soluble vitamins are stored in the body and can build up dangerous levels if large doses are taken.

Since no one food provides your body with all the vitamins and minerals, you need to focus on a healthy mix of foods to provide you with an adequate intake of these essential nutrients.

There are approximately 50 essential nutrients that exist in foods.

The best sources of vitamins and minerals is, and always has been, food!

Food Sources of Healthy Vitamins

Vitamin	Food Sources
Vitamin A	• Deep-coloured fruits and vegetables (spinach, romaine lettuce, broccoli, sweet potatoes, yams, peppers, carrots, apricots) • Eggs • Milk
Vitamin B Complex (e.g. Thiamin (B1), Riboflavin (B2) Peridoxin (B6)Niacin, Vitamin B12, Folic Acid)	• Whole grain breads and cereals, • Green leafy vegetables • Legumes, lean beef
Vitamin C	• Citrus fruits (oranges, grapefruits, lemons) • Tomatoes, Strawberries, Potatoes
Vitamin D	• Fortified milk and milk products
Vitamin E	• Vegetable oils • Margarine
Vitamin K	• Green leafy vegetables (leaf lettuce, spinach, romaine lettuce)

Food Sources of Healthy Minerals

Foods High in Calcium

Milk low-fat (2% M.F. or less)
Yogurt low-fat (2% M.F. or less)
Hard cheese low-fat (20% M.F. or less)
Salmon—canned with bones
Tofu

Foods High in Iron

Lean beef, veal, poultry
Liver, organ meats
Seafood
Legumes
Dark green, leafy vegetables
Dried fruits
Whole grain breads and cereals

Foods High in Zinc

Lean beef, organ meats, turkey
Legumes
Wheat cereals, wheat germ

Foods High in Magnesium

Whole grain cereals, lean meat
Legumes, green vegetables

Other Foods

Salt

Salt is addictive, not because it has a physical pull from the body, but because it has a pull from the taste buds. We may have been brought up with oversalted food, right from day one, if our baby foods contained salt.

When you cut back on salt, your tastes will go through a withdrawal, but they do change. If you taste something salty after being off salt for a while, it almost burns your mouth. But beware, because your tastes do change back if you start to use salt again.

Salt has been linked to both high blood pressure and kidney disease. However, genetics plays an important role too. If either of these diseases occur in your family, you should cut back on salt more than the average person. You don't have to stop using the salt shaker completely. Cutting back on foods that are excessive sources of salt, for instance, snacks such as potato chips, anything pickled or in brine (pickles, olives, sauerkraut) and anything smoked or cured (ham, bacon, bologna, salami, etc.). Changing from canned to frozen or fresh vegetables can also help to considerably lower your sodium intake. There are also many low-sodium versions of some popular high-sodium products, such as low-sodium canned goods, as well as low-sodium teriyaki. soy and other sauces.

Sugar

Sugar contains less than half the calories of fat. It is not the sugar that makes most baked goods and desserts high in calories, it's fat! However, sugar has an addictive effect on the taste buds, and it is what draws us to these high-fat and high-calorie treats.

Sugar also has a physical pull on your body. It sets you up for highs and lows in your blood sugar level. However, be aware that not everyone reacts the same way to this. Some people are more sensitive to sugar than others. Some people can eat a brownie and stop at one. They may not have another sweet thing until the next week. There are others whose blood sugar levels are like roller-coasters and when they eat sugar, it sets them up for overeating.

The first thing you must do is identify how sensitive you are to sugar. Are you the type of person who can stop at one brownie or will it cause your appetite to soar? If you are the type of person who can stop at one sweet, then you can incorporate some sweets into your meal plan.

However, if you are the type of person who can't stop at one dessert, then a little bit does hurt. Do not try to rely on will-power because it rarely works. Satisfy your body's need by feeding it the right things at the right time to keep your blood sugars even and your appetite in control. When you start to eat in this healthy way, you will notice that you won't desire sweets as much. You don't blow good health from one piece of pie. What is important in nutrition is how you eat day by day.

Excess sugar can contribute to elevated blood triglyceride levels. It contributes to dental cavities and if it takes the place of other foods, you can be missing out on important nutrients. Just like salt, sugar is an ingredient in many packaged products. If you read package labels you will find sugar in some very unexpected places.

Caffeine

Caffeine stimulates the nervous system. Some people are not affected at all by small amounts of caffeine, while others become jittery after only one cup of coffee.

For people with ulcers or other stomach problems, caffeine can cause discomfort because it increases the acidity in the stomach. Caffeine binds iron and calcium and slows down their absorption, so try not to drink beverages containing caffeine with your meals.

Coffee is the highest source of caffeine, followed by teas, colas and chocolate. You should have no more than 2-3 daily servings of beverages containing caffeine. Once you begin to cut back on caffeine, you will go through a physical withdrawal just as you do when you cut back on sugar. Caffeine and sugar withdrawal can give you a headache which may last a few days. But don't give up; it will go away and you'll be a lot healthier in the end. You can cut down on the symptoms of withdrawal by eating regular meals and snacks evenly paced throughout the day. Also, withdraw slowly; don't give them up cold turkey.

Are decaffeinated beverages healthy?

Decaffeinated teas and colas are different from decaffeinated coffee. Coffee naturally contains caffeine, as it is in the coffee bean itself. Therefore, to remove the caffeine, it must go through chemical processing. Some coffees are decaffeinated through a natural process called "Swiss water washing," and these are the better ones to choose.

For decaffeinated colas, caffeine is simply not added when they produce the beverage. As for teas, only the part of the leaf that has no caffeine is used so that chemical processing is not necessary.

Do coffee, tea and diet sodas count towards my 6-8 cups water requirement for the day? NO

When it comes to beverages, most of us do not drink enough water. Most of us drink soft drinks, coffees and teas. But water is a vital nutrient. Water is a natural diuretic so it prevents excess fluid retention. The more water you drink, the less water you retain. It is important for healthy-looking skin and for removing waste products from the body.

Alcohol

Alcohol contributes to the problem of overloading calories in the evening, especially if it is mixed with other high-calorie items such as bitter lemon, tonic water, colas and sweet mixes like pina coladas and margaritas.

You can include alcohol in your healthy plan if it is consumed in moderation. A moderate intake means no more than one 355 millilitre (12 ounce) 5% alcoholic beer or 150 millilitres (5 ounce) dry wine or 45 millilitres (1-1/2 ounces) liquor. However, some people find alcohol hard to moderate. More than a moderate intake puts you at risk for high blood pressure, heart disease, stroke and obesity. Alcohol's effects may also increase appetite and set you up for excessive eating.

Alcohol is a concentrated source of calories, especially the sweet liqueurs, sherries, sweet wines and hard liquor. Water down your drinks as much as possible, to give the greatest volume for the least number of calories. Try adding soda water or mineral water to wine, and diet tonic, sugar-free soda or water to hard liquor. Light beer is already watered down, so it is one of the lighter alcoholic beverage choices.

Part III
What Shall I Eat?
(The Healthy Weigh Low-Fat Food Plans)

Keep a Daily Food and Exercise Diary

Keeping a record of the foods you eat daily will increase your awareness of when and what you eat. This increased awareness can help you change unhealthy habits into healthy ones.

Just by taking the time to record what you eat, you will find yourself naturally eating better and getting closer to a healthier you.

All it takes is a few minutes a day!

How to Record in Your Daily Diary

1. Record the time of your meal or snack. Also record the duration (i.e., 1:00-1:30 p.m.). This will help you become aware of problems you may have with eating too quickly.

2. Record all beverages and food consumed. Be specific—record the amount and type of milk (e.g., "250 ml 2% milk" instead of "milk"), or the amount and type of chicken (e.g.,"85 grams boneless, skinless chicken breast" instead of "chicken").

3. Record the exercise you do for the day. Be sure to include the type and the duration (e.g., "jogging for 30 minutes" instead of "jogging").

4. Once you get used to using the daily diary, you can also use it to plan what you will eat and how you will exercise the next day. If you eat or exercise differently than planned, be sure to record the changes.

Week 1 **Day:** **Date:**

Time	Food & Beverage	Amount	Exercise (type)	Duration

Totals:

Number of Servings:

____ lean protein
____ low-fat dairy
____ starchy foods (grains, potato, corn)
____ fruits
____ vegetables
____ added fats
____ other foods

Exercise: ____

Women's Weight-Loss Plan

Totals for the day:

2-1/2	servings protein
2	servings dairy
6	servings starchy foods (grains, potato, corn)
4	servings fruits
free	servings vegetables
2	servings added fats
2	servings other foods

1. Regulate meal and snack times.

2. Combine protein foods and carbohydrate foods at every meal.

3. Divide food into at least 3-5 intakes during the day (e.g., breakfast, lunch, supper and 1-2 snacks).

4. Intakes should not be more than 5 hours apart during the day.

5. Drink 6-8 glasses of water daily.

6. Use as desired: herbs, spices, lemon/lime juice, vinegar, broth soups, mustard, tea, coffee, sugar-free gelatin, sugar-free soft drinks, fat-free Italian dressings, sugar substitutes, extracts (e.g., vanilla).

7. Familiarize yourself with portion size. We do not expect you to go through life weighing and measuring everything you eat. However, we recommend that you weigh food when you first start your plan to familiarize yourself with the right portion sizes for yourself. Our plan will have you eating the right foods at the right times. As a result, you will be satisfied with less food.

My Personalized Food Plan

Create your own personalized food plan.

Take your totals for each category and spread them into meals and 2-3 snacks (an example follows on the next page).

Breakfast

____

____

____

____

____

____

A.M. Snack

____

Lunch

____

____

____

____

____

P.M. Snack

____

Supper

____

____

____

____

____

____

Evening Snack

____

Personalized Meal Plan – Women's Weight Loss

Breakfast

1 serving dairy ______

1 serving starchy foods ______

1 serving fruit ______

A.M. Snack

1 serving fruit ______

Lunch

1 serving protein ______

2 servings starchy foods ______

free servings vegetables ______

1 serving added fat ______

P.M. Snack

1 serving dairy ______

1 serving starchy foods ______

Supper

1-1/2 servings protein ______

2 servings starchy foods ______

free servings vegetables ______

1 serving added fat ______

1 serving fruit ______

Evening Snack

1 serving fruit ______

* 2 servings "other foods" any time during the day

*drink 6-8 glasses of water daily

Serving Size Examples – Women's Weight Loss

1 Serving of Protein:
- 56 grams (2 oz.) fish, skinless poultry or lean meat *or*
- 1-2 eggs *or*
- 250 ml (1 cup) cooked legumes *or*
- 125 ml (1/2 cup) tofu

1 Serving Starchy Foods
Grains
- 125 ml (1/2 cup) cooked rice, barley, couscous or bulgar *or*
- 125 ml (1/2 cup) cooked pasta *or*
- 125 ml (1/2 cup) cereal *or*
- 250 (1 cup) non-cream soup *or*
- 4 crackers *or*
- 1 slice bread or 1/2 roll

Potato
- 1 medium potato

Corn
- 1 ear corn (125 ml/1/2 cup)

1 Serving Added Fats:
- 5 ml (1 t.) oil, mayonnaise, butter or margarine *or*
- 15 ml (1 T.) diet mayonnaise, diet margarine, diet butter, sour cream, nuts, seeds, or regular salad dressing *or*
- 30 ml (2 T.) light salad dressing or peanut butter

1 Serving of Low-Fat Dairy:
- 250 ml (1 cup) low-fat milk or yogurt *or*
- 42 grams (1-1/2 oz.) low-fat cheese *or*
- 125 ml (1/2 cup) low-fat cottage cheese, quark or ricotta

1 Serving Fruit:
- 1 medium fruit; 125 ml (1/2 cup) chopped fruit *or*
- 30 ml (2 T.) dried fruit

1 Serving Vegetables:
(as much as you want)

1 Serving Other Foods:
Snack Foods
- 750 ml (3 cups) air-popped popcorn *or*
- 125 ml (1/2 cup) pretzels *or*
- 125 ml (1/2 cup) no-oil tortilla chips *or*
- 1 sugar-free hot chocolate *or*
- 2 plain cookies *or*
- 1 frozen dessert bar (less than 50 calories each)

Alcohol
- 355 ml (12 oz.) light beer *or*
- 45 ml (3 oz.) dry wine *or*
- 45 ml (3 oz.) hard liquor

Sauces/Spreads
(use in moderation)

A1 Sauce
All-fruit jam
BBQ sauce
Black bean sauce
Chili sauce (no meat)
Chutney
Cocktail sauce
Cooking wine
Enchilada sauce
Extracts (i.e., vanilla)
Soy sauce (low-sodium)
Soup bases (non-cream)
Hoisin sauce
Honey
Honey garlic sauce
Sweet & sour sauce
Honey BBQ sauce
Horseradish
Teriyaki sauce (low-sodium)
Hot sauce
Ketchup
Tomato sauce/paste
Maple syrup
Mint sauce
Mustard
Oyster sauce
Pasta sauce; red
Picante sauce
Plum sauce
Relish
Salsa
Stir-fry sauce
Sugar
Taco sauce

Breakfasts – Women's Weight Loss

Cereal & Fruit
-125 ml (1/2 cup) cereal
-250 ml (1 cup) low-fat milk or yogurt or 125 ml (1/2 cup) low-fat cottage cheese
-1 fresh fruit

Cheese & Toast
-1/2 bagel or 1/2 English muffin *or* 1 slice bread or 2 slices 40-calorie bread
-45 grams (1-1/2 oz.) low-fat cheese or 125 ml (1/2 cup) low-fat cottage cheese
-1 fresh fruit

Milkshake
-250 ml (1 cup) low-fat milk mixed in blender with 3-5 ice cubes, 5 ml (1 t.) vanilla flavouring and 125 ml (1/2 cup) fresh or frozen fruit
-125 ml (1/2 cup) cereal or 1/2 bagel or 1/2 English muffin or 1 slice bread or 2 slices 40-calorie bread
-(optional) 5 ml (1 t.) all-fruit jam

Egg & Toast
-1/2 bagel or 1/2 English muffin or 1 slice bread or 2 slices 40-calorie bread
-1 whole egg or 2 whites (cooked with non-stick spray)
-1 fresh fruit
-(optional) 250 ml (1 cup) vegetables

French Toast
-2 slices 40-calorie bread soaked in egg whites and skim milk and fried using non-stick spray
-30 ml (2 T.) low-calories syrup or 15 ml (1 T.) regular syrup
-1 fresh fruit or 125 ml (1/2 cup) fruit salad
- 125 ml (1/2 cup) low-fat milk

Breakfast Out
-1/2 English muffin or 1/2 bagel or 1 slice toast (no butter or margarine) or 125 ml 1/2 cup) cereal
-1 poached egg or 1 boiled egg or 28 grams (1 oz.) cheese or 250 ml (1 cup) low-fat milk or 250 ml (1 cup) low-fat yogurt
-1 fresh fruit or 125 ml (1/2 cup) fruit salad

Lunches – Women's Weight Loss

Sandwich & Soup Or Salad
-1 roll or 2 slices bread or one 6" pita
-56 grams (2 oz.) lean sliced turkey, chicken, ham or roast beef (mustard, lettuce, tomato)
-all-vegetable salad or "cooked vegetables" (no fat)
- 5 ml (1t.) margarine or butter or 15 ml (1T.) regular salad dressing or 30ml (2T.) light dressing

Salad & Roll
-1 roll or English muffin
-all-vegetable salad
-125 ml (1/2 cup) water-packed tuna or salmon or 180 ml (3/4 cup) cooked legumes or 56 grams (2 oz.) ham or roast beef
-5 ml (1 t.) margarine or butter or mayonnaise or 15 ml (1 T.) regular salad dressing or 30 ml (2 T.) light dressing

Soup & Salad
-4 soda crackers or 4 melba toast
-250 ml (1 cup) non-cream soup
-1 all-vegetable salad topped with 56 grams (2 oz.) lean chicken, turkey, ham, roast beef or 125 ml (1/2 cup) water-packed tuna or salmon (no mayo) or 180

ml (3/4 cup) cooked legumes
-15 ml (1 T.) Parmesan cheese (optional)
-30 ml (2 T.) light dressing

Fast Food Sandwich

Tell the waiter:
No mayonnaise, no butter, no margarine, no special sauce on my sandwich or burger.

Please put the dressing on the side of the salad. Do you have any light salad dressings?

Hold the topping on the frozen yogurt.

Serve my potato plain. Do you have any cottage cheese or yogurt instead of butter or sour cream?

-grilled chicken breast sandwich with lettuce & tomato & mustard (no mayo) and side salad with light dressing
or
-turkey mini sub or snack sub (no cheese, mayo or oil) and side salad with light dressing
or
-single hamburger 56 grams (2 oz.) or junior burger 56 grams (2 oz.) (no mayo) and side salad with light dressing
or
-junior roast beef sandwich (no mayo, no butter) and side salad with light dressing

Fast Food Potato & Salad

Tell the waiter:
Serve my potato plain. Do you have any cottage cheese or yogurt instead of butter or sour cream?

Please serve my salad with dressing on the side. Please bring vinegar or lemon.

-1 baked potato
-125 ml (1/2 cup) low-fat cottage cheese or 250 ml (1 cup) yogurt or chili
-all-vegetable salad
-(optional) 5 ml (1 t.) margarine or butter or 15 ml (1 T.) sour cream or regular salad dressing or 30 ml (2 T.) light salad dressing
or
-1 baked potato (plain)
-1 grilled chicken salad
-(optional) 5 ml (1 t.) margarine or butter or 15 ml (1 T.) sour cream or regular salad dressing or 30 ml (2 T.) light salad dressing

Italian

Tell the waiter:
Prepare my dish without oil, butter, margarine, cream and cheese; sauces to the side.

Please put the dressing on the side of my salad and bring vinegar or lemon.

Can I get a half portion of the entree?

Can you replace the cream sauce with a fat-free tomato sauce?

-appetizer portion of pasta with red clam or marinara or tomato sauce (no oil) and 30 ml (2 T.) Parmesan cheese (optional) + steamed vegetables or all-vegetable salad
-15 ml (1 T.) regular salad dressing or 30 ml (2 T.) light dressing (optional)
or
-250 ml (1 cup) minestrone soup
-1 all-vegetable salad and 30 ml (2 T.) Parmesan cheese (optional)
-15 ml (1 T.) regular salad dressing or 30 ml (2 T.) light dressing (optional)
or

- 1 slice from 35 cm (14") pizza (vegetables and regular cheese) with 1 side salad (no oil)
-15 ml (1 T.) regular salad dressing or 30 ml (2 T.) light dressing (optional)

Chinese

Tell the waiter:
Prepare my dishes with no oil, butter or margarine.

-250 ml (1 cup) hot & sour soup or egg drop soup with 250 ml (1 cup) steamed rice
or
-500 ml (2 cups) vegetable chow mein with chicken, beef or pork + 250 ml (1 cup) steamed rice
or
-500 ml (2 cups) stir-fried vegetables with chicken, beef, tofu or pork (no oil) and 250 ml (1 cup) steamed rice

French/Continental

Tell the waiter:
Prepare my meal without oil, butter, margarine and cream; sauces to the side.

Please put the dressing on the side of the salad. Please bring vinegar or lemon.

Can I get cottage cheese, yogurt or dijon mustard instead of butter or sour cream for my baked potato?

-steamed mussels in broth or tomato sauce (no oil) and 1 roll
or
-56 grams (2 oz.) poached or teriyaki or creole chicken (no skin) or fish with 250 ml (1 cup) steamed rice or baked potato and steamed vegetables or salad (no oil)
-(optional) 5 ml (1 t.) margarine or butter or 15 ml (1 T.) sour cream or regular salad dressing or 30 ml (2 T.) light salad dressing

Chicken

Tell the waiter:
Please put the dressing on the side of the salad. Please bring vinegar or lemon.

Serve the gravy to the side of my chicken or sandwich.

Serve my potato plain. Do you have any cottage cheese or yogurt instead of butter or sour cream?

-chicken sandwich (no gravy) with side salad
-(optional) 15 ml (1 T.) regular salad dressing or 30 ml (2 T.) light dressing
or
-chicken salad with baked potato or roll
-(optional) 5 ml (1 t.) margarine or butter or 15 ml (1 T.) sour cream or regular salad dressing or 30 ml (2 T.) light salad dressing

Suppers – Women's Weight Loss

Chicken

Tell the waiter:
Please put the dressing on the side of the salad. Please bring vinegar or lemon.

Serve the gravy to the side of my chicken or sandwich.
Serve my potato plain. Do you have any cottage cheese or yogurt instead of butter or sour cream?

-1/4 chicken dinner (no skin, no wing) with baked potato and side salad and 1 fruit

-(optional) 5 ml (1 t.) margarine or butter or 15 ml (1 T.) sour cream or regular salad dressing or 30 ml (2 T.) light salad dressing
or
-chicken sandwich (no gravy) with side salad and soup (non-cream) and 1 fruit
-(optional) 15 ml (1 T.) regular salad dressing or 30 ml (2 T.) light dressing
or
-salad topped with chicken strips (no mayo) and soup or baked potato or roll and 1 fruit
-(optional) 5 ml (1 t.) margarine or butter or 15 ml (1 T.) sour cream or regular salad dressing or 30 ml (2 T.) light salad dressing

Fish and Seafood

Tell the waiter:
Prepare my fish and vegetables without oil, butter or margarine; sauces to the side.

Please substitute a baked potato for the french fries. Can I get cottage cheese, yogurt or dijon mustard for my baked potato instead of butter or sour cream?

Please put the dressing on the side of the salad. Please bring vinegar or lemon.

-shrimp cocktail or steamed clams or steamed mussels or Manhattan clam chowder with side salad and roll and 1 fruit
-(optional) 15 ml (1 T.) regular salad dressing or 30 ml (2 T.) light dressing
or
-appetizer portion of fish bouillabaise with side salad and roll and 1 fruit
-(optional) 15 ml (1 T.) regular salad dressing or 30 ml (2 T.) light dressing
or
-85 grams (3 oz.) poached or teriyaki or creole fish with 250 ml (1 cup) rice or 1 baked potato and steamed vegetables and 1 fruit
-(optional) 5 ml (1 t.) margarine or butter or 15 ml (1 T.) sour cream
or
-450 grams (1 lb.) steamed lobster or crab legs and baked potato with side salad and 1 fruit
-(optional) 5 ml (1 t.) margarine or butter or 15 ml (1 T.) sour cream or regular salad dressing or 30 ml (2 T.) light salad dressing

Pizza

Tell the waiter:
Can I get less cheese and double vegetables on my pizza?

Please put the dressing on the side of the salad. Please bring vinegar or lemon.

-1 slice from a 35 cm (14") pizza (vegetable and regular cheese)
-side salad (no oil)
-1 fruit
-(optional) 15 ml (1 T.) regular salad dressing or 30 ml (2 T.) light dressing
or
-1 non-cream soup
-1 personal pan pizza (cheese and vegetables) and side salad (no oil)
-1 fruit
-(optional) 15 ml (1 T.) regular salad dressing or 30 ml (2 T.) light dressing

Fast Food

Tell the waiter:
No mayonnaise, no butter, no margarine or special sauce on my sandwich or burger.

Dressing to the side of the salad. Do you have any light salad dressing?

Hold the topping on the frozen yogurt.

Serve my potato plain. Do you have any cottage cheese or yogurt instead of butter or sour cream?

-1 baked potato topped with 250 ml (1 cup) chili or cottage cheese and 1 all-vegetable salad (no oil)
-1 fruit
-(optional) 15 ml (1 T.) regular salad dressing or 30 ml (2 T.) light dressing
or
-1 baked potato and 1 grilled chicken salad (no oil) and 1 fruit
-(optional) 5 ml (1 t.) margarine or butter or 15 ml (1 T.) sour cream or regular salad dressing or 30 ml (2 T.) light salad dressing
or
-1 McLean (McDonald's) burger or Light (Harvey's) burger or 1 grilled chicken sandwich (no mayo) or 1 Arby's Junior Roast Beef Sandwich (no butter)
-side salad (no oil)
-1 fruit
-(optional) 15 ml (1 T.) regular salad dressing or 30 ml (2 T.) light dressing
or
-1 junior seafood or turkey sub (no cheese, no mayo, no oil, no sauce, mustard only) with 250 ml (1 cup) vegetable soup or 1 side salad (no oil)
-1 fruit
-(optional) 15 ml (1 T.) regular salad dressing or 30 ml (2 T.) light dressing
or
-1 single junior 56 gram (2 oz.) burger (no mayo) with 1 side salad and 1 small frozen yogurt and 1 fruit
-(optional) 15 ml (1 T.) regular salad dressing or 30 ml (2 T.) light dressing

Middle Eastern (Greek, Israeli, Armenian)

Tell the waiter:
Prepare my dish without oil, butter or mayonnaise; sauces to the side.

Please put the dressing, feta cheese and olives on the side of the salad.

Please serve me an appetizer portion and bring it when you bring the others their entree.

Please serve me steamed rice or a plain pita instead of the potatoes. Please serve the vegetables steamed without fat.

-1 pork, chicken or lamb shish kabob (no oil) with 250 ml (1 cup) rice or 1 pita
-steamed vegetables (no oil)
-side salad (no oil)
-1 fruit
-(optional) 15 ml (1 T.) regular salad dressing or 30 ml (2 T.) light dressing
or
-Greek salad (no oil)
-lentil soup
-appetizer portion of dolma (no oil)
-1 fruit
-(optional) 15 ml (1 T.) regular salad dressing or 30 ml (2 T.) light dressing

Chinese

Tell the waiter:
Prepare my dishes without oil, butter or margarine.

-wonton soup or hot & sour soup or egg drop soup and 250 ml (1 cup) stir-fried vegetables (no oil) with chicken, fish, pork or tofu and 125 ml (1/2 cup) steamed rice
-1 fruit
or
-Chinese vegetable soup

-500 ml (2 cups) stir-fried vegetables (no oil) with chicken, fish, pork or tofu and 250 ml (1 cup) steamed rice and 1 fruit
or
-Chinese vegetable soup
-500 ml (2 cups) chow mein (no oil) with chicken, fish, pork or tofu and 250 ml (1 cup) steamed rice and 1 fruit
or
-Chinese vegetable soup
-250 ml (1 cup) moo shi shrimp and broccoli and 250 ml (1 cup) steamed rice and 1 fruit
or
-Chinese vegetable soup
-250 ml (1 cup) beef or shrimp with broccoli and 250 ml (1 cup) steamed rice and 1 fruit
or
-Chinese vegetable soup
-250 ml (1 cup) moo goo gai pan and 250 ml (1 cup) steamed rice and 1 fruit
or
-Chinese vegetable soup
-85 grams (3 oz.) Szechuan fish, pork, chicken or beef (or in blackbean sauce) and 250 ml (1 cup) steamed rice and 500 ml (2 cups) stir-fried vegetables (no oil) and 1 fruit

French/Continental/Canadian

Tell the waiter:
Prepare my meal without oil, butter, margarine and cream; sauces to the side.

Please put the dressing on the side of the salad. Please bring vinegar or lemon.

Can I get cottage cheese, yogurt or dijon mustard for my baked potato instead of butter or sour cream?

-steamed mussels or clams in broth or tomato sauce (no oil) and all-vegetable salad and 1 roll
-1 fruit
-(optional) 15 ml (1 T.) regular salad dressing or 30 ml (2 T.) light dressing
or
-85 grams (3 oz.) poached or teriyaki or creole chicken (no skin) or fish with 250 ml (1 cup) rice or 1 baked potato and steamed vegetables and 1 fruit
-(optional) 5 ml (1 t.) margarine or butter or 15 ml (1 T.) sour cream
or
-85 grams (3 oz.) filet mignon with 1 baked potato and side salad or steamed vegetables and 1 fruit
-(optional) 15 ml (1 T.) regular salad dressing or 30 ml (2 T.) light dressing
or
-500 ml (2 cups) chicken/fish/pork/beef stir-fry (no oil) and 250 ml (1 cup) steamed rice and 1 fruit
or
-250 ml (1 cup) vegetable soup, turkey sandwich or grilled chicken sandwich (no mayo) with side salad and 1 fruit
-(optional) 15 ml (1 T.) regular salad dressing or 30 ml (2 T.) light dressing

Japanese

Tell the waiter:
Prepare my meal without oil, butter or margarine; sauces to the side.

Please put the dressing on the side of the salad. Please bring vinegar or lemon.

-miso soup or suimono soup
-500 ml (2 cups) stir-fried vegetables with chicken, beef or pork (no oil) and 250 ml (1 cup) steamed rice and 1 fruit
or
-miso soup or suimono soup
-yakitori (appetizer portion) and 250 ml (1 cup) steamed rice and 1 fruit

or
-miso soup or suimono soup
-100 grams (4 oz.) sushi and side salad (no oil) and 1 fruit
or
-miso soup or suimono soup
-85 grams (3 oz.) teriyaki beef or chicken or pork or fish with 250 ml (1 cup) steamed rice and 500 ml (2 cups) stir-fried vegetables (no oil) and 1 fruit

Thai

Tell the waiter:
Prepare my dishes without oil, butter or margarine.

Prepare my dish without nuts.

Please put the dressing on the side of the salad. Please bring vinegar or lemon.

-2 beef or chicken satay (no oil, no sauce) with side salad and 250 ml (1 cup) steamed rice and 1 fruit
or
-steamed mussels or clams with side salad and 250 ml (1 cup) steamed rice and 1 fruit
or
-tom yum koong (shrimp soup) or talay thong (seafood soup) with 250 ml (1 cup) steamed rice and side salad and 1 fruit
-(optional) 15 ml (1 T.) regular salad dressing or 30 ml (2 T.) light dressing
or
-85 grams (3 oz.) Thai chicken (no nuts) or beef basil or scallops bamboo or chili beef or ginger pork with 250 ml (1 cup) steamed rice and side salad and 1 fruit
-(optional) 15 ml (1 T.) regular salad dressing or 30 ml (2 T.) light dressing
or
-500 ml (2 cups) poy sian (seafood and vegetables) or pork and string beans with 250 ml (1 cup) steamed rice and 1 fruit

Mexican

Tell the waiter:
Prepare my dishes without oil, butter or margarine, cheese or cream.

Serve the cheese, sour cream, guacamole and refried beans on the side.

Please put extra shredded lettuce, tomatoes and onions on the plate.

Please put the dressing on the side of the salad. Please bring vinegar or lemon.

-gazpacho or black bean soup
-1 chicken taco (no cheese, no oil) and salsa and side salad and 1 fruit
-(optional) 15 ml (1 T.) regular salad dressing or 30 ml (2 T.) light dressing
or
-1 beef or chicken fajita (no oil, no cheese, no sour cream) and tossed side salad and 1 fruit
-(optional) 15 ml (1 T.) regular salad dressing or 30 ml (2 T.) light dressing
or
-1 chicken burrito (cheese on side) with tossed salad and 1 fruit
-(optional) 15 ml (1 T.) regular salad dressing or 30 ml (2 T.) light dressing
or
-250 ml (1 cup) chili con carne with 250 ml (1 cup) Mexican rice (not fried) and side salad and 1 fruit
-(optional) 15 ml (1 T.) regular salad dressing or 30 ml (2 T.) light dressing

Continental

-250 ml (1 cup) cooked rice or pasta or 1 baked potato
-85 grams (3 oz.) skinless poultry or lean meat (beef, lamb, veal, pork) or fish
-vegetables, raw or cooked (no oil)
-1 fruit
or

-375 ml (1-1/2 cups) cooked pasta with 180 ml (3/4 cup) red pasta sauce and 45 ml (3 T.) Parmesan cheese
-vegetables, raw or cooked (no oil)
-1 fruit

Vegetarian
-250 ml (1 cup) cooked rice and 250 ml (1 cup) cooked beans or lentils
-vegetables, raw or cooked (no oil)
-1 fruit
-(optional) 15 ml (1 T.) Parmesan cheese
or
-250 ml (1 cup) vegetable or cabbage or onion soup, extended with 500-750 (2-3 cups) chopped vegetables and 125 ml (1/2 cup) cooked rice or pasta and 250 ml (1 cup) cooked legumes
-spices/herbs to flavour
-30 ml (2 T.) Parmesan cheese
-4 melba toast or soda crackers or 1 slice bread or 1/2 roll
-1 fruit

Italian
Tell the waiter:
Prepare my dish without butter, margarine, cream and cheese; sauces to the side.

Please put the dressing on the side of the salad. Please bring vinegar or lemon.

Can I get a half portion of the entree?

Can you replace the cream sauce with a fat-free tomato sauce?

-appetizer portion of pasta with red clam sauce or marinara sauce, or pasta primavera (red sauce) or shrimp primavera
-side salad or steamed vegetables (no oil)
-1 fruit
-(optional) 15 ml (1 T.) regular salad dressing or 30 ml (2 T.) light dressing
or
-appetizer portion 85 grams (3 oz.) shrimp marinara or filet of sole with tomato sauce
-250 ml (1 cup) pasta with 30-45 ml (2-3 T.) tomato sauce
-side salad or steamed vegetables (no oil)
-1 fruit

Soup & Salad
-250 ml (1 cup) non-cream soup
-4 crackers or 1 slice bread
-1 all-vegetable salad topped with 85 grams (3 oz.) lean chicken, turkey, ham, roast beef or 180 ml (3/4 cup) water-packed tuna or salmon or 250 ml (1 cup) cooked legumes
-1 fruit
-(optional) 15 ml (1 T.) regular salad dressing or 30 ml (2 T.) light dressing

Salad Bar
-fresh vegetables (no oil, no mayo)
-180 ml (3/4 cup) chicken or turkey (no mayo) or cottage cheese or cooked legumes
-125 ml (1/2 cup) fresh fruit salad
-30 ml (2 T.) Parmesan cheese
-30 ml (2 T.) low-calorie dressing
-1 roll or 2 slices bread

Snacks – Women's Weight Loss
(choose any 2 daily)

- 28 grams (1 oz.) low-fat cheese or 125 ml (1/2 cup) low-fat milk or yogurt
- Vegetable sticks—plain or marinated in fat-free Italian dressing
- Vegetable sticks with 125 ml (1/2 cup) low-fat dip

- 125 ml (1/2 cup) low-fat milk blended with 2-3 ice cubes, vanilla flavouring and 15 ml (1T.) maple or chocolate syrup or 125 ml (1/2 cup) fruit

- 1 light hot chocolate

- 1 light fudgsicle

- 250 ml (1 cup) vegetable soup topped with 30 ml (2 T.) Parmesan cheese

- 28 grams (1 oz.) low-fat cheese
  4 crackers or 1 slice bread or 1 fruit *or*
  1 small box raisins

- 125 ml (1/2 cup) low-fat milk or yogurt
  125 ml (1/2 cup) cereal

- 750 ml (3 cups) air-popped popcorn
  30 ml (2 T.) Parmesan cheese

- 1 fruit
  125 ml (1/2 cup) low-fat yogurt

- 1/2 medium baked potato
  30 ml (2 T.) low-fat cottage cheese
  or yogurt topping

- 2 plain cookies
  250 ml (1 cup) low-fat milk

Women's Maintenance/Men's Weight-Loss Plan

Totals for the day:

3	servings protein
3	servings dairy
8	servings starchy foods (grains, potato, corn)
5	servings fruits
free	servings vegetables
3	servings added fats
3	servings other foods

1. Regulate meal and snack times.

2. Combine protein foods and carbohydrate foods at every meal.

3. Divide food into at least 3-5 intakes during the day (e.g., breakfast, lunch, supper and 1-2 snacks).

4. Intakes should not be more than 5 hours apart during the day.

5. Drink 6-8 glasses of water daily.

6. Use as desired: herbs, spices, lemon/lime juice, vinegar, broth soups, mustard, tea, coffee, sugar-free gelatin, sugar-free soft drinks, fat-free Italian dressings, sugar substitutes, extracts (e.g., vanilla).

7. Familiarize yourself with portion size. We do not expect you to go through life weighing and measuring everything you eat. However, we recommend that you weigh food when you first start your plan to familiarize yourself with the right portion sizes for yourself. Our plan will have you eating the right foods at the right times. As a result, you will be satisfied with less food.

My Personalized Food Plan

Create your own personalized food plan.

Take your totals for each category and spread them into meals and 2-3 snacks (an example follows on the next page).

Breakfast

____
____
____
____
____
____

A.M. Snack

____

Lunch

____
____
____
____
____

P.M. Snack

____

Supper

____
____
____
____
____
____

Evening Snack

____

Personalized Meal Plan – Women's Maintenance/Men's Weight Loss

Breakfast

1 serving dairy
2 servings starchy foods
1 serving fruit
1 serving added fat

A.M. Snack

1 serving fruit

Lunch

1 serving dairy
1 serving protein
2 servings starchy foods
free servings vegetables
1 serving added fat
1 serving fruit

P.M. Snack

1 serving dairy
1 serving starchy foods

Supper

2 servings protein
3 servings starchy foods
free servings vegetables
1 serving added fat
1 serving fruit

Evening Snack

1 serving fruit

* 3 servings "other foods" any time during the day

*drink 6-8 glasses of water daily

Serving Size Examples – Women's Maintenance/Men's Weight Loss

1 Serving of Protein:
- 56 grams (2 oz.) fish, skinless poultry or lean meat *or*
- 1-2 eggs *or*
- 250 ml (1 cup) cooked legumes *or*
- 125 ml (1/2 cup) tofu

1 Serving Starchy Foods
Grains
- 125 ml (1/2 cup) cooked rice, barley, couscous or bulgar *or*
- 125 ml (1/2 cup) cooked pasta *or*
- 125 ml (1/2 cup) cereal *or*
- 250 (1 cup) non-cream soup *or*
- 4 crackers *or*
- 1 slice bread or 1/2 roll

Potato
- 1 medium potato

Corn
- 1 ear corn (125 ml/1/2 cup)

1 Serving Added Fats:
- 5 ml (1 t.) oil, mayonnaise, butter or margarine *or*
- 15 ml (1 T.) diet mayonnaise, diet margarine, diet butter, sour cream, nuts, seeds, or regular salad dressing *or*
- 30 ml (2 T.) light salad dressing or peanut butter

1 Serving of Low-Fat Dairy:
- 250 ml (1 cup) low-fat milk or yogurt *or*
- 42 grams (1-1/2 oz.) low-fat cheese *or*
- 125 ml (1/2 cup) low-fat cottage cheese, quark or ricotta

1 Serving Fruit:
- 1 medium fruit; 125 ml (1/2 cup) chopped fruit *or*
- 30 ml (2 T.) dried fruit

1 Serving Vegetables:
(as much as you want)

1 Serving Other Foods:
Snack Foods
- 750 ml (3 cups) air-popped popcorn *or*
- 125 ml (1/2 cup) pretzels *or*
- 125 ml (1/2 cup) no-oil tortilla chips *or*
- 1 sugar-free hot chocolate *or*
- 2 plain cookies *or*
- 1 frozen dessert bar (less than 50 calories each)

Alcohol
- 355 ml (12 oz.) light beer *or*
- 45 ml (3 oz.) dry wine *or*
- 45 ml (3 oz.) hard liquor

Sauces/Spreads
(use in moderation)

A1 Sauce
All-fruit jam
BBQ sauce
Black bean sauce
Chili sauce (no meat)
Chutney
Cocktail sauce
Cooking wine
Enchilada sauce
Extracts (i.e., vanilla)
Soy sauce (low-sodium)
Soup bases (non-cream)
Hoisin sauce
Honey
Honey garlic sauce
Sweet & sour sauce
Honey BBQ sauce
Horseradish
Teriyaki sauce (low-sodium)
Hot sauce
Ketchup
Tomato sauce/paste
Maple syrup
Mint sauce
Mustard
Oyster sauce
Pasta sauce; red
Picante sauce
Plum sauce
Relish
Salsa
Stir-fry sauce
Sugar
Taco sauce

Breakfasts – Women's Maintenance/ Men's Weight Loss

Cereal & Fruit

-125 ml (1/2 cup) cereal
-1 slice toast or 1/2 small bagel or 1/2 English muffin or additional 125 ml (1/2 cup) cereal
-(optional) 5 ml (1 t.) all-fruit jam
-250 ml (1 cup) low-fat milk or yogurt or 125 ml (1/2 cup) low-fat cottage cheese
-1 piece fresh fruit or 125 ml (1/2 cup) fruit salad
- (optional) 5ml (1t.) margarine or butter

Cheese & Toast

-1 small bagel or English muffin or 2 slices bread or 1 roll
-45 grams (1-1/2 oz.) low-fat cheese or 125 ml (1/2 cup) low-fat cottage cheese
-1 piece fresh fruit
- (optional) 5ml (1t.) margarine or butter

Milkshake

-250 ml (1 cup) low-fat milk mixed in blender with 3-5 ice cubes, 5 ml (1 t.) vanilla flavouring and 125 ml (1/2 cup) fresh or frozen fruit
-250 ml (1 cup) cereal or 1 small bagel or 1 English muffin or 2 slices of bread or 1 roll
-(optional) 10 ml (2 t.) all-fruit jam
- (optional) 5ml (1t.) margarine or butter

Egg & Toast

-1 small bagel or English muffin or roll or 2 slices bread
-1 whole egg or 2 whites (cooked with non-stick spray)
-1 fresh fruit
- (optional) 5ml (1t.) margarine or butter
-(optional) 250 ml (1 cup) vegetables

French Toast (or pancakes or waffles)

-2 slices bread soaked in egg whites and skim milk and fried using non-stick spray or two 6" pancakes cooked with non-stick spray or 2 waffles
-30 ml (2 T.) low-calories syrup or 15 ml (1 T.) regular syrup
-1 fresh fruit or 125 ml (1/2 cup) fruit salad
- (optional) 5ml (1t.) margarine or butter

Breakfast Out

-1 English muffin or 1 small bagel or 2 slices toast (no butter or margarine) or 250 ml (1 cup) cereal
-1 poached egg or 1 boiled egg or 28 grams (1 oz.) cheese or 250 ml (1 cup) low-fat milk or 250 ml (1 cup) low-fat yogurt
-1 fresh fruit or 125 ml (1/2 cup) fruit salad
- (optional) 5ml (1t.) margarine or butter

Lunches – Women's Maintenance/ Men's Weight Loss

Sandwich & Soup Or Salad

-1 roll or 2 slices bread or one 6" pita
-56 grams (2 oz.) lean sliced turkey, chicken, ham or roast beef (mustard, lettuce, tomato)
- 250 ml (1 cup) low-fat milk or yogurt or 42 grams (1 1/2 oz.) low-fat cheese
-all-vegetable salad or "cooked vegetables" (no fat) or 250 ml (1 cup) vegetable soup
-1 fruit
-(optional) 5 ml (1 t.) margarine or butter

or mayonnaise or 15 ml (1 T.) light mayonnaise or regular salad dressing or 30 ml (2 T.) light dressing

Salad & Roll

-1 roll or English muffin
-all-vegetable salad
-125 ml (1/2 cup) water-packed tuna or salmon or 250 ml (1 cup) cottage cheese or 180 ml (3/4 cup) cooked legumes or 56 grams (2 oz.) lean sliced chicken, turkey, ham or roast beef
- 250 ml (1 cup) low-fat milk or yogurt or 42 grams (1 1/2 oz.) low-fat cheese
-1 fruit
-(optional) 5 ml (1 t.) margarine or butter or mayonnaise or 15 ml (1 T.) light mayonnaise or regular salad dressing or 30 ml (2 T.) light dressing

Soup & Salad

-1 roll or 2 slices bread
-250 ml (1 cup) non-cream soup
-1 all-vegetable salad topped with 56 grams (2 oz.) lean chicken, turkey, ham, roast beef or 250 ml (1 cup) water-packed tuna or salmon or 125 ml (1/2 cups) cooked legumes
- 250 ml (1 cup) low-fat milk *or*
42 grams (1 1/2 oz.) low-fat cheese
-(optional) 15 ml (1 T.) regular salad dressing or 30 ml (2 T.) light dressing

Fast Food Sandwich

Tell the waiter:
No mayonnaise, no butter, no margarine, no special sauce on my sandwich or burger.

Please put the dressing on the side of the salad. Do you have any light salad dressings?

Hold the topping on the frozen yogurt.

Serve my potato plain. Do you have any cottage cheese or yogurt instead of butter or sour cream?

-grilled chicken breast sandwich with lettuce & tomato & mustard (no mayo) and side salad with light dressing and 1 fruit
or
-seafood or turkey mini sub or snack sub (no cheese, mayo or oil) and side salad with light dressing and 1 fruit
or
-single hamburger 56 grams (2 oz.) or junior burger 56 grams (2 oz.) (no mayo) and side salad with light dressing and 1 fruit and small frozen yogurt
or
-junior roast beef sandwich (no mayo, no butter) and side salad with light dressing and 1 fruit

Fast Food Potato & Salad

Tell the waiter:
Serve my potato plain. Do you have any cottage cheese or yogurt instead of butter or sour cream?

Please serve my salad with dressing on the side. Please bring vinegar or lemon.

-1 medium baked potato
-125 ml (1/2 cup) low-fat cottage cheese or 250 ml (1 cup) yogurt or low-fat milk
-250 ml (1cup) chili or 56 grams (2 oz.) fish, skinless poultry or lean meat
-all-vegetable salad or 250 ml (1 cup) vegetable soup
-1 fruit
-(optional) 5 ml (1 t.) margarine or butter or 15 ml (1 T.) sour cream or regular salad dressing or 30 ml (2 T.) light salad dressing

or
-1 baked potato (plain)
-1 grilled chicken salad (no dressing)
-1 fruit
-(optional) 5 ml (1 t.) margarine or butter or 15 ml (1 T.) sour cream or regular salad dressing or 30 ml (2 T.) light salad dressing

Italian

Tell the waiter:
Prepare my dish without oil, butter, margarine, cream and cheese; sauces to the side.

Please put the dressing on the side of my salad and bring vinegar or lemon.

Can I get a half portion of the entree? Can you replace the cream sauce with a fat-free tomato sauce?

-appetizer portion of pasta with red clam or marinara or tomato sauce (no oil) and 30 ml (2 T.) Parmesan cheese (optional) + steamed vegetables or all-vegetable salad + 1 fruit
-15 ml (1T.) regular salad dressing or 30 ml (2 T.) light dressing (optional)
or
-1 roll
-250 ml (1 cup) minestrone soup
-1 all-vegetable salad and 30 ml (2 T.) Parmesan cheese (optional) + 1 fruit
-(optional) 15 ml (1T.) regular salad dressing or 30 ml (2 T.) light dressing (optional)
or
-1 slice from 35 cm (14") pizza (vegetables and regular cheese) with 1 side salad (no oil) and 1 fruit
-15 ml (1 T.) regular salad dressing or 30 ml (2 T.) light dressing (optional)

Chinese

Tell the waiter:
Prepare my dishes with no oil, butter or margarine.

-250 ml (1 cup) hot & sour soup or egg drop soup with 250 ml (1 cup) steamed rice + 1 fruit
or
-500 ml (2 cups) vegetable chow mein with chicken, beef or pork + 250 ml (1 cup) steamed rice+ 1 fruit
or
-500 ml (2 cups) stir-fried vegetables with chicken, beef, tofu or pork (no oil) and 250 ml (1 cup) steamed rice + 1 fruit

Chicken

Tell the waiter:
Please put the dressing on the side of the salad. Please bring vinegar or lemon.

Serve the gravy to the side of my chicken or sandwich.

Serve my potato plain. Do you have any cottage cheese or yogurt instead of butter or sour cream?

-chicken sandwich (no gravy) with side salad + 1 fruit
-(optional) 15 ml (1 T.) regular salad dressing or 30 ml (2 T.) light dressing
or
-chicken soup or baked potato and salad with 56 grams (2 oz.) chicken strips (no oil) and 1 fruit
- 250 ml (1 cup) low-fat milk or yogurt or 42 grams (1 1/2 oz.) low-fat cheese
-(optional) 5 ml (1 t.) margarine or butter or 15 ml (1 T.) sour cream or regular salad dressing or 30 ml (2 T.) light salad dressing

French/Continental

Tell the waiter:

Prepare my meal without oil, butter, margarine and cream; sauces to the side.

Please put the dressing on the side of the salad. Please bring vinegar or lemon.

Can I get cottage cheese, yogurt or dijon mustard instead of butter or sour cream for my baked potato?

-1 roll
-steamed mussels in broth or tomato sauce (no oil)
-1 side salad (no oil)
-1 fruit
-(optional) 15 ml (1 T.) regular salad dressing or 30 ml (2 T.) light salad dressing
or
-56 grams (2 oz.) poached or teriyaki or creole chicken (no skin) or fish with 250 ml (1 cup) rice or baked potato and steamed vegetables or salad (no oil)
-1 fruit
- 250 ml (1 cup) low-fat milk or yogurt or 42 grams (1 1/2 oz.) low-fat cheese
-(optional) 5 ml (1 t.) butter or margarine or 15 ml (1 T.) sour cream or regular salad dressing or 30 ml (2 T.) light salad dressing

Continental

-250 ml (1 cup) cooked rice or pasta or 1 large baked potato
-85 grams (3 oz.) skinless poultry or lean meat (beef, lamb, veal, pork) or fish
-1 fruit
-(optional) 5 ml (1 t.) butter or margarine or 15 ml (1 T.) sour cream or regular salad dressing or 30 ml (2 T.) light salad dressing
-vegetables, raw or cooked (no oil)
or
-375 ml (1-1/2 cups) cooked pasta with 180 ml (3/4 cup) red pasta sauce and 45 ml (3 T.) Parmesan cheese
-vegetables, raw or cooked (no oil)
-1 fruit
-(optional) 15 ml (1 T.) regular salad dressing or 30 ml (2 T.) light dressing

Vegetarian

-250 ml (1 cup) cooked rice and 250 ml (1 cup) cooked beans or lentils
- 250 ml (1 cup) low-fat milk or yogurt or 42 grams (1 1/2 oz.) low-fat cheese
-vegetables, raw or cooked (no oil)
-1 fruit
-(optional) 30 ml (2 T.) Parmesan cheese
-(optional) 15 ml (1 T.) regular salad dressing or 30 ml (2 T.) light dressing
or
-250 ml (1 cup) non-cream soup, extended with 500-750 ml (2-3 cups) chopped vegetables and 125 ml (1/2 cup) cooked rice or pasta and 250 ml (1 cup) cooked legumes.
-30 ml (2 T.) Parmesan cheese
-1 slice bread or 4 crackers

Italian

Tell the waiter:

Prepare my dish without oil, butter, margarine, cream and cheese; sauces to the side.

Please put the dressing on the side of my salad and bring vinegar or lemon.

Can I get a half portion of the entree?

Can you replace the cream sauce with a fat-free tomato sauce?

-side salad or steamed vegetables (no oil)
-appetizer portion of pasta with red clam

sauce or pasta primavera (with red sauce) or shrimp primavera
-1 fruit
-(optional) 15 ml (1 T.) regular salad dressing or 30 ml (2 T.) light dressing
or
-side salad or steamed vegetables (no oil)
-120 grams (4 oz.) shrimp marinara or filet of sole with tomato sauce
-250 ml (1 cup) cooked pasta with 125 ml (1/2 cup) tomato sauce
-1 fruit
-(optional) 15 ml (1 T.) regular salad dressing or 30 ml (2 T.) light dressing

Salad Bar

-fresh vegetables (no oil, no mayo)
-250 ml (1 cup) legumes or 250 ml (1 cup) chicken or turkey (no mayo) or cottage cheese
-125 ml (1/2 cup) fresh fruit salad
-30 ml (2 T.) Parmesan cheese
-30 ml (2 T.) low-calories dressing
-1 roll or 2 slices bread

Suppers – Women's Maintenance/ Men's Weight Loss

Chicken

Tell the waiter:
Please put the dressing on the side of the salad. Please bring vinegar or lemon.

Serve the gravy to the side of my chicken or sandwich.

Serve my potato plain. Do you have any cottage cheese or yogurt instead of butter or sour cream?

-1 roll
-1/4 chicken dinner (no skin, no wing) with baked potato and side salad and 1 fruit
or
-chicken sandwich (no gravy) with side salad and soup (non-cream) and 1 fruit
-(optional) 15 ml (1 T.) regular salad dressing or 30 ml (2 T.) light dressing
or
-salad topped with chicken strips (no mayo) and soup (non-cream) and 1 baked potato or roll and 1 fruit
-(optional) 5 ml (1 t.) margarine or butter or 15 ml (1 T.) sour cream or regular salad dressing or 30 ml (2 T.) light salad dressing

Fish and Seafood

Tell the waiter:
Prepare my fish and vegetables without oil, butter or margarine; sauces to the side.

Please substitute a baked potato for the french fries. Can I get cottage cheese, yogurt or dijon mustard for my baked potato instead of butter or sour cream?

Please put the dressing on the side of the salad. Please bring vinegar or lemon.

-1 roll or 1 baked potato
-any non-cream soup
-fish bouillabaisse or 565 grams (1-1/4 lb.) steamed lobster or crab and side salad
-1 fruit
-(optional) 5 ml (1 t.) margarine or butter or 15 ml (1 T.) sour cream or regular salad dressing or 30 ml (2 T.) light salad dressing
or
-1 slice bread or 1 small roll
-120 grams (4 oz.) any fish prepared by grilling, broiling, charbroiling, poaching,

steaming, teriyaki in tomato sauce, wine, lemon juice, broth (no oil, butter, margarine or cream)
-250 ml (1 cup) rice or 1 baked potato
-side salad or steamed vegetables (no oil)
-1 fruit
-(optional) 5 ml (1 t.) margarine or butter or 15 ml (1 T.) sour cream or regular salad dressing or 30 ml (2 T.) light salad dressing

Mexican

Tell the waiter:
Prepare my dishes without oil, butter or margarine, cheese or cream.

Serve the cheese, sour cream, guacamole and refried beans on the side.

Please put extra shredded lettuce, tomatoes and onions on the plate.

Please put the dressing on the side of the salad. Please bring vinegar or lemon.

-gazpacho or black bean soup
-side salad (no oil)
-2 chicken tacos with lettuce and tomato (no cheese, no oil, no sour cream)
-1 fruit
-(optional) 15 ml (1 T.) regular salad dressing or 30 ml (2 T.) light dressing
or
-gazpacho or black bean soup
-250 ml (1 cup) chili con carne with 375 ml (1-1/2 cups) Mexican rice (no oil)
-side salad (no oil)
-1 fruit
-(optional) 15 ml (1 T.) regular salad dressing or 30 ml (2 T.) light dressing

Japanese

Tell the waiter:
Prepare my meal without oil, butter or margarine; sauces to the side.

Please put the dressing on the side of the salad. Please bring vinegar or lemon.

-miso soup or suimono soup or su-udon soup
-stir-fried vegetables (no oil)
-yakitori (appetizer portion) and 375 ml (1-1/2 cups) steamed rice or 225 grams (8 oz.) sushi and 1 fruit
or
-120 grams (4 oz.) teriyaki beef or chicken or pork or fish
-165 grams (6 oz.) sushi or 375 ml (1-1/2 cups) steamed rice, stir-fried vegetables (no oil) and 1 fruit
or
-4-6 steamed shrimp dumplings with 125 ml (1/2 cup) steamed rice, stir-fried vegetables (no oil) and 1 fruit

Thai

Tell the waiter:
Prepare my dishes without oil, butter or margarine.

Prepare my dish without nuts.

Please put the dressing on the side of the salad. Please bring vinegar or lemon.

-vegetable soup
-steamed mussels or clams (no oil)
-stir-fried vegetables (no oil)
-375 ml (1-1/2 cups) steamed rice
-1 fruit
or
-any non-cream soup
-pla koong (shrimp salad) or spiced beef salad or yam yai (combination salad); dressing on the side
-250 ml (1 cup) steamed rice
-1 fruit

or
-2 beef or chicken satay (no oil, no sauce)
-375 ml (1-1/2 cups) steamed rice
-stir-fried vegetables (no oil)
-1 fruit

Middle Eastern (Greek, Israeli, Armenian)

Tell the waiter:
Prepare my dish without oil, butter or mayonnaise; sauces to the side.

Please put the dressing, feta cheese and olives on the side of the salad.

Please serve me an appetizer portion and bring it when you bring the others their entree.

Please serve me steamed rice or a plain pita instead of the potatoes. Please serve the vegetables steamed without fat.

-1 pork, chicken or lamb shish kabob (no oil) with 375 ml (1-1/2 cups) rice or 1 pita
-steamed vegetables (no oil)
-side salad (no oil)
-1 fruit
-(optional) 15 ml (1 T.) regular salad dressing or 30 ml (2 T.) light dressing
or
-cucumber and tomato salad (no oil)
-dolma
-250 ml (1 cup) steamed rice
-steamed vegetables
-1 fruit
-(optional) 15 ml (1 T.) regular salad dressing or 30 ml (2 T.) light dressing

Pizza

Tell the waiter:
Can I get less cheese and double vegetables on my pizza?

Please put the dressing on the side of the salad. Please bring vinegar or lemon.

-2 slices from a 35 cm. (14") pizza (vegetable and regular cheese)
-side salad (no oil)
-1 fruit
-(optional) 15 ml (1 T.) regular salad dressing or 30 ml (2 T.) light dressing
or
-1 non-cream soup
-1 personal pan pizza (cheese and vegetables) and side salad (no oil)
-1 fruit
-(optional) 15 ml (1 T.) regular salad dressing or 30 ml (2 T.) light dressing

Fast Food

Tell the waiter:
No mayonnaise, no butter, no margarine or special sauce on my sandwich or burger.

Dressing to the side of the salad. Do you have any light salad dressing?

Hold the topping on the frozen yogurt.

Serve my potato plain. Do you have any cottage cheese or yogurt instead of butter or sour cream?

-1 side salad with light dressing
-1 McLean (McDonald's) Deluxe Burger or Light (Harvey's) burger or grilled chicken sandwich (no mayo) or 1 roast beef sandwich (no butter)
-small frozen yogurt
or
-1 small salad with light dressing
-1 junior seafood or turkey sub (no cheese, no mayo, no oil) or 1 lean roast beef sand wich (no butter, no mayo) or 1 charbroiled 120 gram (4 oz.) burger or 1 Quarter Pounder (McDonald's)
-1 fruit
or

-1 junior roast beef sandwich (no butter) or 1 regular size hot dog or 250 ml (1 cup) chili
-1 baked potato
-1 fruit
-side salad with light dressing
-(optional) 5 ml (1 t.) butter or margarine or 15 ml (1 T.) sour cream

Chinese

Tell the waiter:
Prepare my dishes without oil, butter or margarine.

-wonton soup or hot & sour soup or egg drop soup or chinese vegetable soup
-500 ml (2 cups) chicken or beef or shrimp or pork chow mein
-250 ml (1 cup) steamed rice
-1 fruit
or
-wonton soup or hot & sour soup or egg drop soup or chinese vegetable soup
-500 ml (2 cups) stir-fried vegetables (no oil) with beef, chicken, fish or pork (no oil)
-250 ml (1 cup) steamed rice
-1 fruit
or
-Chinese vegetable soup
-120 grams (4 oz.) Szechuan fish, pork, chicken or beef (or in black bean sauce) and stir-fried vegetables (no oil)
-375 ml (1-1/2 cups) steamed rice
-1 fruit
or
-Chinese vegetable soup
-stir-fried vegetables (no oil) with 250 ml (1 cup) beef & broccoli or chicken & peppers or moo shi shrimp or moo goo gai pan
-250 ml (1 cup) steamed rice
-1 fruit

French/Continental/Canadian

Tell the waiter:
Prepare my meal without oil, butter, margarine and cream; sauces to the side.

Please put the dressing on the side of the salad. Please bring vinegar or lemon.

Can I get cottage cheese, yogurt or dijon mustard for my baked potato instead of butter or sour cream?

-1 roll
-any non-cream soup
-steamed mussels or clams in in broth or tomato sauce (no oil)
-all-vegetable salad (no oil)
-1 fruit
-(optional) 15 ml (1 T.) regular salad dressing or 30 ml (2 T.) light dressing
or
-1 roll or non-cream soup
-120 grams (4 oz.) filet mignon with 1 baked potato or 250 ml (1 cup) rice
-side salad or steamed vegetables (no oil)
-1 fruit
-(optional) 5 ml (1 t.) margarine or butter or 15 ml (1 T.) sour cream or regular salad dressing or 30 ml (2 T.) light dressing
or
-1 roll or non-cream soup
-500 ml (2 cups) chicken/fish/pork/beef stir-fry made without oil
-250 ml (1 cup) steamed rice
-1 fruit
or
-any non-cream soup, turkey sandwich or grilled chicken sandwich (no mayo), side salad (no oil)
-1 fruit
-(optional) 15 ml (1 T.) regular salad dressing or 30 ml (2 T.) light dressing
or
-1 roll
-120 grams (4 oz.) poached or teriyaki or

creole chicken (no skin) or fish with 250 ml (1 cup) rice or 1 baked potato
-steamed vegetables (no oil) or salad (no oil)
-1 fruit
-(optional) 5 ml (1 t.) margarine or butter or 15 ml (1 T.) sour cream or regular salad dressing or 30 ml (2 T.) light dressing

Snacks –Women's Maitenance/ Men's Weight Loss

(choose any 2 daily)

- 45 grams (1-1/2 oz.) low-fat cheese or 250 ml (1 cup) low-fat milk or yogurt
- Vegetable sticks—plain or marinated in fat-free Italian dressing
- Vegetable sticks with 250 ml (1 cup) low-fat dip
- 250 ml (1 cup) low-fat milk blended with 4-5 ice cubes, vanilla flavouring and 15 ml (1T.) maple or chocolate syrup or 125 ml (1/2 cup) fruit
- 250 ml (1 cup) vegetable soup topped with 30 ml (2 T.) Parmesan cheese
- 42 grams (1-1/2 oz.) low-fat cheese
  4 crackers or 1 slice bread
- 250 ml (1 cup) low-fat milk or yogurt
  125 ml (1/2 cup) cereal
- 750 ml (3 cups) air-popped popcorn
  45 ml (3 T.) Parmesan cheese
- 1 fruit
  250 ml (1 cup) low-fat yogurt
- 125 ml (1/2 cup) low-fat frozen yogurt
- 1/2 medium baked potato
  30 ml (2 T.) low-fat cottage cheese or yogurt topping
- 2 plain cookies
  250 ml (1 cup) low-fat milk

Men's Maintenance Plan

Totals for the day:

4	servings protein
3	servings dairy
11	servings starchy foods (grains, potato, corn)
6	servings fruits
free	servings vegetables
4	servings added fats
5	servings other foods

1. Regulate meal and snack times.

2. Combine protein foods and carbohydrate foods at every meal.

3. Divide food into at least 3-5 intakes during the day (e.g., breakfast, lunch, supper and 1-2 snacks).

4. Intakes should not be more than 5 hours apart during the day.

5. Drink 6-8 glasses of water daily.

6. Use as desired: herbs, spices, lemon/lime juice, vinegar, broth soups, mustard, tea, coffee, sugar- free gelatin, sugarfree soft drinks, fat- free Italian dressings, sugar substitutes, extracts (e.g., vanilla).

7. Familiarize yourself with portion size. We do not expect you to go through life weighing and measuring everything you eat. However, we recommend that you weigh food when you first start your plan to familiarize yourself with the right portion sizes for yourself. Our plan will have you eating the right foods at the right times. As a result, you will be satisfied with less food.

My Personalized Food Plan

Create your own personalized food plan.

Take your totals for each category and spread them into meals and 2-3 snacks (an example follows on the next page).

Breakfast

____

____

____

____

____

____

A.M. Snack

____

Lunch

____

____

____

____

____

P.M. Snack

____

Supper

____

____

____

____

____

____

Evening Snack

____

Personalized Meal Plan – Men's Maintenance

Breakfast

1 serving dairy

3 servings starchy foods

1 serving fruit

1 serving added fat

A.M. Snack

1 serving fruit

Lunch

1 serving dairy

1 1/2 servings protein

3 servings starchy foods

free servings vegetables

1 serving added fat

1 serving fruit

P.M. Snack

1 serving dairy

1 serving starchy foods

1 serving fruit

Supper

2-1/2 servings protein

4 servings starchy foods

free servings vegetables

1 serving fruit

2 servings added fats

Evening Snack

1 serving fruit

* 5 servings "other foods" any time during the day

drink 6-8 glasses of water daily

Serving Size Examples

1 Serving of Protein:
- 56 grams (2 oz.) fish, skinless poultry or lean meat *or*
- 1-2 eggs *or*
- 250 ml (1 cup) cooked legumes *or*
- 125 ml (1/2 cup) tofu

1 Serving Starchy Foods
Grains
- 125 ml (1/2 cup) cooked rice, barley, couscous or bulgar *or*
- 125 ml (1/2 cup) cooked pasta *or*
- 125 ml (1/2 cup) cereal *or*
- 250 (1 cup) non-cream soup *or*
- 4 crackers *or*
- 1 slice bread or 1/2 roll

Potato
- 1 medium potato

Corn
- 1 ear corn (125 ml/1/2 cup)

1 Serving Added Fats:
- 5 ml (1 t.) oil, mayonnaise, butter or margarine *or*
- 15 ml (1 T.) diet mayonnaise, diet margarine, diet butter, sour cream, nuts, seeds, or regular salad dressing *or*
- 30 ml (2 T.) light salad dressing or peanut butter

1 Serving of Low-Fat Dairy:
- 250 ml (1 cup) low-fat milk or yogurt *or*
- 42 grams (1-1/2 oz.) low-fat cheese *or*
- 125 ml (1/2 cup) low-fat cottage cheese, quark or ricotta

1 Serving Fruit:
- 1 medium fruit; 125 ml (1/2 cup) chopped fruit *or*
- 30 ml (2 T.) dried fruit

1 Serving Vegetables:
(as much as you want)

1 Serving Other Foods:
Snack Foods
- 750 ml (3 cups) air-popped popcorn *or*
- 125 ml (1/2 cup) pretzels *or*
- 125 ml (1/2 cup) no-oil tortilla chips *or*
- 1 sugar-free hot chocolate *or*
- 2 plain cookies *or*
- 1 frozen dessert bar (less than 50 calories each)

Alcohol
- 355 ml (12 oz.) light beer *or*
- 45 ml (3 oz.) dry wine *or*
- 45 ml (3 oz.) hard liquor

Sauces/Spreads
(use in moderation)

A1 Sauce
All-fruit jam
BBQ sauce
Black bean sauce
Chili sauce (no meat)
Chutney
Cocktail sauce
Cooking wine
Enchilada sauce
Extracts (i.e., vanilla)
Soy sauce (low-sodium)
Soup bases (non-cream)
Hoisin sauce
Honey
Honey garlic sauce
Sweet & sour sauce
Honey BBQ sauce
Horseradish
Teriyaki sauce (low-sodium)
Hot sauce
Ketchup
Tomato sauce/paste
Maple syrup
Mint sauce
Mustard
Oyster sauce
Pasta sauce; red
Picante sauce
Plum sauce
Relish
Salsa
Stir-fry sauce
Sugar
Taco sauce

Breakfasts –Men's Maintenance

Cereal & Fruit

-250 ml (1 cup) cereal
-1 slice toast or 1/2 small bagel or 1/2 English muffin or additional 125 ml (1/2 cup) cereal
-(optional) 5 ml (1 t.) all-fruit jam
-1 piece fresh fruit or 125 ml (1/2 cup) fruit salad
-1 egg or 2 whites or 42 grams (1 1/2 oz.) low-fat cheese or 250 ml (1 cup) low-fat milk or yogurt

Cheese & Toast

-1 large bagel or 3 slices bread or 1 roll
-42 grams (1 1/2 oz.) low-fat cheese or 125 ml (1/2 cup) low-fat cottage cheese
-1 piece fresh fruit

Milkshake

-250 ml (1 cup) low-fat milk mixed in blender with 3-5 ice cubes, 5 ml (1 t.) vanilla flavouring and 125 ml (1/2 cup) fresh or frozen fruit
-375 ml (1 1/2 cups) cereal or 1 large bagel or 1 English muffin or 2 slices of bread or 1 roll

Egg & Toast

-1 large bagel or English muffin or 1 roll or 2 slices bread
-1 whole egg or 2 whites (cooked with non-stick spray) or 42 grams (1-1/2 oz.) low-fat cheese or 250 ml (1 cup) low-fat milk or yogurt
-1 fresh fruit
-cooked or raw vegetables (optional)

French Toast (or pancakes or waffles)

-3 slices bread soaked in egg or egg whites and low-fat milk and fried using non-stick spray or three 6" pancakes cooked with non-stick spray or 2 waffles
-30 ml (2 T.) low-calorie syrup or 15 ml (1 T.) regular syrup
-1 fresh fruit or 125 ml (1/2 cup) fruit salad
-125 ml (1/2 cup) low-fat milk or yogurt

Breakfast Out

-1 large bagel or 3 slices bread
-1 poached egg or 1 scrambled egg (made without oil or butter or margarine) *or*
-1 boiled egg or 28 grams (1 oz.) cheese
-1 fresh fruit or 125 ml (1/2 cup) fruit salad
or
-3 pancakes or waffles topped with 15-30 ml (1-2 T.) syrup and fresh fruit and 250 ml (1 cup) low-fat milk
or
-250 ml (1 cup) cereal with 250 ml (1 cup) low-fat milk or yogurt
-1 slice toast or 1/2 roll or 1/2 bagel
-125 ml (1/2 cup) fresh fruit

Lunches – Men's Maintenance

Sandwich

-500 ml (2 cups) cooked rice or 500 ml (2 cups) cooked pasta or 1 baked potato, large
-85 grams (3 oz.) skinless poultry, lean meat (beef, lamb, veal, pork) or fish
-42 grams (1 1/2 oz.) low-fat cheese or 250 ml (1 cup) low-fat milk or yogurt
-750 ml (3 cups) vegetables, raw or cooked (no oil)
-1 fruit
-(optional) 5 ml (1 t.) margarine or butter or 15 ml (1 T.) sour cream or regular salad dressing or 30 ml (2 T.) light dressing

Sandwich & Soup Or Salad

-1 roll or 2 slices bread or 1 6" pita
-250 ml (1 cup) non-cream soup
-1 all-vegetable salad topped with 85 grams (3 oz.) lean chicken, turkey, ham or roast beef or 180 ml (3/4 cup) water-packed tuna or salmon or cooked legumes
-42 grams (1 1/2 oz.) low-fat cheese or 250 ml (1 cup) low-fat milk or yogurt
-1 fruit
-2 arrowroots or graham wafers or 1 newton
-(optional) 15 ml (1 T.) regular salad dressing or 30 ml (2 T.) light dressing

Fast Food

Tell the server:
No mayonnaise, no butter, no margarine, no special sauce on my sandwich or burger.

Please put the dressing on the side of the salad. Do you have any light salad dressings?
Serve my potato plain. Do you have any cottage cheese or yogurt instead of butter or sour cream?

-1 side salad with light dressing
-1 McLean Deluxe or 1 Light burger or 1 roast beef sandwich (no butter) or 1 grilled chicken sandwich (no mayo)
-1 small frozen yogurt
or
-1 junior roast beef sandwich or 1 regular size hot dog or 250 ml (1 cup) chili
-1 baked potato
-side salad with light dressing
-1 fruit
-(optional) 5 ml (1 t.) margarine or butter or 15 ml (1 T.) sour cream
or
-1 side salad (no oil) or 1 vegetable soup
-1 junior seafood or turkey sub (no mayo, no oil)
-1 fruit
-(optional) 15 ml (1 T.) regular salad dressing or 15 ml (2 T.) light dressing

Italian

Tell the waiter:
Prepare my dish without oil, butter, margarine, cream and cheese; sauces to the side.

Please put the dressing on the side of my salad and bring vinegar or lemon.

Can I get a half portion of the entree?

Can you replace the cream sauce with a fat-free tomato sauce?

-minestrone soup or roll
-side salad or steamed vegetables (no oil)
-appetizer portion pasta with red clam sauce or pasta with marinara sauce or pasta primavera (with red sauce) or shrimp primavera or shrimp marinara
-30 ml (2T.) parmesan cheese
-125 ml (1/2 cup) fruit salad or 1 fruit
-(optional) 15 ml (1 T.) regular salad dressing or 30 ml (2 T.) light dressing

Chinese

Tell the waiter:
Prepare my dishes with no oil, butter or margarine.

-hot & sour soup or Chinese vegetable or egg drop or wonton soup
-500 ml (2 cups) stir-fried vegetables with beef, chicken, fish or pork (no oil)
-250 ml (1 cup) steamed rice
-1 fruit
or

-hot & sour soup or Chinese vegetable or egg drop or wonton soup
-500 ml (2 cups) chow mein (chicken, beef, shrimp or pork)
-250 ml (1 cup) steamed rice
-1 fruit
or
-hot & sour soup or Chinese vegetable or egg drop or wonton soup
-375 ml (1-1/2 cups) stir-fried vegetables (no oil) with 250 ml (1 cup) beef & broccoli or chicken & peppers or moo shi shrimp or moo goo gai pan
-250 ml (1 cup) steamed rice
-1 fruit
or
-hot & sour soup or Chinese vegetable or egg drop or wonton soup
-85 grams (3 oz.) Szechuan fish, pork, chicken or beef (or in black bean sauce)
-250 ml (1 cup) steamed rice
-500 ml (2 cups) stir-fried vegetables (no oil)
-1 fruit

Japanese

Tell the waiter:
Prepare my fish and vegetables without oil, butter or margarine; sauces to the side.

-miso soup or suimono soup or su-udon soup
-500 ml (2 cups) stir-fried vegetables (no oil)
-yakitori (appetizer portion)
-500 ml (2 cups) steamed rice or 165 grams (6 oz.) sushi
-1 fruit
or
-85 grams (3 oz.) teriyaki beef or chicken or pork or fish
-500 ml (2 cups) steamed rice or 165 grams (6 oz.) sushi
-1 fruit
or
-4-6 steamed shrimp dumplings
-250 ml (1 cup) steamed rice
-1 fruit

Pizza

Tell the waiter:
Can I get less cheese and double vegetables on my pizza?

Please serve my salad with dressing on the side. Please bring vinegar or lemon.

-2 slices from a 35 cm (14") pizza (vegetables and regular cheese)
-1 side salad
-1 fruit
-(optional) 15 ml (1 T.) regular salad dressing or 30 ml (2 T.) light dressing
or
-non-cream soup
-personal pan pizza (cheese and vegetables) and side salad
-1 fruit
-(optional) 15 ml (1 T.) regular salad dressing or 30 ml (2 T.) light dressing

Mexican

Tell the waiter:
Prepare my dishes with no oil, butter or margarine, cheese or cream.

Serve the cheese, sour cream, guacamole and refried beans on the side.

Please put extra shredded lettuce, tomatoes and onions on the plate.

Please serve my salad with dressing on the side. Please bring vinegar or lemon.

-gazpacho or black bean soup

-side salad (no oil)
-2 chicken tacos with lettuce and tomato (no oil, no sour cream)
-1 fruit
-(optional) 15 ml (1 T.) regular salad dressing or 30 ml (2 T.) light dressing
or
-250 ml (1 cup) chili con carne with 500 ml (2 cups) steamed Mexican rice (no oil) and vegetables or side salad (no oil)
-1 fruit
-(optional) 15 ml (1 T.) regular salad dressing or 30 ml (2 T.) light dressing

Thai

Tell the waiter:
Prepare my dishes without oil, butter or margarine.

Prepare this dish without nuts.

Please serve my salad with dressing on the side. Please bring vinegar or lemon.

-any non-cream soup
-steamed mussels or clams (no oil)
-500 ml (2 cups) stir-fried vegetables (no oil)
-375 ml (1-1/2 cups) steamed rice
-1 fruit
or
-any non-cream soup
-pla kwong (shrimp salad) or spiced beef salad or yam yai (combination salad, dressing on the side, or poy sian (seafood and vegetables)—no oil
-375 ml (1-1/2 cups) steamed rice
-1 fruit
or
-2 beef or chicken satay (no oil, no sauce)
-500 ml (2 cups) steamed rice
-500 ml (2 cups) stir-fried vegetables (no oil)
-1 fruit

Middle Eastern (Greek/Israeli/Armenian)

Tell the waiter:
Prepare my dish without oil, butter or mayonnaise; sauces to the side.

Please put the dressing, feta cheese and olives on the side of the salad.

Please serve me an appetizer portion and bring it when you bring the others their entree.

Please serve me steamed rice or a plain pita instead of the potatoes.

Please serve the vegetables steamed without fat.

-1 pork, chicken or lamb brochette (no oil)
-steamed vegetables (no oil) or side salad (no oil)
-500 ml (2 cups) steamed rice or 1 large baked potato
-250 ml (1 cup low-fat milk or yogurt
-1 fruit
-(optional) 5 ml (1 t.) margarine or butter or 15 ml (1 T.) regular salad dressing or 30 ml (2 T.) light dressing
or
-1 Gyros
-Greek Salad (no oil)
-1 fruit
-(optional) 15 ml (1 T.) regular salad dressing or 30 ml (2 T.) light dressing

Fish and Seafood

Tell the waiter:
Prepare my fish and vegetables without oil, butter or margarine; sauces to the side.

Please substitute a baked potato for the french fries. Can I get cottage cheese, yogurt or dijon mustard for my baked potato instead of butter or sour cream?

Please serve my salad with dressing on the side. Please bring vinegar or lemon.

-1 roll or baked potato
-any non-cream soup
-fish bouillabaisse or 565 grams (1-1/4 lb.) steamed lobster or crab legs
-1 fruit
-(optional) 5 ml (1 t.) margarine or butter or 15 ml (1 T.) sour cream
or
-120 grams (4 oz.) any fish prepared by grilling, broiling, charbroiling, poaching, steaming, teriyaki, in tomato sauce, wine, lemon juice, broth (no oil, no butter, no margarine, no cream)
-1 large baked potato or 500 ml (2 cups) steamed rice
-side salad or steamed vegetables (no oil)
-1 fruit
-(optional) 5 ml (1 t.) margarine or butter or 15 ml (1 T.) sour cream or regular salad dressing or 30 ml (2 T.) light dressing

Chicken

Tell the waiter:
Serve my salad with dressing on the side. Please bring vinegar or lemon.

Serve the gravy to the side of my chicken or sandwich.

Serve my baked potato plain. Do you have any cottage cheese or yogurt instead of butter or sour cream?

-1 roll
-1/4 chicken dinner (no skin) with baked potato and side salad (no oil)
-1 fruit
-(optional) 5 ml (1 t.) margarine or butter or 15 ml (1 T.) sour cream or regular salad dressing or 30 ml (2 T.) light dressing
or
-chicken sandwich (no gravy) with side salad and soup (non-cream)
-1 fruit
or
-salad topped with chicken strips (no mayo) and soup (non-cream) with baked potato or roll
-(optional) 5 ml (1 t.) margarine or butter or 15 ml (1 T.) sour cream or regular salad dressing or 30 ml (2 T.) light dressing

French/Continental/Canadian

Tell the waiter:
Prepare my meal without oil, butter, margarine or cream; sauces to the side.

Please put the dressing on the side of the salad. Please bring vinegar or lemon.

Can I get cottage cheese, yogurt or dijon mustard instead of butter or sour cream for my baked potato?

-1 roll or baked potato
-any non-cream soup
-steamed mussels or clams in broth or tomato sauce (no oil)
-all-vegetable salad
-1 fruit
-(optional) 5 ml (1 t.) margarine or butter or 15 ml (1 T.) sour cream or regular salad dressing or 30 ml (2 T.) light dressing
or
-1 roll or non-cream soup
-120 grams (4 oz.) poached or teriyaki or creole chicken (no skin) or fish with 250 ml (1 cup) rice or 1 baked potato and steamed vegetables (no oil)
-1 fruit
-(optional) 10 ml (2 t.) margarine or butter or 30 ml (2 T.) sour cream

or
-1 roll or non-cream soup
-120 grams (4 oz.) filet mignon with 1 baked potato and side salad or steamed vegetables (no oil)
-1 fruit
-(optional) 5 ml (1 t.) butter or margarine or 15 ml (2 T.) sour cream
-(optional) 15 ml (1 T.) regular salad dressing or 30 ml (2 T.) light dressing
or
-1 roll or non-cream soup
-turkey sandwich or grilled chicken sandwich (no mayo) or lean roast beef sandwich (no mayo)
-side salad (no oil)
-1 fruit
-(optional) 5 ml (1 t.) butter or margarine or 10 ml (2 t.) light mayonnaise
-(optional) 15 ml (1 T.) regular salad dressing or 30 ml (2 T.) light dressing

Suppers – Men's Maintenance

Continental
-500 ml (2 cups) cooked rice or pasta or 1 large baked potato
-140 grams (5 oz.) skinless poultry or lean meat (beef, lamb, veal, pork) or fish
-vegetables, raw or cooked (no oil)
-1 fruit
-(optional) 5 ml (1 t.) margarine or butter or 15 ml (1 T.) sour cream
-(optional) 15 ml (1 T.) regular salad dressing or 30 ml (2 T.) light dressing

Vegetarian
-500 ml (2 cups) cooked rice and 375 ml (1-1/2 cups) cooked beans or lentils
-vegetables, raw or cooked (no oil)
-30 ml (2 T.) Parmesan cheese (optional)
-1 fruit
-(optional) 30 ml (2 T.) regular salad dressing or 60 ml (4 T.) light dressing

Soup and Salad
-1 roll or 2 slices bread
-250 ml (1 cup) non-cream soup
-1 all-vegetable salad topped with 140 grams (5 oz.) lean chicken, turkey, ham or roast beef or 250 ml (1 cup) water-packed tuna or salmon or 375 ml (1-1/2 cups) cooked legumes
-1 newton or 2 arrowroots or 2 graham wafers
-1 fruit
-(optional) 30 ml (2 T.) regular salad dressing or 60 ml (4 T.) light dressing

Italian
Tell the waiter:
Prepare my dish without oil, butter, margarine, cream and cheese; sauces to the side.

Please put the dressing on the side of my salad. Please bring vinegar or lemon.

Can I get a half portion of the entree?

Can you replace the cream sauce with a fat-free tomato sauce?

-1 roll
-side salad or steamed vegetables (no oil)
-ziti bolognese or pasta with red clam sauce or pasta with marinara sauce or pasta primavera (with red sauce) or shrimp primavera (with red sauce) or shrimp marinara or lobster/shrimp fra diavlo or potato gnocchi with tomato sauce
-1 fruit
-(optional) 15 ml (1 T.) regular salad dressing or 30 ml (2 T.) light dressing

Chinese

Tell the waiter:
Prepare my dishes without oil, butter or margarine.

-any non-cream soup
-500 ml (2 cups) stir-fried vegetables with beef, chicken, fish or pork (no oil)
-375 ml (1 1/2 cups) steamed rice
-2 fortune cookies
-1 fruit
or
-any non-cream soup
-140 grams (5 oz.) pork, chicken, fish or beef in black bean sauce or Szechuan style or "moo shi" style or "with broccoli" or "chop suey" or "with peppers"
-500 ml (2 cups) stir-fried vegetables (no oil)
-250 ml (1 cup) steamed rice
-2 fortune cookies
-1 fruit
or
-any non-cream soup
-500 ml (2 cups) stir-fried vegetables (no oil)
-2 mandarin pancakes
-140 grams (5 oz.) Peking smoked chicken
-1 fruit
or
-any non-cream soup
-500 ml (2 cups) stir-fried vegetables (no oil)
-375 ml (1 1/2 cups) beef, chicken or pork lo mein
-375 ml (1-1/2 cups) steamed rice
-1 fruit

French/Continental/Canadian

Tell the waiter:
Prepare my whole dish and vegetables without oil, butter, margarine and cream; sauces to the side.

Please put the dressing on the side of the salad. Please bring vinegar or lemon.

Can I get cottage cheese, yogurt or dijon mustard instead of butter or sour cream for my baked potato?

-1 roll
-any non-cream soup or small portion of steamed mussels or shrimp cocktail
-140 grams (5 oz.) teriyaki or grilled or poached or creole fish or chicken or 140 grams (5 oz.) filet mignon
-250 ml (1 cup) rice or 1 baked potato
-steamed vegetables and salad (no oil)
-1 fruit
-(optional) 5 ml (1 t.) margarine or butter or 15 ml (1 T.) sour cream
-(optional) 15 ml (1 T.) regular salad dressing or 30 ml (2 T.) light dressing
or
-any non-cream soup
-turkey or grilled chicken sandwich or French dip sandwich (no mayo) or 120 - 140 grams (4-5 oz.) hamburger
-side salad (no oil)
-1 fruit
-(optional) 30 ml (2 T.) regular salad dressing or 60 ml (4 T.) light dressing
or
-1 roll or any non-cream soup
-chicken/fish/pork or beef stir-fry made without oil
-250 ml (1 cup) steamed rice
-1 fruit

Middle Eastern (Greek/Israeli/Armenian)

Tell the waiter:
Prepare my dish without oil, butter or mayonnaise; sauces to the side.

Please put the dressing, feta cheese and olives on the side of the salad.

Please serve me an appetizer portion and bring it when you bring the others their entree.

Please serve me steamed rice or a plain pita instead of the potatoes.
Please serve the vegetables steamed without fat.

-2 pork, chicken or lamb souvlaki (no oil) with 500 ml (2 cups) rice
-steamed vegetables (no oil)
-side salad (no oil)
-1 fruit
-(optional) 15 ml (1 T.) regular salad dressing or 30 ml (2 T.) light dressing
or
-1 roll
-lentil soup
-dolma
-steamed vegetables
-1 fruit

Pizza

Tell the waiter:
Can I get less cheese and double vegetables on my pizza?

Please serve my salad with dressing on the side. Please bring vinegar or lemon.

-2 slices from a 35 cm (14 ") pizza (vegetable and regular cheese)
-side salad (no oil)
-1 fruit
-(optional) 15 ml (1 T.) regular salad dressing or 30 ml (2 T.) light dressing
or
-1 non-cream soup
-1 personal pan pizza (cheese and vegetables)
-side salad (no oil)
-1 fruit
-(optional) 15 ml (1 T.) regular salad dressing or 30 ml (2 T.) light dressing

Chicken

Tell the waiter:
Serve my salad with dressing on the side.
Please bring vinegar or lemon.
Serve the gravy to the side of my chicken or sandwich.

Serve my baked potato plain. Do you have any cottage cheese or yogurt instead of butter or sour cream?

-1 roll
-1/4 chicken dinner (no skin) with baked potato and side salad
-1 fruit
-(optional) 5 ml (1 t.) margarine or butter or 15 ml (1 T.) sour cream
-(optional) 15 ml (1 T.) regular salad dressing or 30 ml (2 T.) light dressing
or
-chicken sandwich (no gravy) with side salad and soup (non-cream)
-1 fruit
or
-salad topped with chicken strips (no mayo) and soup (non-cream) and 1 baked potato or roll
-1 fruit
-(optional) 5 ml (1 t.) margarine or butter or 15 ml (1 T.) sour cream
-(optional) 15 ml (1 T.) regular salad dressing or 30 ml (2 T.) light dressing

Fast Food

Tell the waiter:
No mayonnaise, no butter, no margarine, no special sauce on my sandwich or burger.

Please put the dressing on the side of the salad. Do you have any light salad dressings?

Hold the topping on the frozen yogurt.

Serve my potato plain. Do you have any cottage cheese or yogurt instead of butter or sour cream?

-1 side salad (no oil)
-1 Whopper (no mayo) or 1 Quarter Pounder or 1 lean roast beef sandwich (no butter) or 1 charbroiled 120 grams (4 oz.) burger or 1 grilled chicken sandwich
-1 large baked potato or small non-fat frozen yogurt
-1 fruit
-(optional) 5 ml (1 t.) margarine or butter or 15 ml (1 T.) sour cream
-(optional) 15 ml (1 T.) regular salad dressing or 30 ml (2 T.) light dressing
or
-1 junior turkey, seafood or roast beef sub (no cheese, no mayo, no oil)
-250 ml (1 cup) non-cream soup
-1 side salad
-1 fruit
or
-250 ml (1 cup) chili with baked potato and salad and roll
-1 fruit
-(optional) 5 ml (1 t.) margarine or butter or 15 ml (1 T.) sour cream
-(optional) 15 ml (1 T.) regular salad dressing or 30 ml (2 T.) light dressing

Fish and Seafood

Tell the waiter:
Prepare my fish and vegetables without oil, butter or margarine; sauces to the side. Please substitute a baked potato for the french fries. Can I get cottage cheese, yogurt or dijon mustard for my baked potato instead of butter or sour cream?

Please serve my salad with dressing on the side. Please bring vinegar or lemon.

-1 roll or baked potato
-any non-cream soup or small portion of steamed clams, mussels or oysters or shrimp cocktail
-fish bouillabaisse or 675 grams (1-1/2 lb.) steamed lobster or crab legs
-1 fruit
-(optional) 5 ml (1 t.) margarine or butter or 15 ml (1 T.) sour cream
or
-1 roll
-140 grams (5 oz) any fish prepared by grilling, broiling, charbroiling, poaching, steaming, teriyaki, in tomato sauce, wine, lemon juice, broth (no oil, no butter, no margarine, no cream)
-375 ml (1 1/2 cups) rice or 1 large baked potato
-side salad or steamed vegetables (no oil)
-1 fruit
-(optional) 5 ml (1 t.) margarine or butter or 15 ml (1 T.) sour cream
-(optional) 15 ml (1 T.) regular salad dressing or 30 ml (2 T.) light dressing

Mexican

Tell the waiter:
Prepare my dishes with no oil, butter or margarine, cheese or cream.

Serve the cheese, sour cream, guacamole and refried beans on the side.

Please put extra shredded lettuce, tomatoes and onions on the plate.

Please serve my salad with dressing on the side. Please bring vinegar or lemon.

-gazpacho or black bean soup
-side salad (no oil)
-2 enchiladas (no oil, no cheese, no sour cream) or 2 tacos or 2 fajitas or 2 burritos

or 250 ml (1 cup) chili served with 250 ml (1 cup) Mexican rice (not fried)
-1 fruit
-(optional) 15 ml (1 T.) regular salad dressing or 30 ml (2 T.) light dressing

Japanese

Tell the waiter:
Please serve my salad with the dressing on the side. Please bring vinegar and lemon.

Prepare my dish without oil, butter or margarine.

-miso soup or suimono soup or su-udon soup
-500 ml (2 cups) stir-fried vegetables (no oil)
-yakitori (appetizer portion)
-500 ml (2 cups) steamed rice or 225 (8 oz.) sushi
-1 fruit
or
-120 grams (4 oz.) teriyaki beef or chicken or pork or fish
-500 ml (2 cups) steamed rice or 225 (8 oz.) sushi
-1 fruit
or
-any non-cream soup
-4-6 steamed shrimp dumplings with 500 ml (2 cups) steamed rice
-1 fruit

Thai

Tell the waiter:
Prepare my dishes without oil, butter or margarine.
Prepare this dish without nuts.

Please serve my salad with dressing on the side. Please bring vinegar or lemon.

-2 beef or chicken satay (no oil, no sauce) or steamed mussels or clams (no oil) or any non-cream soup
-pla koong (shrimp salad) or spiced beef salad or yam yai (combination salad), dressing on side, or poy sian (seafood and vegetables)
-375 ml (1-1/2 cups) steamed rice
-1 fruit
or
-steamed mussels or clams (no oil) or any non-cream soup
-140 grams (5 oz.) Thai chicken (no cashews) or 140 grams (5 oz.) sweet & sour chicken or beef basil or scallops bamboo or chili or beef or ginger pork or garlic shrimp or steamed seafood
-375 ml (1 1/2 cups) steamed rice
-500 ml (2 cups) steamed vegetables or stir-fried vegetables (no oil)
-1 fruit

Snacks – Men's Maintenance

(choose any 2 daily)

- 45 grams (1-1/2 oz.) low-fat cheese or 250 ml (1 cup) low-fat milk or yogurt
  1 fruit or 1 small pack raisins or 4 crackers

- 250 ml (1 cup) low-fat frozen yogurt
  2 plain cookies or 30 ml (2 T.) raisins or 1 cone

- 250 ml (1 cup) low-fat milk or yogurt
  125 ml (1/2 cup) cereal or 1 small muffin or 2 plain cookies

- 250 ml (1 cup) vegetable soup topped with 45 ml (3 T.) Parmesan cheese and 4 crackers

- 250 ml (1 cup) low-fat milk or yogurt
  1 fruit

- 750 ml (3 cups) air-popped popcorn
  45 ml (3 T.) Parmesan cheese

- 1 fruit
  250 ml (1 cup) low-fat yogurt

- 250 ml (1 cup) low-fat frozen yogurt

- 250 ml (1 cup) low-fat milk blended with 4-5 ice cubes, vanilla flavouring
  125 ml (1/2 cup) fruit

- 1/2 medium baked potato
  30 ml (2 T.) low-fat cottage cheese or yogurt topping

- 2 plain cookies
  250 ml (1 cup) low-fat milk

Part IV
Enjoy Your Food the Healthy Weigh

Dining Out the Healthy Weigh

In North America, a very large percentage of the food dollar is spent dining out. Dining out is no longer just for very special occasions. Many people today eat out an average of two to three lunches and one to two dinners per week.

Restaurant dining can be a very pleasant experience. It can also be very confusing. Many of our clients report that when they eat out, they are tempted by high-calorie foods, and they feel out of control. This chapter will provide you with all the tools you need to choose healthier foods when you dine out.

Restaurant food can be a high source of hidden fats and calories. Chefs love to make their meals glisten and shine and they do that by adding fat. Would you believe that an order of "grilled fish" can have up to 10 pats of butter added while cooking? That is an extra 50 grams (2 oz.) of fat and an extra 450 calories just for the fat. You could have added three baked potatoes or a banana split to your meal to equal that amount.

One of the main strategies you should use to eat healthier in restaurants is to consume less fat. Never be embarrassed about asking questions or requesting that foods be prepared differently. You are paying for the meal and you have that right.

Eating Out General Guidelines

Order all food without added fat, oil, butter or margarine. Be explicit. Many waiters and chefs do not realize that margarine, olive oil and vegetable oil have just as many calories as butter or lard.

Ask for sauces, salad dressings and toppings on the side and use them sparingly.

Foods that have been prepared the following ways all signal high fat:

alfredo
à la mode
battered
breaded
crispy
creamy
parmigiana
puffed

au lait	basted	escalloped	panfried
au gratin	bisque	flaky	sautéed
au fromage	buttered	hash	stir-fried
béarnaise	casserole	hollandaise	tempura
béchamel			

Appetizers/Beverages

1. Have a roll or slice of bread without butter, margarine or pâté. Ask the waiter to bring you plain bread or rolls if garlic is served.

2. Avoid fried, battered or breaded appetizers, as they are high in fat. Other high-fat choices are those in garlic butter, cream sauce, melted cheese and cheese sauce.

3. If you wish to have an alcoholic beverage, choose one of the following:
   - 125 ml (1/2 cup) of wine
   - 3/4 cup (12 oz.) of beer (preferably "light")
   - 1-1/2 oz. (1/4 cup) of liquor mixed with water, seltzer, tomato juice or a diet beverage

4. The best beverage choices are water, mineral water and seltzer. You can ask the waiter to create a healthy soda by mixing a fruit juice with seltzer.

Entree

1. Order meats, poultry and fish broiled, grilled or poached with no oil, butter or margarine. Preferred methods of preparation are:

• in tomato sauce	• broiled	• BBQ
• in wine sauce	• charbroiled	• kabobs
• in bouillon or broth	• steamed	• en brochette
• in lemon juice	• baked	• poached
• teriyaki		

   Order all other sauces on the side and use them sparingly.

2. For your side dish, a baked potato (with the butter, margarine or sour cream on the side, if desired, and use sparingly) or a side dish of pasta with red sauce is your best bet. Fancy rice dishes are often loaded with fat. If you want rice, order it steamed. You can flavour your baked potato with just a small amount (approximately 5 ml/1 t.) of butter, margarine or sour cream. For additional moistness and flavour you can add salt (in moderation) and pepper, and ask the waiter if the restaurant can provide you with plain yogurt or cottage cheese as a topping.

3. Order vegetables steamed with no sauces, no butter, no oil, no margarine and no cheese.

Salads

1. If you order a salad as your main meal, make sure to include some low-fat protein such as beef, fish, chicken, turkey, cheese, cottage cheese or legumes. If you order a julienne salad, you may want to substitute extra chicken or turkey for the ham and cheese. Remember that 85 grams (3 ounces) is the maximum protein you need. Some of these salads can contain up to 1/2 lb. (8 ounces) of protein, which is too much for you to eat at one time.

If it is a main meal, always include a carbohydrate source with your salad, for example, a roll, a slice of bread, some crackers or a baked potato.

2. **Be sure to have your dressing on the side and use it sparingly**. Flavour the salad with herbs, spices, vinegar or lemon juice. You can extend the dressing they give you as follows: add to 15 ml (1 T.) of dressing, some vinegar or lemon juice, salt, pepper, a little sugar, and a dab of mustard if you wish. Sprinkle the salad with approximately 30 ml (1-2 T.) of Parmesan cheese and then add this dressing mixture on top; delicious, and a great way to cut down on fat and calories. Put aside the extra protein that you don't need (any in excess of 85 grams/3 ounces) before you begin to eat. This avoids temptation later. Ask for a doggie bag!

Dining Out—Sample Menus

Canadian/American

Appetizers

- nachos
- chicken wings
- potato skins
- chicken fingers
- breaded vegetables
- mozzarella sticks
- New England clam chowder
- French onion soup

Main Courses

- salads with dressing already on
- salads made with mayonnaise
- tuna melt
- Reuben sandwich
- Philadelphia cheese steak
- hamburger (if more than 1/4 lb.) (4 oz.)
- bacon burger

- cheeseburger
- hot corned beef or pastrami sandwich
- jumbo hot dog
- seafood salad croissant
- ribs
- 1/2 roasted chicken
- chicken fried steak
- quiche

Side Dishes

- french fries
- creamy coleslaw

Desserts

- ice creams
- sundaes
- mud pie/other pies/cakes

Canadian/American

Good Choice

Tell the waiter: *Prepare my dish without oil, butter or margarine; sauces to the side.*

Please put the dressing on the side of the salad.

Can I get cottage cheese, yogurt or dijon mustard instead of butter or sour cream?

Can you replace the ham and cheese in my julienne salad with extra turkey?

Appetizers

- peel-and-eat shrimp (with cocktail sauce)
- raw or steamed seafood (with cocktail sauce)
- vegetable or minestrone soup
- chicken soup with noodles
- tossed greens (with dressing on the side)

Main Courses

- chef's salad with beef, chicken, fish, turkey (no mayonnaise)—dressing on the side
- turkey sandwich
- grilled chicken breast sandwich (no mayonnaise)

- teriyaki chicken breast
- French dip sandwich
- hamburger 1/4 lb. (4 oz. or less)
- regular-size hot dog 1/8 lb. (2 oz. or less)
- oriental stir-fry (ask for less oil)
- soup and salad (non-creamed soup and dressing on side of salad)

Side Dishes

- baked potato
- rice
- steamed vegetables

Desserts

- sorbet
- fresh fruit
- frozen yogurt

Sample Menu

Order #1

	Tell the waiter:
vegetable salad with 15 ml (1 T.) dressing	*Dressing on the side.*
teriyaki grilled chicken 120 grams 1/4 lb. (46 oz.)	*Grill without oil or fat.*
baked potato	*No butter, margarine or sour cream on my potato. Please bring cottage cheese, yogurt or dijon mustard instead.*
steamed vegetables	*No oil, butter or sauces on the vegetables.*

Order #2

	Tell the waiter:
peel & eat shrimp with cocktail sauce	
oriental stir-fry	*Please stir-fry with little or no oil.*
rice, steamed	
fruit sorbet	

Chinese

✗ Poor Choice

Appetizers
- egg rolls
- spring rolls
- BBQ spare ribs
- fried shrimp
- fried wontons
- pu pu platter

Main Courses
- any dish made with panfried noodles
- any dish fried
- any dish with breaded or battered chicken or fish
- any dish made with cashews or other nuts
- BBQ spare ribs
- fried fish
- fried seafood
- lemon chicken
- duck
- Szechuan orange beef
- pineapple chicken
- Hunan crispy beef
- spicy crispy whole fish
- ginger beef
- General Gau's chicken
- moo shu pork
- Peking duck, chicken or shrimp
- shrimp Cantonese
- pork with garlic sauce

Side Dishes
- fried rice

Desserts
- fried bananas
- ice cream

Chinese

✔ Good Choice

Tell the waiter: *Prepare my dishes with no oil, butter or margarine.*

Appetizers

- teriyaki beef or chicken on skewers
- roast pork strips
- hot & sour soup
- chinese vegetable soup
- wonton soup
- rice and chicken/shrimp soup
- egg drop soup

Main Courses

- stir fried vegetables alone or with beef, pork, chicken or fish (non-battered or non-breaded)
- chow mein (beef/chicken/shrimp/pork/vegetable)
- pony shrimp in black bean sauce
- Szechuan style fresh fish fillets
- roast pork with vegetables
- chicken or vegetable lo mein
- sizzling lamb or sliced chicken
- chop suey
- moo shi shrimp
- beef/shrimp and broccoli
- beef with peppers
- Moo Goo Gai Pan
- steamed dumplings
- steamed fish
- mandarin pancakes
- Peking smoked chicken

Side Dishes

- steamed rice

Desserts

- Lychee nuts
- fortune cookies (limit to 1 or 2)
- fresh fruit cup

Sample Menu

Order # 1

	Tell the waiter:
wonton soup	
stir fried vegetables with pork	*No oil in stir fry.*
steamed rice	
2 fortune cookies	

Order # 2

	Tell the waiter:
teriyaki beef on skewer	*No oil on beef.*
chicken chow mein	*No oil in chow mein.*
chicken steamed dumplings	*No oil in dumplings.*
lychee nuts	

Order # 3

	Tell the waiter:
hot & sour soup	
Peking smoked chicken	*No oil on the chicken.*
mandarin pancakes	
fruit cup	

Fish or Seafood

Appetizers

- fried or buttered fish
- tempura
- clams casino

- New England clam chowder
- fish chowder (in cream)
- fish bisque soup

Main Courses

- any fried or cajun-fried fish
- stuffed fish
- fish in a cream sauce, cheese sauce
- fish in Newburg sauce
- casserole of fish
- lobster or any seafood in a pie

Side Dishes

- french fries
- creamy coleslaw

Desserts

- cakes, pies, ice cream

Fish Or Seafood

Tell the waiter: *Prepare my fish and vegetables without oil, butter or margarine, sauces to the side.*

Please substitute a baked potato for the french fries.

Please serve my salad dressing on the side.

Appetizers

- marinated calamari (with less oil)
- steamed clams or mussels (in tomato sauce or broth)
- shrimp cocktail
- Manhattan clam chowder
- tossed green salad with dressing on the side

Main Courses

- any fish prepared by grilling, broiling, charbroiling, poaching, steaming
- cajun, blackened with teriyaki sauce, wine, lemon juice or broth
- fish on kebobs
- steamed or broiled lobster or crab legs

- fish with tomato sauce
- bouillabaisse (seafood stew in a broth)

Side Dishes

- baked potato
- rice
- steamed vegetable (no butter, oil or margarine)

Desserts

- fresh fruit

Sample Menu

Order #1

	Tell the waiter:
steamed mussels in broth	*No oil or fat in the broth.*
steamed crab legs (6-8)	
baked potato with 5 ml (1 t.) butter, margarine or sour cream	*Butter, margarine or sour cream to the side.*
side salad with 15 ml (1 T.) dressing	*Dressing on the side.*

Order #2

	Tell the waiter:
Manhattan clam chowder	
teriyaki salmon	*No oil, butter or margarine on the salmon.*
rice	
vegetables	
sorbet	

French/Continental

✗ Poor Choice

Appetizers

- anything prepared “au gratin”
- pâté
- escargots
- artichoke hearts
- French onion soup
- cream soup
- croissants

Main Courses

- beef wellington
- New York sirloin
- rib eye steak
- marinated pork chops
- veal oscar
- chicken kiev
- chicken sautéed in olive oil
- duck à l’orange
- stuffed fish
- fish in a cream sauce or gratinée with cheese
- anything in a béchamel sauce
- coquille St. Jacques

Side Dishes

- creamed or fried vegetables
- vegetables gratinée with cheese sauce
- croissants

Desserts

- pies/cakes

French/Continental

Tell the waiter: *Please serve the sauce on the side.*

Grill, bake, broil without oil, butter or margarine.
Please serve the salad dressing on the side.

Please don't add any butter or sour cream to my baked potato.

May I have some cottage cheese, yogurt or dijon mustard for my baked potato?

Can you steam my vegetables without fat?

Appetizers

- grilled fish
- raw vegetables and dip
- tossed salad (dressing on the side)
- grilled asparagus (light on the oil)
- consommé
- gazpacho

Main Courses

- petit filet mignon
- rack of lamb
- poached salmon (dressing on the side)
- blanched fish
- chicken poached in wine

Side Dishes

- steamed vegetables
- baguette (no butter)

Desserts

- fresh fruit or fruit salad or sherbert

Sample Menu

Order #1

	Tell the waiter:
consommé soup	
poached salmon 140 grams (4-6 oz.)	*No oil or fat on the salmon, and put sauce on the side.*
baked potato with 15 ml (1 T.) sour cream	*Sour cream on the side.*
steamed vegetables	*No oil, butter or sauces on the vegetables.*

Order #2

	Tell the waiter:
vegetable salad with 15 ml. (1T.) dressing	*Dressing on the side.*
120 grams (3-4 oz.) filet mignon	*Sauce on the side.*
vegetable of the day	*No oil, butter or sauces on the vegetables.*
potato with 5 ml (1 t.) butter or margarine	*A plain baked potato instead of roasted; butter or sour cream on the side.*

Italian

✗ Poor Choice

Appetizers

- antipasto
- prosciutto
- garlic bread
- marinated mushrooms (in oil)
- fried calamari
- fried mozzarella sticks
- Caesar salad

Main Courses

- cannelloni
- fettucini alfredo
- pasta with white clam sauce
- pasta primavera (made with white sauce)
- lasagna
- ravioli
- veal piccata
- veal marsala
- veal or chicken parmigiana
- veal saltimbocca
- scallops marsala
- shrimp sautéed in oil
- pan broiled steak with marsala sauce
- pan roasted chicken with garlic
- stuffed breaded veal chops
- sautéed chicken or veal
- rolled and stuffed breast of veal

- spaghetti with garlic and oil
- pizza with extra cheese or sausage or pepperoni or bacon

Side Dishes

- vegetables prepared in oil

Dessert

- spumoni
- tortoni
- cannoli

Italian

Tell the waiter: *Prepare my dish without oil, butter or margarine, sauces to the side.*

Please put the dressing on the side of my salad.

Can I get a half portion of pasta?

Can you replace the cream sauce with a tomato sauce?

Appetizers

- pasta fagioli (bean and pasta soup)
- tortellini in broth
- tossed green salad with dressing on the side
- insalata fruitte di mare (marinated seafood on a bed of greens—order with less oil)
- minestrone soup

Main Courses

- ziti bolognese
- pasta with red clam sauce
- pasta with marinara sauce
- pasta primavera (made with red sauce)
- veal or chicken cacciatore
- shrimp primavera
- shrimp marinara
- lobster or shrimp fra diavlo
- potato gnocchi with tomato sauce
- fillet of sole with tomato sauce

Side Dishes

- steamed vegetables

Desserts

- Italian ice
- fresh fruit whip

Sample Menu

Order	Tell the waiter:
vegetable salad with 15 ml (1 T.) dressing and 15 ml (1 T.) Parmesan cheese	*Dressing on the side.*
pasta with red clam sauce	*No oil or butter or margarine on the pasta.*
steamed vegetables	*No oil, butter or sauce on the vegetables.*

Japanese

Poor Choice

Appetizers

- tempura appetizer
- tempura-udon (noodle soup with tempura)

Main Courses

- Agedashi tofu (fried tofu)
- tempura (deep-fried)
- agemono (deep-fried)
- katsu (deep-fried pork)
- uragi (broiled eel)

Desserts

- yokan (sweet bean cake)
- ice cream

Japanese

✔ Good Choice

Tell the waiter: *Please serve my salad with the dressing on the side.*

Prepare my dish without oil, butter or margarine.

Appetizers

- sushi and sashimi (all types)
- yotofu (broiled bean curd)
- shumai (steamed shrimp dumplings)
- ebisu (shrimp in vinegar sauce)
- yakiton
- svimono soup (clear broth)
- miso soup
- su-udon soup (noodles)
- tossed salad (with dressing on side)

Main Courses

- teriyaki chicken, fish, beef
- nabemono (one pot woked dinners)
- shabu-shabu (beef, vegetables, noodles)

Desserts

- fruit

Sample Menu

Order	Tell the waiter:
sushi 170 grams (6 oz.)	
teriyaki beef with vegetables	*No oil or fat.*
steamed rice	

Mexican

✗ Poor Choice

Appetizers

- avocado soup
- nachos
- any appetizer served with cheese, sour cream, olives, guacamole, refried beans

Main Courses

- any main entree served with melted cheese
- tostados
- any main entree topped with sour cream, guacamole or refried beans
- chicken or beef chimichanga
- enchilada el mole
- enchilada rancheras
- flautas con crema
- mole pollo

Side Dishes

- refried beans
- guacamole
- Mexican fried rice

Desserts

- sopaipillas (fried dough rolled in sugar)

Mexican

Good Choice

Tell the waiter: *Prepare my dishes without oil, butter or margarine.*

Serve the cheese on the side.

Serve the sour cream, guacamole and refried beans on the side.

Please put extra shredded lettuce, tomatoes and onion on the platter.

Appetizers

- black bean soup
- gazpacho soup
- tossed salad with dressing or herbs

Main Courses

- enchiladas (without cheese or sour cream)
- tacos (order cheese on the side)
- soft chicken tacos
- taco salad (order without sour cream, guacamole or refried beans)
- fajitas (order with less oil and no sour cream or guacamole)
- chicken or beef burritos (order cheese on the side)
- chili con carne
- Mexican salad (with dressing, sour cream, guacamole and beans on the side and served without the crisp tortilla shell)

Side Dishes

- black beans
- Mexican rice (not fried)
- salsa

Desserts

- flan

Sample Menu

Order #1

	Tell the waiter:
gazpacho soup	
2 chicken tacos with 30 ml (2 T.) cheese and salsa	*Cheese on the side.*
black beans	*No oil or fat on the beans.*
side salad with 15 ml (1 T.) dressing	*Dressing on the side.*

Order #2

	Tell the waiter:
tossed salad	*Dressing on the side.*

beef fajitas	*Prepare with less oil.*
and salsa	*Sour cream and/or guacamole on the side.*
Mexican rice	*Not fried.*

Thai

✗ Poor Choice

Appetizers

- Thai rolls
- tod mun (fried minced fish)
- vegetarian tofu (deep-fried tofu)
- tom ka gai soup (coconut milk soup)

Main Courses

- any dish made with curry sauce
- any dish that is deep-fried
- fried duck
- any dish with peanut sauce or nuts
- spare ribs
- praram long son (fried beef and curry)
- hot Thai cat fish (deep fried)
- pad thai (noodles stir-fried with peanuts, vegetables and shrimp)

Side Dishes

- fried tofu
- fried rice

Desserts

- coconut pudding
- custard
- ice cream

Thai

Tell the waiter: *Prepare my dishes without oil, butter or margarine.*

Prepare this dish without nuts.

Put the dressing on the side of the salad.

Appetizers

- tossed salad (with dressing on the side)
- satay (beef or chicken on skewers; hold the peanut sauce)
- steamed mussels or clams
- seafood kabob
- tom yum koung (soup)
- crystal noodle soup
- talay thong soup
- pok taek soup

Main Courses

- pla koong (shrimp salad)
- spiced beef salad (dressing on side)
- yam yai (combination salad—dressing on side)
- Thai chicken (ask for minimal oil)
- sweet and sour chicken
- beef basil
- scallops bamboo
- pork and string beans
- chili beef
- ginger pork
- garlic shrimp
- poy sian (seafood + vegetables)
- seafood platter (steamed)
- pod jay (vegetables and thai sauce)

Side Dishes

- steamed vegetables
- steamed rice

Desserts

- lychee nuts

Sample Menu

Order #1

	Tell the waiter:
crystal noodle soup	
garlic shrimp	*Very little oil or fat on the shrimp.*

yam yai (combination salad with 15 ml (1 T.) dressing) steamed rice	*Dressing on the side.*

Order #2

	Tell the waiter:
pok taek soup	
pork and string beans	*Prepare without oil.*
steamed rice	

Salad Bar

✗ Poor Choice

- croutons
- salad mixtures made with mayonnaise
  - macaroni salad
  - pasta salad
  - potato salad
  - tuna salad
  - egg salad
  - salmon salad
  - chicken/turkey salad
  - ambrosia salad
- marinated salad in dressing or mayonnaise
- three bean salad in dressing or mayonnaise
- bacon bits
- pepperoni
- crackers
- cheese breads
- sweet breads
- corn relish
- olives
- pickles
- Chinese noodles
- regular dressings
- peanuts
- sesame seeds
- sunflower seeds

Salad Bar

Good Choice

- undressed fresh vegetables
- fresh fruits or fruit salad
- artichokes (no oil)
- chick-peas
- beets
- green peas
- kidney beans (no oil)
- plain bread, rolls, breadsticks

- gelatin with fruit
- fruit salad
- raisins
- hot peppers
- low-calorie dressing
- vinegar
- Parmesan cheese (limit to 30 ml/2T.)
- shredded cheese (limit to 30 ml/2T.)
- cottage cheese (limit to 60 ml/1/4 cup)

Sample Menu

- fresh vegetables
- 60 ml (1/4 cup) chick-peas
- 30 ml (2 T.) Parmesan cheese
- 15 ml (1 T.) dressing
- lemon juice + vinegar
- 4 breadsticks or 1 small roll

Arby's

✗ Poor Choice

- Bacon and Egg Croissant
- Superstuffed Baked Potato
- Chicken Breast Fillet (breaded)
- Super Roast Beef

Arby's

✔ Good Choice

Tell the server: *Please serve my potato with the sour cream or margarine on the side.*

Hold the sauce on the grilled chicken sandwich.

No butter on the bun or my sandwich.

- Baked Potato, plain
- Grilled Chicken Deluxe Sandwich (no sauce)

- Junior Roast Beef sandwich
- Regular Roast Beef sandwich

Sample Menu

Order	Tell the server:
junior roast beef	*No butter on the bun.*
baked potato with 10 ml (2 t.) sour cream or 5 ml (1 t.) butter	*Sour cream (or butter) on the side of the potato.*

Burger King

✗ Poor Choice

- Croissant sandwiches (all varieties)
- Scrambled Egg Platter with Sausages
- Chicken Sandwich (breaded)
- Whopper with Cheese
- Double Whopper with Cheese
- Bacon Double Cheeseburger

Burger King

Good Choice

Tell the server: *No mayonnaise or special sauce on my sandwich or burger.*

Dressing on the side of the salad.

- salad bar with cheese or eggs for protein, crackers for carbohydrates and 15 ml (1 T.) dressing
- B.K. Broilcr
- Hamburger (no mayo; women)
- Whopper (no mayo; men)

Sample Menu

Order	Tell the server:
Hamburger (no mayo)	*No mayonnaise on the Whopper.*
Side salad with 10 ml (2 t.) dressing	*Dressing on the side.*

Harvey's

✗ Poor Choice

- Double Burger
- Super Burger
- Chicken Sandwich (breaded)
- Bacon, Egg, Tomato Sandwich
- Sausage, Egg and Tomato Sandwich
- Bran Muffin

Harvey's

Good Choice

Tell the server: *No mayonnaise on my sandwich.*

Dressing on the side of my salad.

- Light Burger
- Junior Burger
- Grilled Chicken Sandwich (with lettuce, tomato, mustard)
- Hamburger
- Hot Dog
- Side Salad
- Pancakes

Sample Menu

Order

	Tell the server:
Grilled Chicken Sandwich with lettuce, tomato and mustard	*No mayonnaise on the sandwich.*
Side Salad with 30 ml (2 T.) light dressing	

McDonald's

✗ Poor Choice

- Big Mac
- Quarter Pounder with Cheese
- Sausage McMuffin with Egg
- Chicken McNuggets
- Filet-o-Fish sandwich

McDonald's

Tell the server: *Serve my English muffin without butter or margarine.*

Hold the special sauce on my burger.

Hold the topping on the frozen yogurt.

- Chef's Salads; light vinagrette dressing
- English Muffin
- McLean Deluxe
- Hamburger; women
- Quarter Pounder; men
- Low-Fat Frozen Yogurt
- Low-Fat Shake

Sample Menu

Order	Tell the server:
1 McLean Deluxe	
1 Side Salad with 30 ml (2 T.) low-fat dressing	
1 Low-Fat Frozen yogurt	*No topping on the frozen yogurt.*

Pizza Places

✗ Poor Choice

- deep-dish pizza
- double-cheese pizza
- sausage or pepperoni pizza
- Caesar salad

Pizza Places

Good Choice

Tell the server: *Can I get less cheese and double vegetables on my pizza?*

- cheese personal pan pizza
- cheese pizza with vegetables; 2 slices

Sample Menu

Order	Tell the server:
2 slices (from a 14") or 1 personal pan cheese and vegetable pizza (thin and crispy crust)	

1 side salad with 10 ml (2 t.) dressing	*Dressing on the side.*

Submarine Shops

✗ Poor Choice

- deep-fried chicken sub
- tuna sub
- subs larger than 17.5 cms. (7")

Submarine Shops

Good Choice

Tell the server: *No sauce, no oil, no mayonnaise on my sandwich.*

- mini sub or snack sub (turkey, seafood or roast beef)
- no mayo or oil

Sample Menu

Order	Tell the server:
mini turkey sub (with turkey, lettuce, tomato, peppers, onions and mustard) (preferably on a whole wheat bun)	*No sauce, no oil, no mayonnaise, just mustard on the sandwich.*

Swiss Chalet

✗ Poor Choice

- French Fries

- Half Chicken Dinner with fries
- Double Chicken Leg Dinner
- Rib Combo Dinner
- Rib/Chicken Combo Dinner
- Coleslaw

Swiss Chalet

Tell the server: *Serve my salad with dressing on the side.*

Serve my gravy on the side of my chicken or sandwich.

Serve my potato with the sour cream or margarine on the side.

- Baked Potato
- Quarter Chicken Dinner (take off skin)
- any Combo from "Lighter Fare"
- Chicken Soup
- Chalet Salad (with light dressing)
- BBQ Sauce
- Chicken Sandwich (no gravy)
- Roll

Sample Menu

Order

Quarter Chicken Dinner with baked potato and salad; take skin off chicken; use 10 ml (2 t.) dressing on salad; use 10 ml (2 t.) sour cream or 5 ml (1 t.) margarine on the potato

Tell the server:

Nothing on the potato and dressing on the side of the salad.

Taco Bell

✗ Poor Choice

- Taco Salad
- Soft Taco Supreme
- Nachos Supreme
- Mexican Pizza
- Beef Burrito
- Burrito Supreme

Taco Bell

Good Choice

Tell the server: *Serve the guacamole, refried beans and sour cream on the side.*

Serve the cheese on the side.

Serve the dressing on the side of the salad.

- Bean Burrito
- Taco
- Tostada (no beef)
- Pintos and Cheese

Sample Menu

Order

Tell the server:

1 Bean Burrito — *No guacamole or sour cream.*

1 Taco

Wendy's

✗ Poor Choice

- Big Classic
- Fish Filet sandwich
- Hot Stuffed Baked Potatoes
- Taco Salad

Wendy's

Tell the server: *Please serve my potato with the sour cream or margarine on the side.*

Hold the mayonnaise/special sauce on my burger or sandwich.

- Plain Baked Potato
- Chili
- Junior Hamburger Deluxe
- Teriyaki Grilled Chicken
- Grilled Chicken Sandwich (without honey mustard mayo)
- Salad Bar—raw vegetables with chick-peas and low calorie dressing
- Deluxe Garden Salad (no breakstick)
- Grilled Chicken Salad (no breadstick)

Sample Menu

Order	Tell the server:
Grilled ChickenSandwich	*No honey mustard sauce (it contains mayonnaise).*
1 Side Salad with 10 ml (2 t.) dressing	

Hidden Fat Food List

teaspoons of hidden fat

avocado, 1/2 ●●●

bacon, 3 strips ●●●

Beef:

- beef pot pie, 10 cm. (4")
- porterhouse steak, 165 grams (6 oz.)
- rib eye steak, 165 grams (6 oz.)
- sirloin steak, 165 grams (6 oz.)
- T-bone steak, 165 grams (6 oz.)
- salisbury steak, 165 grams (6 oz.)
- ribs, 280 grams (10 oz.)
- swedish meatballs, 336 grams (12 oz.)

Biscuits:

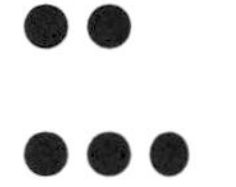

- plain with butter, 110 grams (4 oz.)
- breakfast biscuit with egg and bacon (or sausage and ham)

Bread:

- banana bread 3-3/4 cm. (1 x 1/2" slice)
- bran bread (1 x 1/2" slice)
- cornbread (2" square)

Breakfast plates:

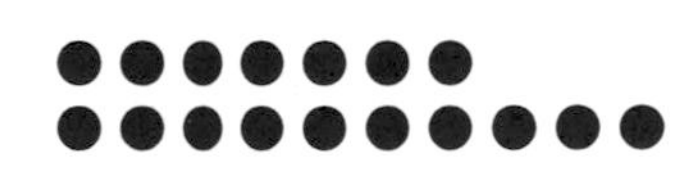

- scrambled egg platter
  - with bacon & toast
  - with sausage & toast

Cake:

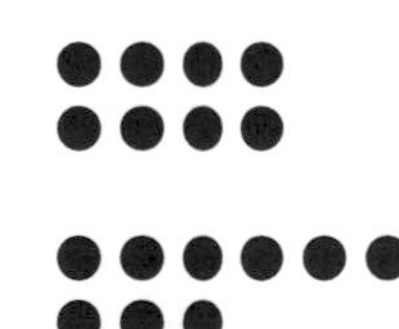

- fudge brownie with nuts
- carrot cake with cream cheese, 22-1/2 cm. (1/12th 9" cake)
- cheesecake, 22-1/2 cm. (1/12th cake)
- coffee cake, 22-1/2 cm. (1/12th 9" cake)
- fruit cake, 1.7 cm. (2/3" slice)

Cereal:

- granola, 125 ml (1/2 cup)
- muesli, 125 ml (1/2 cup)

Cheese:

- cheese fondue, 125 ml (1/2 cup)
- 20% M.F. hard cheese, 28 grams (1 oz.)

4% M.F. creamed cottage cheese, 125 ml (1/2 cup)	●●
Chinese Food:	
beef & broccoli, 250 ml (1 cup)	●●●
1 beef, chicken or pork chow mein, 250 ml (1 cup)	●●●●●
chop suey, 250 ml (1 cup)	●●●
1 egg roll	●●
fried rice, 250 ml (1 cup)	●●●
moo goo guy pan, 250 ml (1 cup)	●●●●●
fried chow mein noodles, 125 ml (1/2 cup)	●●
3 fried wontons	●●●●
lemon chicken, 120 grams (4 oz.)	●●●
Szechuan beef or chicken with noodles, 250 ml (1 cup)	●●●●●
stir-fried beef or chicken (made with oil), 250 ml (1 cup)	●●●
Chicken:	
baked chicken with skin, 85 grams (3 oz.)	●●
chicken à la king, 250 ml (1 cup)	●●●●●
6 chicken nuggets	●●●
1 chicken pot pie, 10 cm. (4")	●●●●●●●
1 chicken sandwich (breaded/fried with cheese)	●●●●●●●●
chicken salad	●●●
1 chicken wing	●
fried chicken, 120 grams (4 oz.)	●●●
extra crispy fried chicken, 120 grams (4 oz.)	●●●●
Chips:	
1 pkg. corn chips, 50 grams (1.75 oz.)	●●●●
1 small pkg. potato chips or cheese balls	●●●
1 small pkg. tortilla chips	●●
chocolate bar	●●●●
cinnamon bun	●●●●●●
club sandwich	●●●
coleslaw, creamed, 125 ml (1/2 cup)	●●
Cookies:	
2 chocolate chip (or 1 large)	●●
1 gourmet chocolate chip	●●●●
2 peanut butter (or 1 large)	●●
2 sandwich cookies	●●

Crackers:
- 5 cheese flavoured crackers ●●
- 5 vegetable flavoured crackers ●●
- 5 peanut butter flavoured crackers ●●
- pita crisps ●●
- bagel chips, 28 grams (1 oz.) ●●
- 5 Tam Tams ●

Croissants:
- plain ●●
- sandwich with egg/cheese ●●●●
- sandwich with bacon, ham or sausage ●●●●●●
- sandwich with ham and cheese ●●●●●

danish ●●●●

donut ●●●●

duck, roasted, 120 grams (4 oz.) ●●●●●●

Omelette:
- plain
- cheese
- western

Breakfast Plate:
- 2 eggs with bacon or sausage or ham and hash browns

egg salad 125 ml (1/2 cup) ●●●

Fish:
- battered fish sandwich (i.e., filet-o-fish or whaler)
- 2 pieces fish and chips
- 1 lunch serving, clams or calamari, breaded and fried
- Lobster Newburg, 250 ml (1 cup)
- 1 frozen "lightly breaded" fish fillet
- fish au gratin, 120 grams (4 oz.)
- fish dijon, 120 grams (4 oz.)
- fish mornay, 120 grams (4 oz.)

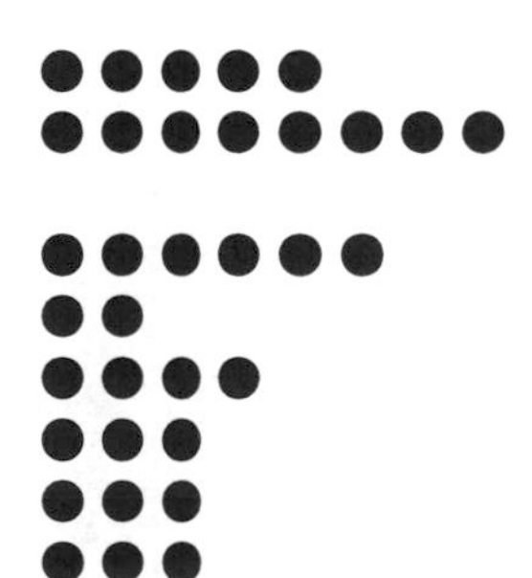

French Fries:
- small order
- large order

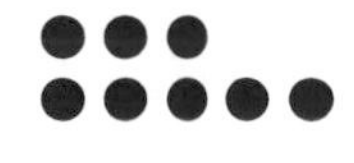

French toast with syrup (2 slices) ●●

Food	
Hamburgers:	
cheeseburger on bun, 120 grams (4 oz.)	●●●●●●
hamburger on bun, 120 grams (4 oz.)	●●●●●
double burger on bun	●●●●●●●●●●
triple burger on bun	●●●●●●●●●●●●●
Big Mac/Big Classic	●●●●●●
Whopper	●●●●●●●
Hot Dogs:	
1 hot dog, regular	●●
1 hot dog, jumbo	●●●
1 super hot dog with cheese or chili	●●●●●●●
franks and beans, 280 grams (10 oz.)	●●●●●
ice cream, 125 ml (1/2 cup)	●●
liver, pan fried, 85 grams (3 oz.)	●●
Mexican	
1 burrito, beef supreme	●●●●●
2 enchiladas, beef	●●●●
2 enchiladas, cheese	●●●●
1 plate nachos (with beef, beans and cheese)	●●●●●●●●
2 tacos, beef	●●●
1 taco salad	●●●●
1 taco light platter	●●●●●●●●●●●●
1 tostada, beef	●●●
Milk Drinks:	
chocolate milk, 250 ml (1 cup)	●●●●
egg nog, 250 ml (1 cup)	●●●●
homo milk, 250 ml (1 cup)	●●
1 regular milkshake	●●●
onion rings (10)	●●●●●
nuts, 60 ml (1/4 cup)—almonds, peanuts, cashews, butternuts, Brazil nuts, macadamia nuts	●●●●
olives (6)	●
Pasta:	
buttered pasta, 250 ml (1 cup)	●●●●
spaghetti & meat sauce, 250 ml (1 cup)	●●
pasta alfredo/white clam sauce/carbonara	●●●●●●●●
lasagna, 280 grams (10 oz.)	●●●●●

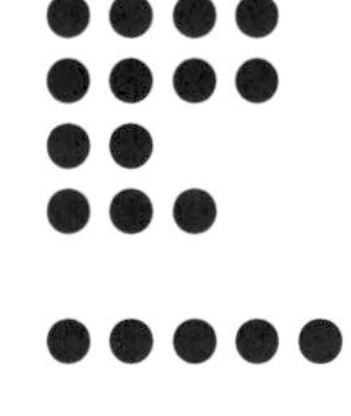

macaroni salad, 250 ml (1 cup) ●●●●●
manicotti & meat sauce, 250 ml (1 cup) ●●●●
pasta salad, 125 ml (1/2 cup) ●●●

2 x 6" pancakes with butter & syrup ●●●●

Pastry/Pie
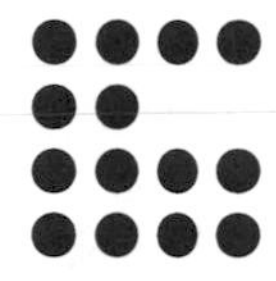
cream pie, 22-1/2 cm. (1/8 x 9" pie) ●●●●
fruit pie, 22-1/2 cm. (1/8 x 9" pie) ●●
pecan or raisin pie, 22-1/2 cm. (1/8 x 9" pie) ●●●●
1 turnover (apple, blueberry or cherry) ●●●●

pâté, 28 grams (1 oz.) ●●●

Pizza (cut from 35 cm (14") size)
2 slices cheese ●●●●
2 slices cheese and pepperoni ●●●●●●
2 slices all-dressed ●●●●●●
2 slices double-cheese ●●●●●●
1 single serving deep-dish ●●●●●●

popcorn, oil popped, no butter, 1 litre (4 cups) ●●●
popcorn, oil popped, with butter, 1 litre (4 cups) ●●●●●●●●●

Potato:

1 stuffed with cheese ●●●●●●●
1 topped with sour cream ●●●●●
mashed potato with milk & butter, 125 ml (1/2 cup) ●
potato salad 125 ml (1/2 cup) ●●●
potato pancakes (fried in oil), 2 x 15 cm. (6") ●●●●●●
scalloped potatoes 125 ml (1/2 cup) ●●●●

quiche (1/6 x 22-1/2 cm. (9") pie) ●●●●●●

roast beef sandwich, 112 grams (4 oz.) ●●●●●

Salad:

Caesar, 500 ml (2 cups) ●●●●●●●●●
Greek, 500 ml (2 cups) ●●●●●
julienne or cobb (with turkey, ham, cheese, and vinaigrette dressing), 500 ml (2 cups) ●●●●●●●●●●●●●

Sauces:
60 ml (1/4 cup):
bearnaise sauce ●●●●●●
cheese sauce

curry sauce	●●●●●●
hollandaise sauce	●●●●●●
mushroom sauce	●●●●●●
sour cream sauce	●●●●●●
white sauce	●●●●●●
1 sausage link (small)	●●
1 scone, 120 grams (4 oz.)	●●●●
smoked meat or pastrami sandwich, 85 grams (3 oz.)	●●●●●
Soup:	
fish chowder (white), 250 ml (1 cup)	●●
cream soups, 250 ml (1 cup)	●●
stuffing, 125 ml (1/2 cup)	●●●
small sundae (hot fudge, no whipped cream or nuts)	●●●
(with whipped cream and nuts)	●●●●●●●●
Turkey:	
meat with skin, roasted 85 grams (3 oz.)	●●
turkey á là king 125 ml (1/2 cup)	●●●●●
1 turkey pot pie, 10 cm. (4")	●●●●●●●
1 turkey wing, 225 grams (1/2 lb.), meat + skin, roasted	●●●●●●
veal parmigiana, 120 grams (4 oz.)	●●●●●
vegetables in cheese sauce, 250 ml (1 cup)	●●●●
yogurt (2% B.F. or more), 250 ml (1 cup)	●●

Grocery Shopping the Healthy Weigh

The way you have been eating in the past has been largely determined by the food you have had in your home.

High-fat, high-calorie foods that tempt you should not be kept in your home. Don't test your willpower. If these foods are available, you may be able to avoid them for a while, but eventually your willpower will break down and then you will probably eat them! Replace these foods with healthier, lower-fat choices. There are many healthy and delicious choices available today, because manufacturers are aware of the strong consumer demand for healthier foods.

Read the labels!

Refer to the list of ingredients

Every packaged food must include a list of ingredients. The ingredient in largest quantity is listed first, while the one in the smallest quantity is last.

The list of ingredients can show you the relative amount of sugar, fat and salt in the product, but beware, because these 3 ingredients can appear on the list disguised with other names.

Sugar can also be referred to as brown sugar, fructose, corn syrup, dextrose, galactose, glucose, honey, lactose, sorbitol, mannitol, maltose or molasses. Each of these names can be listed separately, but added up together, all the sweeteners can make sugar the product's main ingredient.

Fats are those ingredients listed as beef or chicken fat, butter, lard, vegetable oil, shortening, palm and coconut oil. Products that contain them should be used in moderation, especially if they appear near the beginning of the list of ingredients. Remember that high-fat products can make your body fat, so limit the amount you eat.

Sodium can appear on the list of ingredients as baking powder, baking soda (sodium bicarbonate), sodium chloride, sodium citrate, sodium nitrate, sodium benzoate, monosodium glutamate (MSG) or brine. If nutrition information is provided, look for the number of milligrams (mg) of sodium. Your daily requirement for sodium is 1000-3000 milligrams daily, but the average intake is about 4000-6000 milligrams daily. You must also consider that some foods are very high in sodium, such as pickles, sauerkraut, cheese and smoked and cured meats. The sodium in foods will not cause you to gain fat, but it can cause water retention in some people.

Additives cover a wide range of ingredients from flavours, colours and preservatives, to vitamins, minerals, sugar, salt and fat. They serve a wide variety of purposes and they are not all bad. They are used in a wide variety of nutritious convenience foods, such as canned fruits and vegetables, packaged breads and cereals. High standards of food quality would not be possible without additives.

Don't be fooled by the additive names used on some labels. For example, if you read an ingredient list that says "water, starches, cellulose, pectin, fructose, sucrose, glucose, malic acid, citric acid, succinic acid, anisyl propionate, amyl acetate, ascorbic acid, beta carotene, riboflavin, thiamin, niacin, phosphorus, potassium," would you think this product is full of additives? It's not. It is actually the content of a natural healthy food—cantaloupe!

All products do not have the same portion size. For example, some cereals have 60 millimetres (1/4 cup) listed as a serving while others have 375 millimetres (1-1/2 cups) as a serving. Therefore, if you compare only calories from one product to the next, you could be making a mistake, because the portion sizes can be different.

Nutrition Information

"Reduced calorie," "No cholesterol," "High fibre," "Less sodium," "90% fat-free." All of these and other nutrition claims should be investigated. For example, a packaged turkey cold cut labelled as 90% fat-free means that 10% of the product by weight is fat and that's a lot of fat! To determine whether a product is truly low in fat, you should determine the percentage of calories that comes from fat (not the percentage of weight that is fat). The healthy guideline is to choose products that contain less than 30% of their calories as fat.

We hope that, in the future, manufacturers will list the percentage of calories that are fat right on the label. Meanwhile, refer to the following chart.

If one serving provides:	It should contain no more than:
50 calories	1.5 grams of fat
100 calories	3.0 grams of fat
150 calories	5.0 grams of fat
200 calories	6.0 grams of fat
250 calories	8.0 grams of fat
300 calories	9.0 grams of fat
350 calories	11.5 grams of fat
400 calories	12.0 grams of fat
450 calories	15.0 grams of fat

Diet Foods

Diet foods are products in which an ingredient has been restricted or changed. However, so-called "diet foods" are not necessarily low in calories, fat or sugar. Chocolate bars labelled "dietetic" are often higher in fat and calories than regular chocolate bars. Some frozen diet entrées are higher in fat than their regular counterparts. Calories may be reduced because a serving size is smaller, but the food may still be high in fat. Some light cheeses contain only 1 gram of fat less than the regular variety, but still contribute nearly 50% of the calories from fat. Even though they may be sugar-free, some "light" or "sugar-free" desserts are just as high or higher in fat than their regular counterparts. Don't be misled by "no cholesterol" or "100% vegetable shortening." These labels do not necessarily mean that the product is low in saturated or total fat.

So, read your labels carefully! The shopping list at the end of this chapter will help you choose some of the better products on the market, but there are new items introduced daily. It's a good idea to become familiar with reading labels; they cannot help you if you don't read them.

There are many foods and ingredients on the market today that are good-tasting, attractive and indeed low-calorie, low-fat, low-sodium or low in sugar. Many of these foods can reduce the anxiety of "doing without" and enable you to successfully control your food and calorie intake.

Protein Foods

1) Meat (Fresh or Frozen)

Select lean, well-trimmed cuts. Fat is marbled throughout meat, so use your eyes to determine the least amount of white marbling. Also, the higher the grade (the better the quality), the more cholesterol and fat it contains. Meat of lower quality graded "select" has less fat than "choice" or "prime" grades. Trim as much visible fat off the meat as possible before cooking, so that it will not be absorbed into the meat. Marinate less fatty cuts to make them tender. Prepared meats in pastry, patties or sauce signal high fat, so eat them sparingly.

Good choices are:

a) Beef
- Flank steak
- Ground beef (lean or extra lean)
- Round (all cuts)
- Sirloin

b) Lamb
- Lamb loin
- Leg of lamb

c) Pork
- Pork loin chops
- Pork tenderloin

d) Veal
- Veal chops
- Lean ground veal

2) Poultry

Poultry can be a source of less fat than red meat, provided the skin is removed prior to cooking and low-fat ingredients and preparation methods are used. Avoid ready-made poultry in pastry, patties, nuggets, breading or sauce. Plain, unbasted and utility poultry has less fat than basted. Don't be fooled by ground chicken or turkey; they can contain more fat than ground beef. Ask about which parts of the bird have been ground up, and avoid those that have included the fat and skin.

Good choices are:

Chicken—no skin (or remove prior to cooking)
Turkey—no skin (or remove prior to cooking)

3) Fresh or Frozen Fish

The best choices for fish are plain; fresh or frozen; or canned in water or broth, as those are the lowest in fat.

The high-fat choices are those that are breaded, battered in sauces, with cheese, in patties, cakes, sticks, nuggets, pâtés, in salad mixtures or in pastry.

Good choices (fresh fish) are:

Bass	* Herring	Shark
* Blue	Lobster	Shrimp
Caviar	* Mackerel	Smelt
Clams	Mussels	Snapper
Cod	Perch	Sole
Crab	Oysters	Squid
Dolphin	Pike	Sturgeon
Flounder	Pollock	Swordfish
Gefilte fish	Salmon	Trout
Grouper	* Sardines	* Tuna
Haddock	Scallops	Turbot
	Whitefish	

The fish that are starred (*) are those that are higher in a very healthy fish oil called "omega 3 fatty acids." This type of fish oil has been shown to protect against heart disease.

Good choices (frozen fish) are:

—any fish listed above frozen without salt, sauce or cheese

4) Packaged Luncheon Meats

Use packaged meats in moderation due to their high fat and high sodium content. They are also high in nitrites, which have been shown to cause cancer. Choose fresh luncheon meats from the deli counter instead.

Canadian or back bacon is leaner than side bacon. To reduce the fat even more, trim prior to cooking.

5) Deli Counter

Most deli products are high in fat and salt, so they should be eaten in moderation. Choose items that are not premixed with mayonnaise, oil and sauce, and not in pastry or breading.

Good choices are:

Lean chicken breast
Lean ham (is higher in sodium)
Lean roast beef
Lean turkey breast
Part skim milk cheese (less than 20% B.F.)

6) Canned Meat, Fish and Poultry

Choose products packed in water or broth whenever possible. If oil-packed products are used, rinse and drain the product well. The edible bones of canned sardines and salmon are high in calcium, which is good for your bones and teeth.

Good choices are:

Baby clams
Chicken/turkey packed in water
Cocktail shrimp
Crab meat
Mackerel
Oysters packed in water
Salmon (low-sodium also available)
(high in calcium if eaten with the bones)
Tuna—packed in water

7) Eggs

If your cholesterol levels are normal, there is no need to cut eggs out of your diet. Three to four eggs weekly are all right to have on the prudent diet. If you are on a low-cholesterol diet, you can replace whole eggs with egg whites or egg substitutes. Don't be fooled by health claims made about brown eggs. Brown and white eggs have the same nutritional value.

8) Legumes (dried beans, peas), Canned Beans, Peanut Butter

Legumes are a high-fibre, low-fat extension or replacement for meat and fish. To make them a complete protein choice, combine them with any grain (rice, bread, etc.), lean protein food (meat, fish, poultry), low-fat dairy food (milk, cheese, yogurt), nuts or seeds.

Good legume choices are:

Black beans
Black-eyed peas
Chick-peas
Kidney beans
Lentils
Lima beans
Mung beans
Navy beans
Pinto beans
Soybeans
Split peas
Canned beans in tomato sauce (no pork)
Tofu (high in calcium)

If you do not have time to cook the legumes yourself, you can purchase pre-cooked legumes in cans.

9) Frozen Dinners

Even though the "light" frozen dinners can be less than 300 calories, they can still be high in fat. In some instances, the calories are lower because the portion sizes are smaller. Choose dinners with less than 9 grams of fat for each 300 calories. Dinners in cream sauces, cheese sauces, breadings, batters, pastry and pie crusts signal high fat.

Dairy Products

To determine the amount of fat in calcium foods, look for the percentage of milk fat (%M.F.), percentage of butterfat (%B.F.) or, in French, percentage of matiére grasse (%M.G.), written on the label.

1) Milk

Choose non-fat and low-fat milk. Specialty milk beverages such as eggnog and chocolate milk are higher in fat, sugar and calories.

Good choices are:

Buttermilk (made from skim or low fat)
Evaporated skim milk
Milk— skim, 1%, 2%, lactose reduced
Skim milk powder

2) Yogurt

Choose products with 1% M.F. (milk fat) or less. It is best to buy plain yogurt and add your own fruit. You can also add a tablespoon of all-fruit jam to plain low-fat yogurt.

Good choices are:

Astro fat-free and cholesterol free (0.1% M.F.)
Astro naturally light (1% M.F.)
Beatrice diet (0.1% M.F.)
Beatrice light (0.4% M.F.)
Delisle light (1% M.F.)
Nordica light (0.1% M.F.)
Sealtest Light n' Lively (0.9% M.F.)
Sealtest Light n' Lively diet (0.04% M.F.)
Silhouette light (0.1% M.F.)
Western (0.1% M.F.)
Western (1.1% M.F.)
Yoplait light (0.1% M.F.)

3) Cheese

Choose cheeses that have less than 20% butterfat. Avoid processed varieties, as these are higher in sodium.

Good Choices are:

Colby light
Cottage cheese (1% or 2% M.F.)
Cottage cheese pressed (0.5% or 1% M.F.)
Gouda light
Jarlsberg light
Reduced Calories Laughing Cow cheese
Mozzarella, part skim
Parmesan, grated
Quark
Ricotta, low-fat
Swiss light

Starchy Foods

1) Cold Cereals

As a rule with cereals, the shorter the list of ingredients the more nutritious the product.

Aim for cereals with less than 2 grams of fat, less than 5 grams of sugar and more than 2 grams of fibre per serving.

You can increase the fibre content of low-fibre cereals by mixing them with a high-fibre cereal or adding fruit.

Note the portion size listed on the nutrition information chart.

The usual serving size is 30 grams (1 ounce) by weight, which can range from 60 millilitres (1/4 cup) for granola to 125 millilitres (1/2 cup) for bran cereals, to 500 millilitres (2 cups) for puffed cereals. Look for the words "whole wheat," "whole grain," "whole corn," "oat bran," "oats," "whole millet" or "whole barley" at the beginning of the list of ingredients. Avoid cereals in which sugar (or honey, corn syrup, fructose, molasses) is near the beginning of the list. Some pre-sweetened cereals have as much as 20 millilitres (4 teaspoons) added sugar per cup. Granola and even "light granola" are not good choices, since they are high in both sugar and fat.

Good choices are:

- All Bran
- Balance
- 100% Bran
- Bran Buds
- Bran Flakes
- Cheerios—plain
- Chex—all varieties
- Fibre One
- Frosted Mini Wheats
- Fruitful Bran
- Grapenuts
- Mini Wheats
- Nutrigrain
- Puffed Rice
- Puffed Wheat
- Raisin Bran
- Shredded Wheat
- Shredded Wheat n' Bran
- Special K
- Total
- Wheetabix Whole Wheat cereal
- Wheaties

2) Hot Cereals

Choose plain varieties without added sugar. The more processed the cereal, the less nutritious it is.

Good choices are:

- Corn grits
- Cornmeal
- Cream of Rice
- Cream of Wheat
- Farina
- Oatbran
- Oatmeal/rolled oats
- Red River
- Rice bran

3) Breads

White breads are not as high in fibre or nutrients as whole grain breads. Better choices are a multigrain variety, 60% or 100% whole wheat. Look for the words "whole grain" or "whole wheat" first on the list of ingredients. Croissants, sweet breads, Danish and cheese breads are high in fat and are not the healthiest choices.

Good choices are:

Bagels (preferably whole wheat)
Bran bread
Cracked wheat bread
English muffins (preferably whole wheat)
French stick (preferably whole wheat)
Italian bread (enriched)
Multigrain bread
Oatbran bread (made from whole grain or whole wheat flour)
Pita bread (preferably whole wheat)
Pumpernickel bread
Rye bread
Sourdough bread
Unsalted tortillas (corn or whole wheat without fat)
Vienna bread
100% whole wheat bread
60% whole wheat bread

4) Crackers

Crackers advertised as "buttery" or "rich", and those containing cheese, vegetable or meat flavours are higher in fat and calories than plain crackers.

Choose crackers with no added fat or with fat listed near the end of the list of ingredients. Aim for those with less than 2 grams of fat per serving.

Avoid crackers containing saturated fats such as butter, lard, palm oil, palm kernel oil, coconut oil and hydrogenated oils.

Good choices are:

Breadsticks (plain, onion, sesame)
Canapes
Crispbread
Flatbreads
Matzo
Melba toast
Rice cakes
Rusks
Wasa (all varieties)
Zwieback toast

5) Pasta Products

Whole wheat pasta is the best nutritional choice of the pasta products. Coloured pasta is made with vegetable pulp, but is not much more nutritious than plain white pasta.

For pasta mixes, read the list of ingredients and choose those without added cheese, oil, lard or butter. Do not add fat to the products, even if instructions call for it. The finished products will be just as good without the fat. For canned pasta products, choose those in tomato-based sauces.

Good choices are:

Whole wheat pastas

6) Rice Products

Choose converted, wild and brown rice. Avoid rice mixes with hidden fat or cheese in the list of ingredients.

Good choices are:

Brown rice
Converted rice
Wild rice

7) Other Grains

Other grains can be used as part of a meal or to extend a meal.

Good choices are:

Barley
Bulgur
Cornmeal
Corn tortillas
Couscous
Wheat bran
Wheat germ

8) Non-Cream Soups

High-fat soups are those that are chowdered, creamed or bisqued, and those that contain a lot of meat. If you are concerned about the fat in soups, refrigerate them prior to use. When you open the can, the fat will have settled on the top, and you can remove it prior to cooking. Soups are often high in sodium, but there are low-sodium versions of many of the ones listed below.

Good choices are:

Beef Barley
Beef noodle/beef vegetable/beef rice
Chicken noodle/chicken vegetable (non-creamed)/ chicken gumbo/chicken rice
Lentil

Manhattan clam chowder
Minestrone
Pea (no pork, made with water)
Scotch broth
Won Ton
Vegetable (non-creamed)

9) Mixes: Cake, Quick Breads and Pancakes

Most cake and quick bread mixes are high in fat, sugar and calories. The best choice of cake mix is angel food cake, as it contains little fat and, as a result, is quite low in calories.

Good choices are:

Aunt Jemima—original pancake mix
whole wheat pancake & waffle mix
angel food cake mix
low-fat muffin mix

10) Frozen Bakery and Breakfast Items

Choose those with less than 5 grams of fat per serving.

Good choices are:

Bagels—all varieties

11. Potatoes and Corn

Potatoes and corn are considered "the starchy vegetables" since they contain less water than the other vegetables. Sweet potatoes and corn are rich in vitamin A.

Good choices are:

Potatoes
Sweet potatoes
Corn

Vegetables and Corn

1) Vegetables

Vegetables are a powerhouse of vitamins and minerals. As a rule, the deeper the colour, the more nutrients they contain. Choose vegetables that are deep green, deep orange, deep red and deep yellow in colour. Cruciferous vegetables are those belonging to the cabbage family, such as cabbage, broccoli, Brussel sprouts and cauliflower. This group of vegetables contains a substance called "indoles" which has been shown to protect against cancer. Fresh vegetables are higher in fibre than their juices, so choose them instead of juice whenever possible.

Best choices are:

Deep-coloured vegetables (Vitamin A-rich)	Vitamin C-rich vegetables	Cruciferous vegetables
Asparagus	Peppers	Broccoli
Broccoli	Tomatoes	Brussel sprouts
Carrots		Cabbage
Green beans		Cauliflower
Parsley		
Peas		
Peppers		
Romaine lettuce		
Shallots		
Spinach		
Squash		
Tomatoes		
Yams		

2) Fruits

Fresh fruits are higher in fibre than their juices, so choose them instead of juice whenever possible. Dried fruits are very concentrated in sugar, so limit the amount you eat.

As a rule, the deeper the colour of the fruit, the more nutrients it contains.

Best choices are:

Deep-coloured fruits (Vitamin A-rich)	Vitamin C-rich fruits
Apricots	Grapefruit
Berries	Lemons
Cherries	Limes
Grapes	Oranges
Kiwi	Strawberries
Melons	Kiwi
Nectarines	
Oranges	
Peaches	
Strawberries	

3) Frozen and Canned Vegetables

Frozen vegetables are just as nutritious as fresh, provided the vegetables have no added salt, sauce or cheese.

Canned vegetables are not as high in fibre as fresh or frozen, and they are higher in salt. However, they are just as high in vitamins and minerals and they are convenient to have on hand. Low-sodium varieties of canned vegetables are also available.

Good choices are:

Frozen vegetables (no added salt, sauce or cheese)
Canned vegetables (non-creamed and without oil)

4) Frozen and Canned Fruit

Frozen fruits are almost as nutritious as fresh provided they have no added sugar.

Canned fruits are not as high in fibre as fresh or frozen fruits, especially if they have been pulverized into sauce (i.e., applesauce, etc.). However, they are just as high in vitamins and minerals and they are convenient to have on hand.

Choose:

Unsweetened frozen fruits
Canned fruits (in water or own juice)

Added Fats

Fats

Use as little added fat as possible. Saturated fats are the worst types because they contribute to increased blood cholesterol levels.

Oils

Choose oils highest in polyunsaturated and monounsaturated fats, and lowest in saturated fat (less than 2 grams of saturated fat per 15 millilitres (1 tablespoon). Note that some oils are labelled "light." This does not mean light in calories or fat. It means light in colour or taste.

Good choices are:

Canola (rapeseed)
Olive
Peanut
Corn
Safflower
Soybean
Sunflower

Peanut Butter

Choose natural peanut butter with no added sugar, salt or fat. With natural peanut butter, the fat floats on the top. You can lower the fat content by pouring the fat off. To increase the sweetness, spread all-fruit jam on top.

Good choices are:

Natural 100% peanuts

Margarines

When liquid vegetable oils are partially hydrogenated to make margarines, substances called trans fatty acids are formed. New studies indicate that these acids behave like saturated fats in the body, increasing the risk of heart disease. To reduce your intake of trans fatty acids choose margarines with an acceptable liquid oil, such as canola oil as the first ingredient. The softer and more liquid the margarine, the better. The harder the margarine, the more saturated it is. Margarine has the same number of calories as butter and oil, unless it is a calorie-reduced type.

Better choices are:

Becel / Becel light
Country Crock Calorie Reduced Diet Margarine
Fleishmann's corn oil soft margarines
Imperial margarine
Mazola light corn oil spread

Salad Dressings

Choose dressings with no oil. Avoid creamy dressings, as they are higher in fat and you might tend to use more since they are thicker. Even some reduced calorie creamy dressings can be high in fat. Read the labels and choose those with less than 20 calories per 15 millilitres (1 tablespoon) serving.

Good choices are:

Fat-free dressings—all varieties
No-oil dressings—all varieties
Light Italian dressing

Other Foods

Low-Fat Sauces

Some sauces have more fat than others. Choose the fat-free varieties, such as the ones listed below. However, some contain more sodium (salt) than others. Choose low-sodium varieties as much as possible. If you do choose the higher-sodium variety, do not add additional salt in preparation or at the table.

The flavoured salts (seasoning salts, celery salt, garlic salt, etc.) are all high in sodium, so use them in moderation. Flavour food with plain herbs and spices (garlic, thyme, rosemary, etc.), lemons, limes, low-sodium soup bases, wines and vinegars.

Cooking wine adds a wonderful flavour to food. The alcohol is burned off when heated, and therefore most of the calories are burned off as well.

Good choices are:

Angostura bitters
Angostura—low-sodium soy & teriyaki sauce
Black bean sauce
Chili sauce
Chinese spice
Cocktail sauce
Cooking wine
Enchilada sauce
Flavour extracts (vanilla, almond, maple, etc.)
Hoisin sauce
Horseradish
Hot sauce
Ketchup
Lemon juice
Lime juice
Mint sauce
Mustards (any flavour)
* Oyster sauce
Picante sauce
Red pasta sauce (any, without meat)
Red pepper sauce
Relish (all varieties)
Salad dressings, no oil
Salsa
Soup bases (chicken, turkey, beef, onion, seafood)
* Soya sauce
Spices, herbs—powdered with salt
Stir-fry sauce
Taco sauce
* Teriyaki sauce

Tomato paste
Tomato sauce
Vinegar
Worcestershire sauce

* Use in moderation since can be high in sodium, but in small amounts can give food a delicious flavour. Low-sodium versions are also available.

Low-fat Snack Foods

Most snack foods are high in fat, so use in moderation.

Better choices are:
Air-popped popcorn (no added oil)
Hot chocolate, sugar-free
No-oil tortilla chips
Pretzels sticks, twists, thins (preferably non-salted)

Cookies

Read the label to check the type of fat used. Avoid cookies with tropical oils (palm, coconut), hydrogenated oil, hydrogenated fat, butter or lard.

Better choices are:
Animal crackers
Anisette toast or sponge
Arrowroots
Fig bars
Gingersnaps
Graham crackers
Newtons
Social tea biscuits
Vanilla wafers

Frozen Treats

Even though some of the frozen treats listed below contain milk or yogurt, they are not classified as "dairy foods." This is because their high sugar content classifies them as carbohydrate foods. Some frozen treats contain a lot of fat, but the ones listed below contain the least amount.

Frozen Fruit Bars
Low-Fat Frozen Yogurt
No-Fat Frozen Yogurt
Sorbet, water ices
Sherbet
Ice Milk

Grocery List

Fruits/Vegetables

Fruits

Fresh

- ❍ apples
- ❍ apricots
- ❍ bananas
- ❍ berries
- ❍ cherries
- ❍ grapes
- ❍ grapefruit
- ❍ kiwi
- ❍ lemons/limes
- ❍ melon
- ❍ nectarines
- ❍ oranges
- ❍ peaches
- ❍ strawberries
- ❍ *canned in own juice or water*
- ❍ *frozen unsweetened*
- ❍ *dried*
- ❍ dates
- ❍ prunes
- ❍ mixed
- ❍ raisins
- ❍ ________
- ❍ ________

Vegetables

- ❍ asparagus
- ❍ broccoli
- ❍ brussel sprouts
- ❍ cabbage
- ❍ carrots
- ❍ cauliflower
- ❍ celery
- ❍ cucumber
- ❍ eggplant
- ❍ garlic cloves
- ❍ green beans
- ❍ mushrooms
- ❍ onions
- ❍ parsley
- ❍ peas
- ❍ peppers
- ❍ romaine lettuce
- ❍ shallots
- ❍ snow peas
- ❍ spinach
- ❍ squash
- ❍ tomatoes
- ❍ turnips
- ❍ zucchini
- ❍ vegetables—canned
- ❍ vegetables—frozen
- ❍ ________
- ❍ ________

Starchy Foods

Breads/Quick Breads

- ❍ whole wheat 100%—sliced
- ❍ whole wheat English muffins/rolls
- ❍ bagels
- ❍ ________
- ❍ ________

Cereals—Cold

- ❍ All Bran
- ❍ Balance
- ❍ 100% Bran
- ❍ Bran Bud
- ❍ Bran Flakes
- ❍ Cheerios
- ❍ Chex
- ❍ Fiber One
- ❍ Frosted Mini Wheats
- ❍ Fruitful Bran
- ❍ Grapenuts
- ❍ Mini Wheats
- ❍ Nutrigrain
- ❍ Product 19
- ❍ Puffed Wheat
- ❍ Puffed Rice
- ❍ Raisin Bran
- ❍ Shredded Wheat
- ❍ Shredded Wheat & Bran
- ❍ Special K
- ❍ Total
- ❍ Wheaties
- ❍ Wheatabix
- ❍ ________
- ❍ ________

Cereals—Hot

- ❍ Cream of Wheat
- ❍ Farina
- ❍ Oatbran
- ❍ Oatmeal
- ❍ Rolled Oats
- ❍ Red River
- ❍ ________
- ❍ ________

Crackers

- ❍ breadsticks
- ❍ canapés
- ❍ crispbread
- ❍ matzo
- ❍ melba toast
- ❍ rice cakes
- ❍ rusks
- ❍ flatbreads
- ❍ Wasa
- ❍ Zwieback toast
- ❍ ________
- ❍ ________

Pasta—Whole Wheat

- ❍ ________
- ❍ ________

Rice

- ❍ brown
- ❍ wild

Other Grains

- ❍ barley
- ❍ bulgur/kasha
- ❍ cornmeal
- ❍ couscous
- ❍ wheat bran
- ❍ wheat germ
- ❍ ________
- ❍ ________
- ❍ waffles
- ❍ pancakes

- ❍ **Potatoes**
- ❍ **Corn**

Beans/Fish/Poultry/Meat/Eggs

Beans and Peas

- ❍ black
- ❍ chick-peas

- ❍ kidney
- ❍ lentils
- ❍ mung
- ❍ navy
- ❍ pinto
- ❍ soy
- ❍ split

❍ **Tofu**

Fish
- ❍ fresh
- ❍ frozen
- ❍ canned/water-packed

Poultry—no skin
- ❍ chicken
- ❍ turkey

Beef—lean
- ❍ lean ground
- ❍ flank
- ❍ round
- ❍ sirloin

Lamb
- ❍ leg
- ❍ loin chops

Veal
- ❍ chops (leg, loin or shoulder)

Pork
- ❍ loin chops
- ❍ tenderloin

Deli
- ❍ chicken/turkey breast
- ❍ lean roast beef
- ❍ Skim Milk Cheese

Eggs
- ❍ egg substitutes
- ❍ ________
- ❍ ________

Milk/Yogurt/Cheese

Cheese
- ❍ low-fat 20% M.F. or less
- ❍ colby light
- ❍ cottage cheese (1-2%)
- ❍ gouda light
- ❍ Jarlsberg light
- ❍ Reduced Calories Laughing Cow
- ❍ mozzarella part skim
- ❍ quark
- ❍ ricotta (5%)
- ❍ Swiss light
- ❍ fat-free cheese
- ❍ ________
- ❍ ________

Milk
- ❍ skim or 1% or buttermilk

Yogurt
- ❍ low-fat (1% M.F. or less)
- ❍ ________
- ❍ ________

Added Fats
- ❍ light sour cream
- ❍ light cream-cheese—fat free
- ❍ diet
- ❍ light
- ❍ soft margarine
- ❍ light mayonnaise—fat-free

Peanut Butter
- ❍ natural 100% peanuts

Salad Dressing
- ❍ light
- ❍ oil-free
- ❍ ________
- ❍ ________

Other Foods

Desserts/Snacks

Cookies
- ❍ animal crackers
- ❍ arrowroots
- ❍ gingersnaps
- ❍ graham crackers
- ❍ newtons
- ❍ social tea
- ❍ vanilla wafers
- ❍ ________

Popcorn
- ❍ kernels
- ❍ light microwave

❍ **Pretzels**—unsalted

Frozen Desserts
- ❍ frozen Dole fruit bars
- ❍ frozen yogurt (non-fat/low-fat)
- ❍ light Fudgesiscles/creamsicles/ popsicles
- ❍ sorbet/sherbet/ice milk

Sauces

- ❍ A1 sauce
- ❍ BBQ
- ❍ blackbean
- ❍ chili sauce

- ❍ chutney
- ❍ cocktail sauce
- ❍ enchilada sauce
- ❍ hoisin sauce
- ❍ honey BBQ sauce
- ❍ honey garlic sauce
- ❍ horseradish
- ❍ hot sauce
- ❍ marinara sauce
- ❍ mint sauce
- ❍ mustard
- ❍ oyster sauce
- ❍ picante sauce
- ❍ red pasta sauce
- ❍ relish
- ❍ salsa
- ❍ soya sauce (low sodium)
- ❍ stir-fry sauce
- ❍ sweet & sour sauce
- ❍ taco sauce
- ❍ teriyaki sauce (low sodium)
- ❍ tomato sauce
- ❍ vinegar
- ❍ ________
- ❍ ________

Seasonings

- ❍ allspice
- ❍ angostura bitters
- ❍ basil
- ❍ black pepper
- ❍ bouillon cubes
- ❍ cayenne pepper
- ❍ celery seed
- ❍ chili powder
- ❍ Chinese spice
- ❍ cinnamon
- ❍ curry
- ❍ dill
- ❍ garlic powder
- ❍ ginger
- ❍ lemon juice
- ❍ lime juice
- ❍ nutmeg
- ❍ oregano
- ❍ onion powder
- ❍ paprika
- ❍ parsley
- ❍ rosemary
- ❍ tobasco sauce
- ❍ Worcestershire sauce
- ❍ vanilla
- ❍ ________
- ❍ ________
- ❍ ________

Miscellaneous

- ❍ all-fruit jams
- ❍ baking soda
- ❍ cornstarch
- ❍ baking powder
- ❍ cooking spray—non-stick
- ❍ flour—whole wheat
- ❍ honey sugar
- ❍ maple syrup

Soups

- ❍ beef broth/consommé
- ❍ beef
- ❍ noodle/rice/barley
- ❍ chicken noodle/rice
- ❍ lentil
- ❍ Manhattan clam chowder
- ❍ minestrone
- ❍ onion
- ❍ pea (no pork)
- ❍ scotch broth
- ❍ vegetable
- ❍ wonton
- ❍ ________
- ❍ ________
- ❍ ________
- ❍ ________

Cooking the Healthy Weigh

Healthy food does not have to be boring. You can cook delicious meals that are quick and easy to prepare and don't compromise your commitment to health and weight control.

In this chapter you will learn how to cook with much less fat, salt and sugar. The results will be so delicious, there will be no reason to go back to your old way of cooking.

We realize that these days most people don't have the time to spend all afternoon preparing food in the kitchen. With that in mind, we have made all of our recipes easy to prepare.

Plan Ahead

Human nature dictates that if you don't have the right things to eat close at hand, you are going to reach for the wrong things. When you come home after a long day, prevent yourself from being tempted to have a quick burger or a TV dinner or to order in from a restaurant. By having healthier foods ready to eat, you will make it very easy to eat the Healthy Weigh.

Take the time to prepare some of the healthy ingredients you will need for the week ahead. It does not take much time to do and it will prevent you from reaching for the wrong things later on.

Some Suggestions for Plan-Ahead Food

• Clean and cut vegetables, such as carrots, celery, zucchini, peppers, mushrooms and baby corns, and marinate them in our delicious, low-fat marinade. Marinated vegetables are great to have available as a snack or as part of a meal.

• Wash lettuce and place it in plastic bags with absorbent paper inside. It will remain fresh in these bags for 3 to 4 days and it is ready to use for a salad.

• Prepare a low-fat dip to be used with vegetables.

• Prepare a container of The Best Teriyaki Marinade* (page 161) or have a commercial sauce available to be used as marinade for meat, fish or poultry.

• Precook a few pieces of meat, fish or poultry for the week ahead. Either use The Best Teriyaki Marinade* (page 161) or choose any of our delicious marinade recipes. Divide them into individual portions and freeze them for use later in the week.

• Prepare a pasta sauce or have a commercial sauce available to be used on fish, chicken or pasta.

• Prepare a pot of brown or wild rice and freeze in portions for the week.

• Boil some legumes (soybeans, pinto beans, black-eyed peas, white beans, navy beans, kidney beans) or purchase pre-cooked canned legumes to have on hand.

• Bake some potatoes so that they are ready to use.

How to Change Your Favourite Recipes

To Reduce the Amount of Salt

To replace or cut back on salt in recipes, herbs and spices should be used as much as possible. Refer to our handy list "How to Flavour with Herbs and Spices" (page 142) which gives suggestions on how to season foods without salt. You can change the character of any dish just by changing the spice: oregano for Italian, tarragon for French, curry for Indian, saffron for Spanish, and cumin and chili powder for Mexican. Experiment with fresh herbs. They add incredible flavour to foods.

Cutting back on salt may be difficult at first, but your taste buds will get used to less salt and you will lose your taste for it.

To Reduce the Amount of Sugar

Vanilla extract and/or cinnamon can make a dish seem sweeter even without adding extra sugar. You can also simply cut the sugar in most recipes by 1/3.

To Reduce the Amount of Fat

Reduce the amount of butter, margarine and oil called for in the recipe. You will not be able to tell that they are missing. Most recipes call for more fat than is necessary.

For Sautéeing or Stir-Frying

Instead of using oil, use non-stick cookware or use non-stick spray and cook over low heat. To prevent sticking, place water, defatted stock or wine in the pan instead of oil, butter or margarine. Start with the onions. When onions are cooked slowly, they release their own moisture and prevent other foods from sticking. Onions also add a wonderful flavour to foods.

For Baking, Broiling, Poaching or Steaming

You can save yourself time from cleaning dirty pans by placing your food in foil. Add any stock, herbs, spices or other seasonings to the food and seal the food in the foil like a pouch. Your finished product will also be very moist.

To Make Fat-Free Gravy

Pour the meat drippings into a bowl and place in the refrigerator for a few hours. The fat will solidify on top and you can easily remove it. To speed this process, place the bowl in the freezer, or put ice cubes into the liquid. The fat will solidify much faster.

Combine 15 millilitres (1 tablespoon) of cornstarch with 30 millilitres (2 tablespoons) cold water. Mix into a paste and add to 250 millimetres (one cup) of the defatted drippings. Simmer until thickened and season to taste (without fat).

To Make Fat-Free Salad Dressing

Add only a fraction of the oil called for in the recipe. Instead of 250 millilitres (1 cup) of oil, use 20 millilitres (1-2 tablespoons). Your dressing will still be delicious! You can also replace some of the oil with lemon juice, extra vinegar or water.

To Make Low-Fat Dips

Replace the sour cream in your recipe with low-fat yogurt or cottage cheese. You can blend the cottage cheese first to make it smoother.

To Make Non-Fat Cream

Add dry skim milk powder to less water than is called for. This will make a thicker "creamier" consistency without fat. You can also use evaporated milk as a substitute for cream.

How to Flavour with Herbs and Spices

For Meat, Fowl, Fish and Egg Dishes:

Beef:	dry mustard, marjoram, nutmeg, onion, sage, poppy seeds, tabasco, cumin, fresh parsley, thyme, pepper, bay leaf, dill, chives, curry, garlic, paprika
Ground beef:	chili powder, oregano, allspice, basil, savory, ground rosemary
Beef stew:	caraway seeds, sage, bay leaves, allspice, basil, a small onion stuffed with whole cloves
Pork:	onion, garlic, sage, ginger, marjoram, paprika, thyme, fresh parsley, rosemary, poppy seeds, tabasco, applesauce, spiced apples
Ground pork:	allspice, basil, cloves

Fresh pork roast:	rub with ground coriander before cooking or rub with mixture of sage, basil and savory
Lamb:	fresh mint, garlic, rosemary, curry, sweet basil, broiled pineapple rings, dried apricots, fresh parsley
Roast lamb:	sprinkle with rosemary before cooking
Lamb chops:	add marjoram while cooking, sprinkle chopped basil leaves on chops before broiling
Lamb stew:	allspice, basil, bay leaves, caraway seeds, sage, cloves, cumin, marjoram, onion, paprika, ginger, poppy seeds
Veal:	bay leaf, ginger, marjoram, curry, cumin, onion, paprika, thyme, rosemary, poppy seeds, fresh parsley, tabasco, currant jelly, spiced apricots
Veal stew:	allspice, basil, bay leaves, caraway seeds, sage
Ground veal:	basil, chives, cloves, garlic, ginger
Liver:	sweet basil
Chicken:	bay leaves, curry, lemon juice, ginger, paprika, fresh parsley, rosemary, sage, mushrooms, thyme, honey mustard, cranberry sauce, apricot sauce, pineapple
Fish:	dry mustard, paprika, curry, bay leaf, lemon juice, basil, fresh parsley, rosemary.
Broiled fish:	when almost finished cooking sprinkle with chervil
Fish cocktail:	basil
Fish sauces:	dill
Fish dressing:	sage, saffron, turmeric
Scrambled eggs:	savory
Other egg dishes:	pepper, green pepper, mushrooms, dry mustard, paprika, curry, chives, basil, thyme, chervil

For Potato Substitutes:

Rice:	add a pinch of saffron or turmeric before boiling
Spaghetti/noodles:	poppy seed or caraway seed blended with noodles
Macaroni:	dill seed, poppy seed
Vegetables	chives, cider vinegar, curry powder, garlic, lemon juice, onion, paprika, fresh parsley, pimento, chili powder, cumin, caraway seeds
Asparagus:	lemon juice, vinegar, caraway seeds
Beans, green:	marjoram, lemon juice, nutmeg, dill seed, mushrooms, sage, savory
Beans, lima:	rosemary, savory
Broccoli:	lemon juice
Cabbage:	low-fat mustard dressing, dill seed, lemon juice and sugar, caraway seeds, mixed pickling spices
Carrots:	parsley, mint, nutmeg, glazed with a pinch of sugar, pinch of thyme added during cooking
Cauliflower:	nutmeg
Corn:	green peppers, tomatoes
Onions:	thyme
Peas:	fresh mint, mushrooms, parsley, onion, thyme, rosemary, savory
Potatoes:	parsley, mace, chopped green pepper, onion, rosemary (added to water during cooking)
Potato Salad:	dill seed
Squash:	ginger, mace, savory
Sweet potatoes:	candied or glazed with cinnamon and nutmeg, escalloped with apples and sugar
Tomatoes, canned:	sweet basil, thyme, oregano, allspice, bay leaves, curry powder, dill, garlic, sage, savory
Tomatoes, fresh:	sprinkle with thyme on bed of lettuce

Fruit:	almond extract, cinnamon, ginger, nutmeg, peppermint extract, cloves (peaches; allspice)
Desserts:	cake: mace, nutmeg; sweets: mace; cinnamon, nutmeg; puddings and custards: almond or peppermint extract, nutmeg
Hot breads:	mace, sage
Cottage cheese:	nutmeg, caraway seeds
Salad dressing:	small amount of Tabasco
Tomato sauce:	allspice, oregano

Recipe Modification for Lowering Fat and Increasing Fibre

For	Try
1 whole egg	60 ml (1/4 cup) egg substitute or 1 egg white + 5 ml (1 t.) vegetable oil or 2 egg whites
250 ml (1 cup) butter	250 ml (1 cup) margarine
250 ml (1 cup) shortening or lard	180 ml (3/4 cup) vegetable oil
125 ml (1/2 cup) shortening	80 ml (1/3 cup) vegetable oil
250 ml (1 cup) whole milk	250 ml (1 cup) skim milk
250 ml (1 cup) light cream	250 ml (1 cup) evaporated skim milk or 45 ml (3 T.) oil and skim milk to equal 250 ml (1 cup)
250 ml (1 cup) heavy cream	250 ml (1 cup) evaporated milk or 160 ml (2/3 cup) skim and 80 ml (1/3 cup) oil
250 ml (1 cup) sour cream	250 ml (1 cup) plain yogurt or 250 ml (1 cup) blenderized low-fat cottage cheese (with lemon juice)
30 g (1 oz.) regular cheese	30 g (1 oz.) low-calorie or skim milk cheese
30 ml (2 T.) flour (as thickener)	15 ml (1 T.) cornstarch or arrowroot

15 ml (1 T.) salad dressing	15 ml (1 T.) low-calorie salad dressing
30 g (1 oz.) (1 square) baking chocolate	45 ml (3 T.) powdered cocoa and 15 ml (1 T.) oil
30 g (1 oz.) bacon (2 strips)	30 g (1 oz.) lean Canadian bacon or 30 g (1 oz.) lean ham
250 ml (1 cup) all-purpose flour	250 ml (1 cup) whole wheat flour minus 30 ml (2 T.); also decrease the amount of oil called for in the recipe by 15 ml (1 T.) and increase the liquid called for by 20-25 ml (4-5 t.); or use 125 ml (1/2 cup) white + 125 ml (1/2 cup) whole wheat flour; or use 180 ml (3/4 cup) white and 60 ml (1/4 cup) wheat germ and/or bran
White rice	Brown rice
Sugar	Reduce amount. Reduction can be up to 1/2 of the original amount. Use no more than 60 ml (1/4 cup) of added sweetener (sugar, honey, molasses, etc.) per 250 ml (1 cup) of flour.
Fat	Use no more than 7 ml (1-1/2 t.) of added oil or fat per 250 ml (1 cup) of flour; compensate by increasing low-fat moisture ingredient, such as buttermilk, to add moistness.
Salt	Reduce amount, try spices and herbs.

Part V: Recipes

Soups

Chinese Noodle Soup

375 ml (1-1/2 cups)	sliced mushrooms
2 cloves	garlic, minced
1 litre (4 cups)	liquid chicken stock
250 ml (1 cup)	oriental noodles; uncooked
15 ml (1 T.)	sherry
10 ml (2 t.)	rice vinegar (optional)
125 ml (1/2 cup)	chopped scallions

Place all ingredients in a large soup pot and bring to a boil. Cover and reduce heat. Simmer for 5 to 10 minutes until vegetables and noodles are tender.

Makes 1 litre (4 cups) = 4 - 250 ml (1 cup) servings.

Per 250 ml (1 cup) serving:

calories: 95
fat: 2.0 g
protein: 7.5 g
carbohydrates: 11.0 g
sodium: 825 mg
fibre: 1.0 g
cholesterol: 9 mg

Gazpacho

125 ml (1/2 cup)	finely chopped seedless cucumber
60 ml (1/4 cup)	finely chopped onions
250 ml (1 cup)	finely chopped tomatoes
125 ml (1/2 cup)	finely chopped red peppers
125 ml (1/2 cup)	finely chopped green peppers
500 ml (2 cups)	tomato juice or Clamato juice
2 ml (1/2 t.)	Worcestershire sauce
30 ml (2 T.)	red wine vinegar
15 ml (1 T.)	lemon juice
1 clove	garlic, minced
2 ml (1/2 t.)	salt
2 ml (1/2 t.)	hot pepper sauce or ground pepper

Mix all the chopped vegetables together in a bowl and put half aside. Blend the other half with the tomato juice, Worcestershire sauce, vinegar, lemon juice and garlic in a blender until fairly smooth. Transfer into a bowl and season with the salt and pepper. Add the reserved chopped vegetables. Chill. Serve soup cold.

Makes 4 - 250 ml (1 cup) servings.

Per 250 ml (1 cup) serving:

calories: 60
fat: 0.47 g
protein: 2.36 g
carbohydrates: 14.6 g
sodium: 768 mg
fibre: 3.0 g
cholesterol: 0

Japanese Vegetable Soup

1-1/2 litres (6 cups)	liquid chicken broth
80 ml (1/3 cup)	dry sherry
20 ml (4 t.)	low sodium soy sauce
500-700 ml (2-3 cups)	frozen oriental mixed vegetables

Place chicken broth, sherry and soy sauce in a pot. Bring to a boil. Add frozen vegetables and simmer until vegetables are tender.

Makes 8 - 250 ml (1 cup) servings.

Per 250 ml (1 cup) serving:

calories: 64
fat: 1.2 g
protein: 5.3 g
carbohydrates: 6.7 g
sodium: 667 mg
fibre: 1.6 g
cholesterol: 0

Dressing and Dips

Creamy Caesar Dressing

250 ml (1 cup)	Creamy Garlic Dressing*
60 ml (1/4 cup)	grated Parmesan cheese
60 ml (1/4 cup)	water

Follow recipe for Creamy Garlic Dressing* (page 157). Add the Parmesan cheese and the additional water and mix.

Makes 500 ml (2 cups) = 16 - 30 ml (2 T.) servings.

Per 30 ml (2 T.) serving:

calories: 27
fat: 2.1 g
protein: 1.1 g
carbohydrates: 1.3 g
sodium: 96 mg
fibre: 0.1 g
cholesterol: 1 mg

Creamy Garlic Dressing

160 ml (2/3 cup)	low-fat plain yogurt
125 ml (1/2 cup)	light mayonnaise
5 ml (1 t.)	dry mustard
125 ml (1/2 cup)	chopped fresh parsley
3 cloves	garlic, minced
2 ml (1/2 t.)	salt
45 ml (3 T.)	water
15 ml (1 T.)	balsamic vinegar

Mix all ingredients together in a bowl and chill.

Makes 375 ml (1-1/2 cups) = 12 - 30 ml (2 T.) servings.

Per 30 ml (2 T.) serving:

calories: 41
fat: 3.3 g
protein: 0.9 g
carbohydrates: 2.5 g
sodium: 160 mg
fibre: 0.2 g
cholesterol: 0

Herb Dip

125 ml (1/2 cup)	low-fat plain yogurt
250 ml (1 cup)	low-fat cottage cheese
30 ml (2 T.)	chopped fresh parsley
30 ml (2 T)	chopped scallions
1 ml (1/4 t.)	paprika
1 clove	garlic, minced
5 ml (1 t.)	dried basil

Blend all ingredients in a blender or food processor until smooth.

Serve with vegetables.

Makes 430 ml (1-3/4 cups) dip= 6 - 60 ml (1/4 cup) servings.

Per 60 ml (1/4 cup) serving:

calories: 51
fat: 0.6 g
protein: 7.5 g
carbohydrates: 3.9 g
sodium: 218 mg
fibre: 0.2 g
cholesterol: 2 mg

Honey Mustard Dip

250 ml (1 cup)	tofu
60 ml (1/4 cup)	thawed frozen orange juice concentrate
40 ml (2-1/2 T.)	light mayonnaise
15 ml (1 T.)	honey mustard

Blend all ingredients until smooth. Serve with fresh vegetables.

Makes 250 ml (1 cup) = 8 - 30 ml (2 T.) servings.

Per 30 ml (2 T.) serving:

calories: 81
fat: 4.5 g
protein: 5.5 g
carbohydrates: 6.2 g
sodium: 61 mg
fibre: 0.1 g
cholesterol: 0

Light Guacamole Dip

1-120 g (4 oz.) block	firm-style tofu
one-half	medium avocado, ripe
60 ml (1/4 cup)	diced onions
2 cloves	garlic, minced
125 ml (1/2 cup)	diced tomatoes
60 ml (1/4 cup)	diced green peppers
30 ml (2 T.)	canned green chili peppers
	juice of one-half lemon
1 ml (1/4 t.)	hot sauce

Blend tofu, avocado, onions and garlic in food processor or blender until smooth. Transfer to a bowl and add rest of ingredients. Stir to combine.

Makes 375 ml (1-1/2 cups) dip= 6 - 60 ml (1/4 cup) servings.

Per 60 ml (1/4 cup) serving:

calories: 66
fat: 4.3 g
protein: 3.7 g
carbohydrates: 5.3 g
sodium: 6 mg
fibre: 0.9 g
cholesterol: 0

Onion Dip

250 ml (1 cup)	low-fat cottage cheese
80 ml (1/3 cup)	chopped scallions or green onions
60 ml (1/4 cup)	low-fat milk
60 ml (1/4 cup)	chopped fresh parsley
to taste	salt and pepper

Blend the first four ingredients in a food processor or blender until smooth. Season with salt and pepper to taste.

Makes 375 ml (1-1/2 cups) = 6 - 60 ml (1/4 cup) servings.

Per 60 ml (1/4 cup) serving:

calories: 42
fat: 0.1 g
protein: 7.9 g
carbohydrates: 2.5 g
sodium: 81 mg
fibre: 0.2 g
cholesterol: 0

Spinach Dip

1 - 280 g (10 oz.) pkg.	frozen chopped spinach
250 ml (1 cup)	chopped scallions
180 ml (3/4 cup)	chopped water chestnuts
1 pkg.	vegetable soup mix
60 ml (1/4 cup)	light mayonnaise
300 ml (1-1/4 cups)	plain low-fat yogurt

Thaw spinach and squeeze out water. Combine all ingredients and refrigerate for at least 2 to 3 hours prior to serving.

Makes 875 ml (3-1/2 cups) dip.

Per 30 ml (2 T.) serving:

calories: 22
fat: 1.0 g
protein: 1.0 g
carbohydrates: 2.7 g
sodium: 98 mg
fibre: 0.5 g
cholesterol: 0

Vinaigrette Dressing

80 ml (1/3 cup)	olive or canola oil
125 ml (1/2 cup)	water
60 ml (1/4 cup)	balsamic vinegar
2-3 cloves	garlic, minced
5 ml (1 t.)	dry mustard
15 ml (1 T.)	sugar
to taste	salt and pepper

Combine all ingredients and chill.

Variations

Parmesan Vinaigrette:	add 30 ml (2 T.) grated Parmesan cheese
Poppy Seed Dressing:	add 15 ml (1 T.) poppy seeds

Makes 250 ml (1 cup) = 16 - 15 ml (1 T.) servings.

Per 15 ml (1 T.) serving:

calories: 54
fat: 5.7 g
protein: 0.1 g
carbohydrates: 1.1 g
sodium: 12 mg
fibre: 0
cholesterol: 0

Sauces and Marinades

Apricot Sauce
for chicken, turkey or veal

250 ml (1 cup)	oil-free catalina dressing
125 ml (1/2 cup)	all-fruit apricot jam
1-35 g pkg (1.25 oz.)	dried onion soup mix

Mix catalina dressing, apricot jam and onion soup mix in a bowl. Store in refrigerator.

Makes 375 ml (1-1/2 cups) sauce = 12 - 30 ml (2 T.) servings.

Per 30 ml (2 T.) serving:

calories: 51
fat: 2.5 g
protein: 0.53 g
carbohydrates: 7.2 g
sodium: 756 mg
fibre: 0.37 g
cholesterol: 1.5 mg

Easy Tomato Salsa Sauce
for fish, chicken or turkey

125 ml (1/2 cup)	mild salsa
60 ml (1/4 cup)	tomato paste
10 ml (2 t.)	sugar

Mix ingredients together in bowl.

Makes 180 ml (3/4 cup) = 3 - 60 ml (1/4 cup) servings.

Per 60 ml (1/4 cup) serving:

calories: 37
fat: 0.5 g
protein: 1.2 g
carbohydrates: 8.5 g
sodium: 25 mg
fibre: 1.8 g
cholesterol: 0

Honey Garlic Sauce

for chicken or pork

15 ml (1 T.)	cornstarch
15 ml (1 T.)	water
160 ml (2/3 cup)	low-sodium soy sauce
125 ml (1/2 cup)	honey
15 ml (1 T.)	balsamic vinegar
10 ml (2 t.)	powdered ginger
3-5 cloves	garlic, minced

In a small bowl, mix the cornstarch and water to make a paste and set aside. Combine the remaining 5 ingredients in a saucepan and heat until boiling. Add the cornstarch mixture and continue to heat, stirring constantly until thickened. Allow sauce to cool before marinating chicken or pork.

Makes 320 ml (1-1/3 cups) sauce = 12 - 30 ml (2 T.) servings.

Per 30 ml (1 T.) serving:

calories: 56
fat: 0.03 g
protein: 0.79 g
carbohydrates: 14 g
sodium: 434 mg
fibre: 0.06 g
cholesterol: 0

Honey Mustard Glaze

for fish or chicken

125 ml (1/2 cup)	light mayonnaise
125 ml (1/2 cup)	honey mustard
30 ml (2 T.)	lemon juice
2-4 cloves	garlic, minced

Makes 250 ml (1 cup) = 8 - 30 ml (2 T.) servings.

Per 30 ml (2 T.) serving:

calories: 75
fat: 5.5 g
protein: 0.8 g
carbohydrates: 6.6 g
sodium: 307 mg
fibre: 0.5 g
cholesterol: 0

Indian Sauce

for fish, chicken, turkey or pork

2	hard-cooked eggs, chopped (optional)
5 ml (1 t.)	salt
2 ml (1/2 t.)	pepper
5 ml (1 t.)	curry powder
60 ml (1/4 cup)	balsamic vinegar
60 ml (1/4 cup)	canola or olive oil
60 ml (1/4 cup)	chutney

Combine all ingredients and chill.

Makes 250 ml (1 cup) = 8 - 30 ml (2 T.) servings.

Per 30 ml (2 T.) serving:

calories: 91
fat: 8.3 g
protein: 1.7 g
carbohydrates: 2.9 g
sodium: 347 mg
fibre: 0.2 g
cholesterol: 53 mg

Oriental Marinade

for meat, chicken or fish

125 ml (1/2 cup)	pineapple juice
125 ml (1/2 cup)	sherry
125 ml (1/2 cup)	low-sodium soy sauce
2 cloves	garlic, minced
45 ml (3 T.)	parsley, fresh, chopped

Makes 375 ml (1-1/2 cups) marinade.

Per 30 ml (2 T.) serving:

calories: 19.7
fat: 0.02 g
protein: 0.63 g
carbohydrates: 2.76 g
sodium: 181 mg
fibre: 0.06 g
cholesterol: 0

Piquant Tomato Sauce

5 ml (1 t.) olive oil
3 cloves garlic, minced
60 ml (1/4 cup) chopped onions
1-795 ml (28 oz.) can plum tomatoes, drained and chopped
1-170 ml (6 oz.) can tomato paste
125 ml (1/2 cup) liquid chicken broth
30 ml (2 T.) chopped green olives
15 ml (1 T.) sugar
15 ml (1 T.) chopped fresh parsley
15 ml (1 T.) chopped fresh basil or 5 ml (1 t.) dried basil
leaves
2 bay leaves
to taste salt and pepper

Add oil to non-stick pan or one sprayed with non-stick spray.

Heat and add garlic and onions. Sauté for 2 minutes or until lightly browned. Add next 9 ingredients and simmer, uncovered, for 20 minutes until thickened. Season with salt and pepper to taste.

Makes 500 ml (2 cups) sauce = 4 - 125 ml (1/2 cup) servings.

Per 125 ml (1/2 cup) serving:

calories: 124
fat: 2.6 g
protein: 4.9 g
carbohydrates: 24.5 g
sodium: 515 mg
fibre: 4.7 g
cholesterol: 0

The Best Teriyaki Marinade

250 ml (1 cup)	low-sodium teriyaki sauce
15 ml (1 T.)	sherry
5 ml (1 t.)	honey
2-3 cloves	garlic, minced
10 ml (2 t.)	minced fresh ginger

Mix all ingredients together and store in the refrigerator.

Makes 250 ml (1 cup).

Per 15 ml (1 T.) serving:

calories: 35
fat: 0.01 g
protein: 1.2 g
carbohydrates: 7.9 g
sodium: 44 mg
fibre: 0.05 g
cholesterol: 0

Vegetable and Salads

Baked Vegetables

2	ears of corn
2	medium potatoes, partially cooked
2	medium purple onions, sliced
2	medium red peppers, sliced into strips
2	medium green peppers, sliced into strips
500 ml (2 cups)	diagonally sliced carrots, approx. 3 carrots
4 cloves	garlic, minced
30 ml (2 T.)	low-sodium teriyaki sauce
5 ml (1 t.)	olive oil
30 ml (2 T.)	lemon juice
30 ml (2 T.)	chopped fresh parsley
10 ml (2 t.)	oregano or basil

Remove husk and silk from corn and cut into 4 equal pieces. Cut potatoes into 8 pieces. Place corn, potatoes, onion, peppers and carrots into a bowl. Add garlic, teriyaki sauce, olive oil, lemon juice, parsley and basil. Toss well.

Divide mixture and place each half on top of a large piece of foil. Gather corner of foil and twist to seal.

Place packages on BBQ or in oven and bake for approximately 15 to 20 minutes until potatoes are done.

Remove the package and pierce the foil with a knife or fork to release the steam.

Makes approximately 4 servings.

Per serving:

calories: 162
fat: 1.6 g
protein: 5.1 g
carbohydrates: 35 g
sodium: 265 mg
fibre: 4.4 g
cholesterol: 0

Chinese Chicken Salad

500 ml (2 cups)	diced cooked chicken
1 litre (4 cups)	shredded iceberg lettuce
250 ml (1 cup)	shredded carrots
125 ml (1/2 cup)	chopped green onions
60 ml (1/4 cup)	low-sodium soy sauce
80 ml (1/3 cup)	white vinegar
30 ml (2 T.)	sesame seeds, toasted
2 ml (1/2 t.)	ground ginger
15 ml (1 T.)	sugar
30 ml (2 T.)	chopped fresh parsley

Place diced chicken in a mixing bowl. Add the lettuce, carrot and green onion. In a separate bowl combine the soy sauce, vinegar, sesame seeds, ginger and sugar. Stir until the sugar is dissolved. Pour over the chicken/vegetable mixture. Cover and marinate for 1 to 2 hours in refrigerator. Toss in parsley just prior to serving.

Makes 6 - 250 ml (1 cup) servings.

Per serving:

calories: 141
fat: 4.1 g
protein: 18.3 g
carbohydrates: 7.9 g
sodium: 211 mg
fibre: 1.6 g
cholesterol: 45 mg

Couscous and Chick-Pea Salad

Salad

400 ml (1-2/3 cups)	chicken broth
250 ml (1 cup)	couscous
80 ml (1/3 cup)	chick-peas
60 ml (1/4 cup)	diced carrots
160 ml (2/3 cup)	frozen peas and carrots, thawed
60 ml (1/4 cup)	diced green or red pepper
15 ml (1 T.)	minced purple onions
30 ml (2 T.)	currants
2 ml (1/2 t.)	dried basil
2 ml (1/2 t.)	dried thyme

For a curry flavour, replace the basil and thyme with 5 ml (1 t.) curry powder.

Dressing

30 ml (2 T.)	red wine vinegar
15 ml (1 T.)	olive oil
to taste	salt and pepper

For a different flavour, replace the red wine vinegar with apple cider, vinegar or malt vinegar.

Bring chicken broth to a boil. Add couscous. Cover pot and remove from heat. Let stand, covered for 5 minutes. Fluff with a fork. Add chickpeas and the remaining 7 ingredients. In a separate bowl combine the vinegar, oil, salt and pepper, and stir well. Just before serving, add the dressing to the salad and toss.

Makes 4 - 250 ml (1 cup) servings.

Per 250 ml (1 cup) serving:

calories: 288
fat: 2.1 g
protein: 12.6 g
carbohydrates: 54.5 g
sodium: 354 mg
fibre: 1.3 g
cholesterol: 0

Easy Italian Vegetables

750 ml (3 cups)	any combination of vegetables
125 ml (1/2 cup)	red pasta sauce or commercial variety
5 ml (1 t.)	granulated sugar
60 ml (1/4 cup)	grated Parmesan cheese

Steam or microwave vegetables until tender crisp. Drain well. Add the pasta sauce, sugar and grated Parmesan cheese.

Great vegetables with this recipe are:

- fresh zucchini slices
- fresh broccoli florets
- fresh cauliflower
- fresh mushrooms
- fresh carrots
- fresh green beans
- diced onions added to another vegetables
- frozen Italian mixed vegetables
- frozen California mixed vegetables

Makes 2 - 250 ml (1 cup) servings.

Per 250 ml (1 cup) servings:

calories: 197
protein: 11.4 g
fat: 5.3 g
carbohydrates: 30.7 g
sodium: 556 mg
fibre: 4.5 g
cholesterol: 9.8 mg

Easy Tuna-Vegetable Delight

1 recipe	Easy Italian Vegetables*
60 ml (1/4 cup)	water-packed solid white tuna

Complete the recipe for Easy Italian Vegetables* (page 171). Add the tuna and toss.

Makes 2 - 250 ml (1 cup) servings.

Per 250 ml (1 cup) serving:

calories: 223
fat: 5.4 g
protein: 17.3 g
carbohydrates: 30.7 g
sodium: 566 mg
fibre: 4.5 g
cholesterol: 13.5 mg

Greek Salad with Spinach

2 litres (8 cups)	
or 1 - 10 oz. bag	loosely packed, chopped fresh spinach
125 ml (1/2 cup)	peeled, seeded and coarsely chopped cucumber
1/2	purple onion, thinly sliced in rings
1	tomato, sliced
120 g (4 oz.)	crumbled feta cheese
80 ml (1/3 cup)	balsamic vinegar
10 ml (2 t.)	dried oregano
60 ml (1/4 cup)	sherry
45 ml (3 T.)	water

Remove large stems from spinach; tear spinach into bite-size pieces and place in a large bowl. Add next 4 ingredients; toss and set aside. Combine remaining ingredients and stir well. Just prior to serving, pour over salad or have on the side.

Makes 8 - 250 ml (1 cup) servings.

Per serving:

calories: 66
fat: 4.1 g
protein: 4.1 g
carbohydrates: 5.3 g
sodium: 211 mg
fibre: 2.0 g
cholesterol: 12 mg

Low-Fat Caesar Salad

2 cloves	garlic, minced
30 ml (2 T.)	water
45 ml (3 T.)	olive oil
5 ml (1 t.)	Worcestershire sauce
2 ml (1/2 t.)	dry mustard
6	anchovy fillets, washed, drained and mashed
to taste	salt and pepper
	juice of 1 lemon
1 large head	romaine lettuce, shredded
45 ml (3 T)	grated Parmesan cheese

Combine all ingredients except lettuce and cheese in a large salad bowl.

Just before serving, add lettuce and Parmesan cheese and toss until well covered.

Makes 4 - 250 ml (1 cup) servings.

Per 250 ml (1 cup) serving:

calories: 141
fat: 12.5 g
protein: 5.0 g
carbohydrates: 3.4 g
sodium: 347 mg
fibre: 1.1 g
cholesterol: 8 mg

Low-Fat Coleslaw

1 litre (4 cups)	
or 1-227 g (8 oz.)pkg.	shredded cabbage
125 ml (1/2 cup)	shredded carrots (optional)

Dressing:

30 ml (2 T.)	lemon juice
30 ml (2 T.)	balsamic vinegar
60 ml (1/4 cup)	water
30 ml (2 T.)	granulated sugar
15 ml (1 T.)	olive oil
2 ml (1/2 t.)	mustard
to taste	salt and pepper

Combine cabbage, and carrot in salad bowl.

Combine dressing ingredients. Pour over salad and toss.

Makes 4 - 180 ml (3/4 cup) servings.

Per 180 ml (3/4 cup) serving:

calories: 76
fat: 3.4 g
protein: 0.9 g
carbohydrates: 12.0 g
sodium: 22 mg
fibre: 1.5 g
cholesterol: 0

Low-Fat Stir-Fry

Stir-Fry Sauce:

5 ml (1 t.)	minced garlic
45 ml (3 T.)	low-sodium soy sauce
45 ml (3 T.)	dry sherry
30 ml (2 T.)	cornstarch
5 ml (1 t.)	ginger
30 ml (2 T.)	sugar
30 ml (2 T.)	water
5 ml (1 t.)	dried chicken soup base

Mix all ingredients together in a small bowl and set aside.

Vegetables

125 ml (1/2 cup)	liquid chicken stock
2 to 2-1/2 litres (8-10 cups)	mixed vegetables (chopped or sliced)

Try any of the following delicious variations:

- onions, peppers, carrots and zucchini
- cabbage, broccoli, water chestnuts and snowpeas
- broccoli, cauliflower, green beans, onions and red peppers
- carrots, broccoli, mushrooms and baby corn
- bean sprouts, mushrooms, spinach, snowpeas and red peppers
- frozen oriental mixed vegetables

Heat chicken stock in a large non-stick pan (or wok) or one sprayed with non-stick spray. If using onions, add the onions first and then add the vegetables that take the longest to cook (i.e. carrots, broccoli, cauliflower, cabbage). Keep stirring the mixture as it cooks. Add more liquid chicken stock 15 ml (1 T.) at a time if the vegetables begin to stick. Then add the other vegetables and the stir-fry sauce. Keep stirring over heat until the vegetables are tender crisp.

Makes 4 - 250 ml (1 cup) servings.

Per 250 ml (1 cup) serving:

calories: 187
protein: 5.1 g
fat: 1.4 g
carbohydrates: 40 g
sodium: 685 mg
fibre: 5.6 g
cholesterol: 0.51 mg

Marinated Vegetables

6-8	carrots, peeled and cut into sticks
1	zucchini, cut into sticks or slices
1/2 head	cauliflower, cut into chunks
one-half	onion, sliced
1 398 ml (14 oz.) can	baby corns, drained
1 398 ml (14 oz.) can	artichoke hearts or hearts of palm, cut into halves
1	green or red pepper
12	cherry tomatoes
250 ml (1 cup)	light Italian or oil-free Italian dressing
3 large cloves	garlic, minced
15 ml (1 T.)	sugar
20 ml (4 t.)	dried dill
10 ml (2 t.)	dricd basil

The dill and basil can be replaced with 30 ml (2 T.) Greek salad spice.

Wash and cut up the vegetables. Dry them well and place them in a large bowl. In a separate bowl, mix together the salad dressing, garlic and spices and pour them onto the vegetables. Toss well. Cover and store in the refrigerator.

Variations:

You can use any combination of vegetables. Some vegetable suggestions are mushrooms, green beans, seedless cucumber, broccoli.

Makes approximately 14 - 250 ml (1 cup) servings.

Per 250 ml (1 cup) serving:

calories: 81
fat: 1.09 g
protein: 3.21 g
carbohydrates: 17.76 g
sodium: 294 mg
fibre: 2.9 g
cholesterol: 1.1 mg

Oriental Chicken Salad with Fruit

125 ml (1/2 cup)	diced chicken
30 ml (2 T.)	rice vinegar
15 ml (1 T.)	teriyaki sauce
20 ml (4 t.)	dry sherry
625 ml (2-1/2 cups)	shredded romaine or boston lettuce or spinach
250 ml (1 cup)	melon cubes or pineapple cubes
125 ml (1/2 cup)	sliced red or green pepper
125 ml (1/2 cup)	sliced or shredded carrot
60 ml (1/4 cup)	diagonally cut scallions
60 ml (1/4 cup)	water chestnuts, drained

Combine chicken, vinegar, teriyaki sauce and dry sherry in a bowl and set aside.

Line serving platter with lettuce or spinach. Place melon or pineapple cubes, peppers, carrots, scallions and water chestnuts on top. Using a slotted spoon, place chicken on salad. Drizzle sherry mixture over salad.

Makes 2 - 350 ml (1-1/2 cups) servings.

Per serving:

calories: 189
fat: 2.5 g
protein: 16.5 g
carbohydrates: 26.3 g
sodium: 413 mg
fibre: 4.9 g
cholesterol: 33 mg

Oriental Salad with Beef

10 ml (2 t.)	rice vinegar
10 ml (2 t.)	low-sodium soy sauce
5 ml (1 t.)	sesame oil or peanut oil
60 g (2 oz.)	cooked roast beef, cut into strips
250 ml (1 cup)	cooked brown rice, chilled
125 ml (1/2 cup)	canned mandarin orange sections with
30 ml (2 T.)	juice
60 ml (1/4 cup)	diced red peppers
30 ml (2 T.)	sliced scallion
30 ml (2 T.)	sesame seeds, toasted

In a medium mixing bowl, combine vinegar, soy sauce, and oil. Add beef and coat well. Cover and refrigerate for 20 minutes.

Add remaining ingredients to beef mixture and toss to combine.

Makes 2 - 250 ml (1 cup) servings.

Per 250 ml (1 cup) serving:

calories: 312
fat: 11.2 g
protein: 14.8 g
carbohydrates: 39.5 g
sodium: 289 mg
fibre: 2.0 g
cholesterol: 25 mg

Ratatouille

5 ml (1 t.)	olive oil
1 medium	eggplant, peeled and cut into 2.5 cm (1") squares
2 medium	zucchini, unpeeled, sliced thin
2	ripe tomatoes, chopped
2	green peppers, cut into strips
2	red peppers, cut into strips
15 ml (1 T.)	lemon juice
15 ml (1 T.)	red wine vinegar
2	bay leaves
125 ml (1/2 cup)	chopped fresh parsley
4 cloves	garlic, minced
15 ml (1 T.)	sugar
5 ml (1 t.)	thyme
2 ml (1/2 t.)	oregano
5 ml (1 t.)	basil
5 ml (1 t.)	salt
1-284 ml (10 oz.) can	peeled small tomatoes
1-284 ml (10 oz.) can	sliced mushrooms, drained

Heat olive oil in large non-stick saucepan or one sprayed with non-stick spray. Sauté eggplant, zucchini, tomatoes, onions and peppers until tender.

Add remaining ingredients and simmer, stirring frequently for 10 minutes.

Can be stored in the refrigerator for 4 to 5 days.

Makes 2 litres (8 cups) = 8 - 250 ml (1 cup) servings.

Per 250 ml (1 cup) serving:

calories: 55
fat: 1.0 g
protein: 2.2 g
carbohydrates: 11.7 g
sodium: 517 mg
fibre: 2.7 g
cholesterol: 0

Tuna Primavera Salad

500 ml (2 cups)	cooked pasta (medium-size shells)
125 ml (1/2 cup)	sliced carrots
125 ml (1/2 cup)	frozen green peas, thawed
125 ml (1/2 cup)	sliced red peppers
30 ml (2 T.)	diagonally sliced scallions
1-198 g (7 oz.)	water-packed tuna
80 ml (1/3 cup)	oil-free Italian dressing
2 ml (1/2 t.)	dill
2 ml (1/2 t.)	oregano
2 ml (1/2 t.)	basil

Combine cooked, drained pasta with the rest of the ingredients and toss.

Makes 4 - 250 ml (1 cup) servings.

Per 250 ml (1 cup) serving:

calories: 219
fat: 2.0 g
protein: 21.5 g
carbohydrates: 28.5 g
sodium: 346 mg
fibre: 1.5 g
cholesterol: 39 mg

Grains & Starchy Vegetables

Couscous

500 ml (2 cups)	liquid chicken stock
375 ml (1-1/2 cups)	couscous (dry)
to taste	pepper

Place chicken stock in a saucepan and bring to a boil. Add couscous and stir. Remove from heat, cover and let stand for 5 minutes. Fluff with a fork and serve.

Variation

Raisin and Curry Couscous: Just prior to serving toss in 60 ml (1/4 cup) currants or raisins, 5 ml (1 t.) curry powder and (optional) 2 ml (1/2 t.) cumin.

Makes 750 ml (3 cups) = 6 - 125 ml (1/2 cup) servings.

Per 125 ml (1/2 cup) portion:

Without raisins	Raisins and curry	
	Raisins	Seedless raisins
calories: 196.1	200.7	218.3
fat: 0.80 g	0.90 g	0.91 g
protein: 7.92 g	8.06 g	8.21 g
carbohydrates: 37.88 g	38.87 g	43.55 g
sodium: 277 mg	278 mg	279 mg
fibre: 0	1.07 g	0.32 g
cholesterol: 0	0	0

Healthy Potato Salad

Salad:

1 kg (2 lb.)	15-20 small red potatoes* (unpeeled)
80 ml (1/3 cup)	chopped red onions
180 ml (3/4 cup)	chopped, fresh parsley
to taste	salt and pepper

Dressing:

125 ml (1/2 cup)	red wine or balsamic vinegar
25 ml (1-1/2 T.)	dijon mustard
15 ml (1 T.)	olive oil
5 ml (1 t.)	sugar

(* Red potatoes are the most colourful, but you can use any potato.)

Cook potatoes in boiling water until soft. Drain, dry and cut potatoes into long 1-1/4 cm. long (1/2") slices. Combine the potatoes, onions, parsley, salt and pepper in a bowl. Mix the dressing and pour over the warm potatoes. Toss. Marinate in refrigerator for 1 to 2 hours prior to serving.

Makes 8 - 250 ml (1 cup) servings.

Per 250 ml (1 cup) serving:

calories: 117
fat: 1.9 g
protein: 3.1 g
carbohydrates: 23 g
sodium: 52 mg
fibre: 2.4 g
cholesterol: 0

Healthy Topped Baked Potato

1 medium	baked potato
80 ml (1/3 cup)	low-fat cottage cheese
30 ml (2 T.)	chopped scallions or fresh parsley

Bake the potato unwrapped at 220°C (425°F) for 50 to 60 minutes.

Cut the potato in half lengthwise and puff up the insides with a fork. Add the cottage cheese and top with the scallions or parsley.

The cottage cheese and scallions can be replaced with any of:

125 ml (1/2 cup)	low-fat yogurt
30 ml (2 T.)	Parmesan cheese
30 ml (2 T.)	low-fat cheddar cheese and 60 ml (1/4 cup) cooked broccoli
60 ml (1/2 cup)	red pasta sauce and 15 ml (1 T.) grated Parmesan cheese

Makes 1 baked potato serving.

Per 1 baked potato serving:

Cottage cheese & scallions		Parmesan	Tomato sauce & Parmesan
calories:	205	199	241
fat:	1.0 g	3.8 g	5.0 g
protein:	13.0 g	8.0 g	6.7 g
carbohydrates:	36.6 g	34.1 g	43.9 g
sodium:	328 mg	231 mg	432 mg
fibre:	3.6 g	3.4 g	3.4 g
cholesterol:	3 mg	9 mg	4 mg

Cheese & broccoli		Yogurt
calories:	200	210
fat:	3.0 g	0.3 g
protein:	8.5 g	9.6 g
carbohydrates: 3.0 g	43.0 g	
sodium:	18.8 mg	99 mg
fibre:	4.9 g	3.4 g
cholesterol: 02 mg		

Low-Fat Fries

1 medium	Yukon Gold* potato
to taste	salt and pepper

(*Any type of potato can be used but Yukon Gold are the tastiest for this recipe.)

Boil the whole, unpeeled potato in water until almost fully cooked (approximately ten minutes).

Dry the potato and slice into 1 cm (1/2") coins. Spread coins on a non-stick baking sheet or one sprayed with non-stick spray. Sprinkle with seasonings and bake at 230°C (450°F) for 15 to 20 minutes until browned and cooked through.

Makes 2 servings.

Per serving:

calories: 55
fat: 0.1 g
protein: 1.6 g
carbohydrates: 12.4 g
sodium: 5 mg
fibre: 1.2 g
cholesterol: 0

Low-Fat Herbed Bruschetta

2-3	medium-size tomatoes, diced= approx. 500 ml (2 cups)
2 cloves	garlic, minced
10 ml (2 t.)	dried basil or 45 ml (3 T.) fresh basil
2 ml (1/2 t.)	salt
2 ml (1/2 t.)	pepper
15 ml (1 T.)	olive oil
1	thin French baguette or vienna-style baguette
30 ml (2 T.)	grated Parmesan cheese

Combine tomatoes, garlic, basil, salt and pepper and oil in a bowl.

Slice bread into 2.5 cm (1") thick slices. Place on a baking sheet and broil until lightly browned on both sides. Spoon tomato mixture on top of each slice. Sprinkle with Parmesan cheese and broil for 1 minute.

Makes approximately 16-18 1 slice servings.

Per 1 slice serving:

calories: 73
fat: 1.7 g
protein: 2.3 g
carbohydrates: 12.1 g
sodium: 179 mg
fibre: 0.6 g
cholesterol: 9 mg

Orange Almond Rice

125 ml (1/2 cup)	orange juice
375 ml (1-1/2 cups)	water
5 ml (1 t.)	sugar
2 ml (1/2 t.)	nutmeg
250 ml (1 cup)	brown rice
60 ml (1/4 cup)	sliced almonds

Combine the orange juice, water, sugar and nutmeg in a saucepan. Bring to a boil and add the rice. Stir and continue boiling for 1 minute. Lower heat, cover and simmer for 40 to 50 minutes until ready. Add more water if needed. Just prior to serving, toss in the almonds.

Makes 4 to 125 ml (1/2 cup) servings.

Per 125 ml (1/2 cup) serving:

calories: 238
fat: 4.9 g
protein: 5.4 g
carbohydrates: 43.4 g
sodium: 7 mg
fibre: 2.3 g
cholesterol: 0

Roast Potatoes

1 kg (2 lb.)	small red potatoes
250 ml (1 cup) + 60 ml (1/4 cup)	liquid chicken broth, divided
5 ml (1 t.)	minced garlic
60 ml (1/4 cup)	chopped fresh parsley
1 ml (1/4 t.)	paprika
125 ml (1/2 cup)	chopped onion

Scrub and wash potatoes but leave peel on. Slice in half and arrange on a non-stick pan or one sprayed with non-stick spray. In a bowl, mix chicken broth, garlic, parsley, paprika and chopped onion. Pour mixture over potatoes and bake at 230°C (450°F). Baste twice while cooking. Remove after 60 minutes and pour on an additional 60 ml (1/4 cup). Sprinkle salt and pepper to taste and broil 3 to 5 minutes until browned.

Microwave directions:

Use a microwavable dish and microwave, uncovered, at high power for 10 minutes or until tender.

Makes 6 - 125 ml (1/2 cup) servings.

Per 125 ml (1/2 cup) serving:

calories: 139
fat: 0.5 g
protein: 5.0 g
carbohydrates: 29.5 g
sodium: 182 mg
fibre: 3.1 g
cholesterol: 0

Wild Rice and Vegetables

325 ml (2-1/3 cups)	liquid chicken broth
1 ml (1/4 t.)	black pepper
125 ml (1/2 cup)	chopped onions
1-284 ml (10 oz.) can	sliced mushrooms, drained
60 ml (1/4 cup)	diced red peppers
180 ml (3/4 cup)	brown rice
60 ml (1/4 cup)	wild rice

Combine broth, pepper, onions, mushrooms and peppers in a saucepan. Bring to a boil and add rices. Boil for 30 seconds and reduce heat. Cover and simmer for 40 to 50 minutes until the liquid is absorbed.

Makes 6 - 125 ml (1/2 cup) servings.

Per 125 ml (1/2 cup) serving:

calories: 138
fat: 1.3 g
protein: 5.2 g
carbohydrates: 27.1 g
sodium: 182 mg
fibre: 2.1 g
cholesterol: 0

Fish and Seafood

Easy Broiled Salmon or Halibut Steaks

4 -120 g (4 oz.)	salmon or halibut steaks
125 ml (1/2 cup)	light Italian dressing
2 cloves	garlic, minced
5 ml (1 t.)	tarragon
1 ml (1/4 t.)	pepper

Mix the dressing with the spices in a bowl. Marinate steaks in the mixture for at least 2 hours or overnight. Place steaks on a cooking rack sprayed with non-stick spray. Broil for approximately 5 to 8 minutes until fish flakes. Do not turn fish over.

Variations:

Marinate fish as in recipe above. When fish is on the rack ready to be broiled, sprinkle on 125 ml (1/2 cup) breadcrumbs or 30 ml (2 T.) sesame seeds.

or

Serve with our Easy Tomato Salsa Sauce* (page 162).

Makes 4 (1 piece) servings.

Per serving:

calories: 189.8
fat: 8.59 g
protein: 24.08 g
carbohydrates: 2.77 g
sodium: 497 mg
fibre: 0.11 g
cholesterol: 67.9 mg

Easy Oriental Shrimp or Salmon

(or other fish)

1/2 kg (1 lb.)	shrimp, deveined, or salmon, halibut or other fish
125 ml (1/2 cup)	President's Choice Memories of Kyoto
125 ml (1/2 cup)	President's Choice Memories of Singapore

Marinate fish in sauces for 1 to 6 hours. Reserve marinade.

Place the fish in a pan sprayed with non-stick spray. Coat the fish with the reserved marinade and broil 3 to 8 minutes depending on the fish, until the shrimp are opaque or other fish flakes easily.

Makes 4 servings.

Per 85 g (3 oz.) serving:

calories: 254
protein: 24.2 g
carbohydrates: 34 g
fat: 1.5 g
sodium: 790 mg
fibre: 0
cholesterol: 221 mg

Easy Shrimp Stir-Fry

1 recipe	Low-Fat Stir-Fry*
450 g (1 lb.)	raw, deveined shrimp, peeled

Follow recipe for Low-Fat Stir-Fry* (page 176) but after adding the onions to the skillet, add the shrimp and cook for 2 to 3 minutes until shrimp are opaque. Then add the other vegetables and proceed with the recipe.

Makes 4 - 250 ml (1 cup) servings.

Per 250 ml (1 cup) serving:

calories: 399
fat: 3.5 g
protein: 38 g
carbohydrates: 53 g
sodium: 937 mg
fibre: 7.5 g
cholesterol: 292 mg

Honey Mustard Glazed Fish

250 ml (1 cup)	Honey Mustard Glaze*
8 - 120 g (4 oz.)	fish fillets or steaks

Prepare recipe for Honey Mustard Glaze* (page 164). Place fish in a non-stick pan or one sprayed with non-stick spray. Spoon onto each fillet, 30 ml (2 T.) dressing.

Bake at 180°C (350°F) for 15 to 20 minutes until fish is flaky.

Makes 8 servings.

Per serving:

calories: 163
fat: 5.2 g
protein: 23.4 g
carbohydrates: 5.2 g
sodium: 324 mg
fibre: 0.4 g
cholesterol:

Lemon Fish and Vegetables

400 g (14 oz.) pkg.	frozen fish fillets, thawed
280 g (10 oz.) pkg.	frozen cut broccoli
125 ml (1/2 cup)	diced yellow or red peppers
5 ml (1 t.)	lemon peel
30 ml (2 T.)	lemon juice
15 ml (1 T.)	sugar
15 ml (1 T.)	cornstarch
15 ml (1 T.)	low-sodium soy sauce
125 ml (1/2 cup)	water

Cut fish into 4 pieces. Spray a baking dish with non-stick spray and place fish into it. Bake at 180°C (350°F) for 20 to 30 minutes or until fish flakes or microwave 6 minutes.

Steam the broccoli and peppers in a saucepan until tender crisp. Put aside. In another saucepan place the lemon peel, lemon juice, sugar, cornstarch, soy sauce and water. Cook over medium heat, stirring constantly until thickened. Pour half of the sauce over the vegetables and toss. Transfer vegetables to a platter and place fish on top of the vegetables. Pour the remaining sauce over the fish.

Makes 3 servings.

Per serving:

calories: 175
fat: 13.4 g
protein: 1.3 g
carbohydrates: 13.4 g
sodium: 187 mg
fibre: 3.2 g
cholesterol: 76 mg

Oriental Shrimp

5 ml (1 t.)	olive or canola oil
1/2 kg (1 lb.)	shelled and deveined large shrimp
250 ml (1 cup)	diagonally sliced scallions
125 ml (1/2 cup)	chicken broth
15 ml (1 T.)	hoisin sauce
2 ml (1/2 t.)	cornstarch
	red peppers for garnish

In a non-stick pan or one sprayed with non-stick spray, add oil and heat. Add shrimp and scallions and cook until shrimp are pink and tender (approximately 3 to 5 minutes).

Combine the chicken broth, hoisin sauce and cornstarch in a bowl and mix well. Add to shrimp and cook, stirring constantly until mixture thickens.

Garnish with red pepper.

Makes 4 servings.

Per serving:

calories: 161
fat: 3.5 g
protein: 27.6 g
carbohydrates: 3.8 g
sodium: 343 mg
fibre: 0.6 g
cholesterol: 196 mg

Poached Salmon or Halibut

5 ml (1 t.)	olive or canola oil
125 ml (1/2 cup)	chopped onions
2 cloves	garlic, minced
5 ml (1 t.)	dill
1 ml (1/4 t.)	pepper
500 ml (2 cups)	chicken stock
250 ml (1 cup)	cooking wine (optional)
4	salmon or halibut steaks (or any other fish fillets) - 120 g (4 oz.) each

In a non-stick skillet or one sprayed with non-stick spray, add the oil and heat. Stir in the onions, garlic and spices and sauté slightly. Add the stock (and the wine if desired) and bring to a boil. Add the fish. Cover and simmer for 6 to 8 minutes, or until the fish flakes.

Makes 4 - 90 g (3 oz.) servings.

Per serving:

calories: 197
fat: 8.8 g
protein: 24.8 g
carbohydrates: 3.1 g
sodium: 459 mg
fibre: 0.4 g
cholesterol: 60 mg

Teriyaki Shrimp or Salmon

(or other fish)

250 ml (1 cup)	The Best Teriyaki Marinade*
450 g (1 lb.)	deveined shrimp or salmon, halibut or other fish fillet

Prepare The Best Teriyaki Marinade* (page 167) and cool completely prior to marinating.

Marinate fish for at least 2 hours or overnight.

Place the fish on a cooking rack sprayed with non-stick spray. Coat the fish with the thickened sauce and broil 3 to 8 minutes, depending on the fish, until the shrimp are opaque or other fish flakes easily.

Makes 4 servings.

Per serving:

calories: 249
protein: 28 g
carbohydrates: 31 g
fat: 1.24 g
sodium: 441 mg
fibre: 0.18 g
cholesterol: 219 mg

Beef, Lamb and Pork

Easy Lamb and Apricot Kabobs

3-1/4 kg (1.5 lb.)	boneless, lean lamb leg or loin
12	dried apricots
125 ml (1/2 cup)	President's Choice Memories of Kyoto
125 ml (1/2 cup)	President's Choice Memories of Singapore
6	kabob sticks

Cut lamb into 2-1/2 cm. (1") cubes and place into bowl. Add dried apricots and sauces. Marinate for 1 to 6 hours. Reserve marinade. Place lamb and apricots onto skewers and bake at 180°C (350°F) until desired doneness (basting frequently with marinade).

Makes 6 servings.

Per 1 kabob serving:

calories: 316
fat: 54. g
protein: 24 g
carbohydrates: 41 g
sodium: 549 mg
fibre: 0
cholesterol: 72 mg

Easy Onion Pot Roast or Brisket

3 cloves	garlic, minced
1-35 g (1-1/4 oz.) pkg.	dried onion soup mix
5 ml (1 t.)	dijon mustard
45 ml (3 T.)	ketchup
5 ml (1 t.)	thyme
2 ml (1/2 t.)	pepper
125 ml (1/2 cup)	water
1-900 g (2 lb.)	boneless short rib roast or lean brisket
15 ml (1 T.)	cornstarch
15 ml (1 T.)	cold water

Make a paste of the garlic, onion soup mix, dijon mustard, ketchup and spices. Put aside.

Place 125 ml (1/2 cup) water in the bottom of a casserole dish. Place the roast in the pan and brush it with the paste mixture.

Cover and cook in a 165°C (325°F) oven for 2-1/2 to 3 hours or until meat is tender.

Gravy

Collect drippings into measuring cup. Add water, if necessary to make 250 ml (1 cup). Spoon off fat from top of liquid and discard. Dissolve cornstarch in the cold water and stir into liquid. Place in a saucepan and cook until gravy thickens.

Slice roast or brisket (against the grain) and serve with gravy.

Makes 8 - 90 g (3 oz.) servings.

Per serving:

calories: 203
fat: 8.7 g
protein: 24.2 g
carbohydrates: 6.1 g
sodium: 643 mg
fibre: 0.4 g
cholesterol: 56 mg

Japanese-Style Flank Steak

3/4 kg. (1-1/2 lb.)	lean flank steak
60 ml (1/4 cup)	finely chopped green onions
60 ml (1/4 cup)	low-sodium soy sauce
30 ml (2 T.)	water
30 ml (2 T.)	sherry
3 cloves	garlic, minced
30 ml (2 T.)	water
1 ml (1/4 tsp.)	coarsely ground pepper

Trim fat from steak. Combine steak and next 7 ingredients in a large, zip-top plastic bag. Seal bag and marinate in refrigerator for 6 hours.

Remove steak from bag, and reserve marinade. Place steak on a rack coated with cooking spray and place rack in a roasting pan. Brush half of reserved marinade over steak. Broil 5 to 7 minutes. Turn steak over, and brush with remaining marinade. Broil 5 minutes or until desired degree of doneness. Cut steak diagonally across grain into thin slices.

Makes 6 - 90 g (3 oz.) servings.

Per serving:

calories: 215
fat: 9.3 g
protein: 28 g
carbohydrates: 2.0 g
sodium: 236 mg
fibre: 0.15 g
cholesterol: 50 mg

Luscious Lamb Chops

6-120 g (4 oz.)	bone-in loin lamb chops
60 ml (1/4 cup)	oil-free catalina dressing
10 ml (2 t.)	dijon mustard
5 ml (1 t.)	dried rosemary
1 ml (1/4 t.)	pepper
2 ml (1/2 t.)	thyme

Trim fat from lamb chops. Arrange chops in a single layer on broiler pan sprayed with non-stick spray.

Mix rest of ingredients in a separate bowl and spread half the mixture over chops.

Broil for 5 minutes. Turn and brush with rest of sauce. Broil for 3 to 5 minutes longer or until desired doneness.

Makes 6 - 90 g (3 oz.) servings.

Per serving:

calories: 175
fat: 6.5 g
protein: 25.6 g
carbohydrates: 2.2 g
sodium: 285 mg
fibre: 0.2 g
cholesterol: 96 mg

Marinated Pork and Mushrooms

30 ml (2 T.)	teriyaki sauce
20 ml (4 t.)	dark corn syrup
20 ml (4 t.)	dry sherry
20 ml (4 t.)	lemon juice
20 ml (4 t.)	rice vinegar
2 cloves	garlic , minced
5 ml (1 t.)	ground ginger
450 g (1 lb.)	lean pork tenderloin, thinly sliced
5 ml (1 t.)	olive or canola oil
250 ml (1 cup)	sliced mushrooms
250 ml (1 cup)	sliced scallions
15 ml (1 T.)	cornstarch
15 ml (1 T.)	cold water
125 ml (1/2 cup)	diced tomatoes

Mix first 7 ingredients in a large bowl. Add pork slices and turn to coat both sides. Cover bowl and marinate in refrigerator for at least one hour or overnight.

Heat oil in a non-stick skillet or one sprayed with non-stick spray. Sauté the mushrooms and scallions for 3 to 5 minutes, stirring constantly, until tender. Add the pork and the marinade and continue cooking for 2 to 3 minutes.

Make a paste by mixing the cornstarch and water and add to the skillet. Bring to a boil and add the tomatoes. Sauté for another minute until the pork is fully cooked and the vegetables are tender.

Makes 4 - 90 g (3 oz.) servings.

Per serving:

calories: 235
fat: 7.8 g
protein: 26.5 g
carbohydrates: 14.1 g
sodium: 428 mg
fibre: 1.4 g
cholesterol: 65 mg

Pepper Steak

60 ml (1/4 cup)	water
45 ml (3 T.)	low-sodium soy sauce
30 ml (2 T.)	chili sauce
30 ml (2 T.)	ketchup
1 clove	garlic, minced
5 ml (1 t.)	ground pepper
30 ml (2 T.)	sherry
10 ml (2 t.)	canola or olive oil
125 ml (1/2 cup)	diced onions
2	green, yellow or red peppers, cut into strips
450 g (1 lb)	boneless round steak, trimmed of fat, cut into thin 5 cm (2") strips
10 ml (2 t.)	cornstarch
60 ml (1/4 cup)	water

Mix first 7 ingredients in a bowl and set aside.

Place oil in a non-stick pan or one sprayed with non-stick spray. Heat slightly. Add onions and sauté for 1 to 2 minutes until softened. Add peppers and sauté another 4 to 5 minutes until slightly tender. Add steak strips and cook until browned. Stir in soy sauce mixture. Let it come to a slow boil. In a separate bowl, mix cornstarch and water to make a paste. Add to skillet and continue cooking until sauce thickens.

Makes 4 - 90 g (3 oz.) servings.

Per serving:

calories: 222.6
fat: 7.86 g
protein: 26.66 g
carbohydrates: 9.56 g
sodium: 349 mg
cholesterol: 49.5 mg

Skewered Lamb Kabobs

450 g (1 lb.)	boneless lamb (trimmed of visible fat), cut into 2.5 cm (1") cubes
2	onions, cut into large chunks
8-12	cherry tomatoes
1	small eggplant, peeled and cut into large cubes
12	whole large mushrooms
1	green pepper, cut into large chunks
1	red pepper, cut into large chunks

Marinade:

5 ml (1 t.)	olive or canola oil
45 ml (3 T.)	water
60 ml (1/4 cup)	lemon juice
125 ml (1/2 cup)	red or white wine
5 ml (1 t.)	granulated sugar
to taste	salt and pepper
1 clove	garlic, minced
3	bay leaves

In a bowl, combine ingredients for marinade. Place meat and vegetables into marinade, cover and leave in refrigerator to marinate for 4 to 6 hours, turning meat occasionally.

Alternate the lamb cubes with the vegetables on the skewers. BBQ or broil, brushing meat and vegetables with marinade and turning often as they cook. Cook to desired degree of doneness.

Makes 4 - 90 g (3 oz.) servings.

Per Serving:

calories: 242
fat: 6.6 g
protein: 25.6 g
carbohydrates: 16.4 g
sodium: 276 mg
fibre: 3.0 g
cholesterol: 72 mg

Teriyaki Beef or Pork and Broccoli

250 ml (1 cup)	The Best Teriyaki Marinade*
450 g (1 lb.)	boneless round steak or pork tenderloin, cut
into thin strips	
10 ml (2 t.)	olive or canola oil
750 ml (3 cups)	frozen or fresh broccoli

Prepare The Best Teriyaki Marinade* (page 167) and cool completely prior to marinating.

Place beef or pork in pan lined with aluminum foil. Pour teriyaki marinade over beef or pork and cover. Place in refrigerator and marinate for 2 to 6 hours.

Place oil in non-stick skillet or one sprayed with non-stick spray. Stir-fry broccoli until tender crisp (about 5 minutes). If the broccoli sticks, add a little bit of water. Add the beef or pork and the marinade to the skillet and stir-fry until beef or pork is browned.

Makes 4 - 180 ml (3/4 cup) servings:

Per 180 ml (3/4 cup) serving:

calories: 363
fat: 8.2 g
protein: 35 g
carbohydrates: 40 g
sodium: 297 mg
fibre: 6.1 g
cholesterol: 49 mg

Terrific Meat Loaf or Hamburger Patties or Meatballs

450 g (1 lb.)	ground round beef
125 ml (1/2 cup)	dried breadcrumbs
60 ml (1/4 cup)	finely chopped onions
60 ml (1/4 cup)	ketchup
1	egg, slightly beaten
30 ml (2 T.)	water
7 ml (1-1/2 t.)	Worcestershire sauce
5 ml (1 t.)	dry mustard
2 ml (1/2 t.)	black pepper
5 ml (1 t.)	salt

Mix all ingredients together in a large bowl.

Meatloaf: Place in loaf pan 1.5 l (6 cup) and bake at 180°C (350°F) for 60 minutes.

Hamburgers: Shape into 5 patties and grill or bake at 180°C (350°F) for 20 minutes or until desired doneness.

Meatballs: Shape into 2.5 cm (1") meatballs and bake at 180°C (350°F) for 20 minutes or until desired doneness.

Makes 5 - 90 g (3 oz.) servings.

Per 90 g (3 oz.) serving:

calories: 220
fat: 4.9 g
protein: 29 g
carbohydrates: 13.5 g
sodium: 836 mg
fibre: 0.66 g
cholesterol: 93 mg

Chicken & Turkey

Apricot Chicken, Turkey or Veal

6 - 180 g (6 oz.)	bone-in veal chops or bone-in skinless chicken breasts
or	
6 - 120 g (4 oz.)	boneless, skinless chicken or turkey cutlets
180 ml (3/4 cup)	Apricot Sauce* (1/2 recipe)

Prepare recipe for Apricot Sauce* (page 162). Place the veal, chicken or turkey in a baking pan and dry well so that the sauce sticks. Pour 30 ml (2 T.) onto each piece of veal, chicken or turkey and bake at 180°C (350°F) until meat or poultry is cooked through. Baste a few times while baking.

Chicken breasts: 45 to 50 minutes

Veal chops: 25 to 30 minutes

Boneless chicken or turkey cutlets: 15 to 20 minutes

The meat can be broiled for the last 2 to 3 minutes so that the sauce caramelizes.

Makes 6 (1 piece) servings.

Per (1 piece) serving:

calories: 24 g
fat: 4.8 g
protein: 42.1 g
carbohydrates: 7.2 g
sodium: 871 mg
fibre: 0.4 g
cholesterol: 105 mg

Breaded Chicken, Turkey or Fish

250 ml (1 cup)	dry breadcrumbs
2 cloves	garlic, minced
2 ml (1/2 t.)	salt
2	egg whites
1	juice of half lemon
6 -180 g (6 oz.)	bone-in, skinless chicken breast halves
or	
6 -120 g (4 oz.)	turkey cutlets
or	
6 - 120 g (4 oz.)	fish fillets or steaks

Combine breadcrumbs, garlic and salt in a large zip-top plastic bag.

Combine egg whites with lemon juice. Brush over chicken or turkey or fish and place one piece at a time into bag with breadcrumbs. Shake to coat.

Place coated pieces in a non-stick baking pan or one sprayed with non-stick spray. Sprinkle remaining crumbs over chicken, turkey or fish.

Bake uncovered at 180°C (350°F) for 45 to 50 minutes for the chicken or 20 to 30 minutes for the turkey or fish.

Makes 6 (1 piece) servings.

Per (1 piece) serving: (Analysis based on chicken)

calories: 282
fat: 3.1 g
protein: 45 g
carbohydrates: 15.4 g
sodium: 405 mg
fibre: 0.32 g
cholesterol: 104 mg

Breaded Honey Mustard Chicken

4-180 g (6 oz.)	bone-in, skinless chicken breast halves
125 ml (1/2 cup)	Honey Mustard Glaze*
250 ml (1 cup)	cornflake crumbs (optional)

Place chicken in a non-stick baking dish or one sprayed with non-stick spray. Spoon 30 ml (2 T.) Honey Mustard Glaze (page 164) on top of each breast. Sprinkle with crumbs (if using). Bake at 180°C (350°F) for 45 to 50 minutes until chicken is no longer pink inside.

Makes 4 (1 piece) servings.

Per (1 piece) serving:

calories: 287
fat: 6.8 g
protein: 42 g
carbohydrates: 11.9 g
sodium: 442 mg
fibre: 0.59 g
cholesterol: 104 mg

Chicken or Turkey Hawaiian

450 g (1 lb.)	boneless, skinless chicken or turkey breast cut into 2.5 cm. (1") cubes
2 small	sweet potatoes, cut into 2.5 cm. (1") cubes
15 ml (1 T.)	soy sauce
1-568 ml (20 oz.) can	unsweetened pineapple juice, drained (reserve juice)
1/4 kg (1/2 lb.)	snowpeas
1	red pepper, cut into 8 large chunks
125 ml (1/2 cup)	chopped onion
1 ml (1/4 t.)	ginger

Sauté chicken or turkey in a non-stick skillet or one sprayed with non-stick spray until cooked (about 3 to 5 minutes).

Add sweet potato cubes and enough water to just cover. Cook until potatoes are tender (approximately 15 minutes). Add soy sauce, pineapple juice, snowpeas, pepper and onion. Simmer for another 10 minutes. Add pineapple chunks and ginger.

Makes 4 - 250 ml (1 cup) servings.

Per 250 ml (1 cup) serving:

calories: 379
fat: 8.8 g
protein: 38 g
carbohydrates: 36 g
sodium: 425 mg
fibre: 5.5 g
cholesterol: 100 mg

Easy Chicken with Peppers

125 ml (1/2 cup)	The Best Teriyaki Marinade*
225 g (1/2 lb.)	boneless, skinless chicken breast
1	large red pepper, cut into strips
1	large green pepper, cut into strips
5 ml (1 t.)	canola or olive oil
60 ml (1/4 cup)	chopped onions
1 clove	garlic, minced
10 ml (2 t.)	cornstarch
10 ml (2 t.)	water

Prepare recipe for The Best Teriyaki Marinade* (page 167) and cool completely prior to marinating. Marinate the diced chicken and peppers for at least 3 hours or overnight in a covered bowl in the refrigerator.

Place the oil in a non-stick skillet or one sprayed with non-stick spray. Sauté onion and garlic for 1 to 2 minutes until onions are golden.

Add the peppers and chicken mixture and stir-fry for 3 to 4 minutes until peppers are tender crisp and chicken is no longer pink inside.

If a thicker consistency of sauce is needed, make a paste of cornstarch and water. Add to the stir-fry and cook until thickened.

Makes 2 - 250 ml (1 cup) servings.

Per 250 ml (1 cup) serving:

calories: 318
fat: 3.6 g
protein: 31.6 g
carbohydrates: 41 g
sodium: 264 mg
fibre: 1.24 g
cholesterol: 64 mg

Easy Chicken Stir-Fry

1 recipe	Low-Fat Stir-Fry*
350 g (3/4 lb.)	boneless, skinless chicken breast, cut into strips or cubes

Follow recipe for Low-Fat Stir-Fry* (page 176) but after adding the onions to the skillet, add the chicken and stir-fry for 3 to 5 minutes until almost cooked. Then proceed with the recipe.

Makes 4 - 250 ml (1 cup) servings.

Per 250 ml (1 cup) serving:

calories: 284
fat: 2.5 g
protein: 25 g
carbohydrates: 40 g
sodium: 741 mg
fibre: 5.6 g
cholesterol: 51 mg

Easy Honey Mustard Chicken

250 ml (1 cup)	Honey Mustard Glaze*
8 - 180 g (6 oz.)	bone-in skinless chicken breast

Prepare recipe for Honey Mustard Glaze* (page 164). Place chicken, or fish in a baking pan or on a rack and brush 30 ml (2 T.) glaze onto each piece. Bake at 180°C (350°F) until chicken is no longer pink (45 to 50 minutes) or until fish flakes (15 to 20 minutes).

Makes 8 (1 piece) servings.

Per (1 piece) serving:

calories: 257
fat: 6.6 g
protein: 42.2 g
carbohydrates: 5.2 g
sodium: 359 mg
fibre: 0.4 g
cholesterol: 104 mg

Honey Garlic Chicken or Pork

4-100 g (6 oz.)	bone-in, skinless chicken breast halves
or	
4	pork chops
or	
750 g (1-1/2 lb.)	pork tenderloin
250 ml (1 cup)	Honey Garlic Sauce* or commercial variety ("VH" brand)

Prepare recipe for Honey Garlic Sauce* (page 163). Cool the sauce completely before marinating the chicken or pork. Once cooled, marinate the skinless chicken or pork for at least 2 hours or overnight.

Bake at 180°C (350°F) until chicken is no longer pink inside (45 to 50 minutes) or the pork is of desired doneness (approximately 15 to 20 minutes).

Makes 6 servings.

Per serving:

calories: 171
fat: 0.88 g
protein: 16 g
carbohydrates: 24 g
sodium: 406 mg
fibre: 0.12 g
cholesterol: 38 mg

Indian Chicken, Turkey, Fish, Beef or Pork

6 - 180 g (6 oz.)	bone-in, skinless chicken breasts or bone-in pork chops
	or
3/4 kg (1-1/2 lb)	boneless round or beef tenderloin or pork tenderloin, boneless turkey or chicken cutlets or fish fillets
250 ml (1 cup)	Indian Sauce*

Prepare recipe for Indian Sauce* (page 164). Place meat, poultry or fish in baking pan and dry well so that the sauce sticks. Brush 30 ml (2 T.) onto each piece and bake at 180°C (350°F) until chicken is no longer pink inside, fish flakes or meat is no longer red inside.

Chicken breasts: 45 to 50 minutes.

Beef, pork, turkey, or chicken cutlets or fish fillets: 15 to 20 minutes.

Makes 6 (1 piece) servings.

Per 1 piece serving:

calories: 293
fat: 10.9 g
protein: 43 g
carbohydrates: 3.0 g
sodium: 478 mg
fibre: 0.2 g
cholesterol: 160 mg

Orange Turkey Cutlets

10 ml (2 t.)	cornstarch
30 ml (2 T.)	cold water
250 ml (1 cup)	orange juice
30 ml (2 T.)	grated orange rind
2 cloves	garlic, minced
20 ml (4 t.)	dried tarragon
5 ml (1 t.)	ground pepper
4 - 120 g (4 oz.)	turkey cutlets
	orange slices for garnish

Mix cornstarch and water to make a paste. Set aside. Place the orange juice, orange rind, garlic, tarragon and pepper in a large skillet. Add the cornstarch paste. Mix well. Add the turkey cutlets and poach in sauce until no longer pink (approximately 10 to 15 minutes).

Garnish with orange slices.

Makes 4 (1 piece) servings.

Per (1 piece) serving:

calories: 256
fat: 6.2 g
protein: 36.3 g
carbohydrates: 12.3 g
sodium: 86 mg
fibre: 1.1 g
cholesterol: 91 mg

Teriyaki Chicken

250 ml (1 cup)	The Best Teriyaki Marinade*
4-180 g (6 oz.)	bone-in, skinless chicken breast halves
	or
8	skinless chicken thighs

Prepare The Best Teriyaki Marinade* (page 167) and cool completely prior to marinating.

Place chicken in pan lined with aluminum foil. Add teriyaki marinade and cover pan. Refrigerate and marinate for 2 to 6 hours.

Bake chicken in 180°C (350°F) oven for 45 to 50 minutes or until chicken is no longer pink inside.

Makes 4 servings.

Per serving:

calories: 336
fat: 2.26 g
protein: 46 g
carbohydrates: 31.8 g
sodium: 306 mg
fibre: 0.18 g
cholesterol: 104 mg

Sophie's Spring Rolls

8 large or 20 small (appetizer size)	rice paper crêpes
250 ml (1 cup)	fresh bean sprouts
3	green onions, chopped
60 ml (1/4 cup)	tofu, sliced into small pieces
8	water chestnuts, sliced
3	eggs, beaten, and cooked in a non-stick skillet until set and sliced into small pieces
60 ml (1/4 cup)	shredded carrots
225 g (1/2 lb.)	chicken breasts, cooked and shredded
60 ml (1/4 cup)	chopped coriander leaves
	lettuce
	carrot and cucumber slices for garnish

Prepare all the vegetables.

Separate rice paper crêpes and dip one at a time into hot water (as hot as your hands can take). Once they start to soften, drain and place on a clean damp tea towel.

Fill rice paper crêpes with vegetables, chicken, egg, tofu and spices. Add hoison sauce, ginger sauce, President's Choice Kyoto Sauce or Honey Garlic Sauce* (page 163).

Roll up tightly and tuck in the ends. Cover with a damp tea-towel until ready to serve. Can be prepared up to 8 hours in advance.

Serve with a dipping sauce such as hoisin sauce, ginger sauce, President's Choice Kyoto Sauce or Honey Garlic Sauce.

Makes 8-10 servings.

Per serving:

calories: 123
fat: 3.1 g
protein: 11.9 g
carbohydrates: 11.9 g
sodium: 55 mg
fibre: 1.1 g
cholesterol: 97 mg

Pasta

Chicken or Seafood Primavera

1 recipe	Pasta Primavera*
750 ml (3 cups)	shrimp, or scallops, or clams, or diced chicken

Follow recipe for Pasta Primavera* (page 220), but omit Parmesan cheese. Instead, add cooked shrimp, Scallops, Clams, or diced chicken to the sauce.

Makes 6 servings.

Per serving 180 ml (3/4 cup) pasta and 250 ml (1 cup) sauce:

	Shrimp	Scallops	Clams	Chicken
calories:	403	381	437	443
fat:		5.5 g	4.6 g	5.7 g 6.9 g
protein:	28.4 g	23.1 g	32.5 g	35.6 g
carbohydrates:	62.2 g	64.5 g	65.8 g	61.4 g
sodium:	509 mg	497 mg	476 mg	440 mg
fibre:	6.2 g	7.0 g	6.2 g	6.2 g
cholesterol:	130 mg	23 mg	56 mg	67 mg

Light Fettucini Alfredo

180 ml (3/4 cup)	1% or 2% cottage cheese
80 ml (1/3 cup)	low-fat milk
80 ml (1/3 cup)	grated Parmesan cheese
1	egg
250 g (1/2 lb.)	fettucini
to taste	salt and pepper
80 ml (1/3 cup)	chopped fresh parsley

In food processor or with mixer, blend the cheeses, milk and egg until smooth. Set aside. Boil the pasta in water, drain and return pasta to saucepan. Add the blended cheese mixture to the pasta. Cook over medium heat for 1 minute stirring constantly until cheese mixture thickens slightly. Sprinkle with parsley.

Makes 6 - 250 ml (1 cup) servings.

Variation:

Fettucini Vegetable Alfredo: add cooked diced green and red peppers, broccoli, onions and zucchini to the thickened cheese pasta mixture just prior to serving.

Per 250 ml (1 cup) serving:

calories: 286
fat: 4.6 g
protein: 16.2 g
carbohydrates: 44 g
sodium: 250 mg
fibre: 0.15 g
cholesterol: 97 mg

Pasta Primavera

10 ml (2 t.)	olive oil
250 ml (1 cup)	chopped onions
250 ml (1 cup)	diced carrots
250 ml (1 cup)	broccoli florets
250 ml (1 cup)	diced red peppers
250 ml (1 cup)	sliced zucchini
250 ml (1 cup)	sliced fresh mushrooms
750 ml (3 cups)	Piquant Tomato Sauce* (page 166) or commercial variety of pasta sauce
1 litre (4 cups)	whole wheat fettucini or spaghetti
80 ml (1/3 cup)	Parmesan cheese

In a non-stick skillet or one sprayed with non-stick spray, heat the oil. Add the onions and sauté for 2 minutes. Add the carrots and sauté until tender. Then add the broccoli, peppers, zucchini and mushrooms. Once the vegetables are tender crisp, add the pasta sauce.

Boil the pasta, drain and serve topped with vegetable sauce. Sprinkle Parmesan cheese on top of sauce.

Makes 6 servings.

Per serving 375 ml (1-1/2 cup) pasta and 180 ml (3/4 cup) sauce and 30 ml (2 T.) Parmesan cheese:

calories: 297
fat: 5.5 g
protein: 11.6 g
carbohydrates: 53.6 g
sodium: 482 mg
fibre: 7.3 g
cholesterol: 392 mg

Pasta Parmesan with Shrimp or Chicken and Vegetables

450 g (1 lb.)	pasta (fettucini or penne or linguini)
10 ml (2 t.)	olive oil
1	red pepper, diced
375 ml (1-1/2 cups)	sliced mushrooms
2 cloves	garlic, minced
900 g (2 lb.)	large raw shrimp, or diced raw chicken
60 ml (1/4 cup)	chicken broth heated
60 ml (1/4 cup)	grated Parmesan cheese
80 ml (1/3 cup)	chopped fresh parsley
to taste	salt and pepper

Cook pasta in boiling water, drain and set aside. Add 5 ml (1 t.) of the oil to a non-stick skillet or one sprayed with non-stick spray. Add peppers and sauté until tender crisp. Then add the mushrooms and sauté for another 2 minutes. Transfer to bowl. In the same skillet add the other 5 ml (1 t.) of oil and garlic. Then add the shrimp or chicken and stir fry until cooked. If stir-frying chicken, add 15 ml (1 T.) chicken broth to pan.

Add mushroom combination to chicken (or shrimp) and heat through. Add chicken broth, Parmesan cheese, parsley and spices. Stir. Add to pasta. Toss. Serve immediately.

Makes 8 servings.

Per serving:

calories: 330
fat: 5.7 g
protein: 34.3 g
carbohydrates: 33.8 g
sodium: 289 mg
fibre: 0.3 g
cholesterol: 238 mg

Pasta with Fish and Piquant Tomato Sauce

500 ml (2 cups)	Piquant Tomato Sauce* or commercial brand tomato sauce
125 ml (1/2 cup)	breadcrumbs
45 ml (3 T.)	grated Parmesan cheese
15 ml (1 T.)	chopped fresh parsley
1 clove	garlic, minced
550 g (1 1/4 lb.)	fish—divided into 6 portions
30 ml (2 T.)	dijon mustard
15 ml (1 T.)	honey
225 g (1/2 lb.)	pasta

Delicious fish in this recipe are swordfish steaks, halibut steaks, scallops or shrimps.

Prepare one recipe of Piquant Tomato Sauce* (page 166). Set aside.

In a bowl, mix together the breadcrumbs, cheese, parsley and garlic. Set aside.

Place fish in a broiler pan sprayed with non-stick spray. Broil fish until opaque. Mix together dijon mustard and honey and brush over fish. Then sprinkle fish with the breadcrumb mixture. Broil. Set aside.

Before putting fish back into oven, boil the pasta in water and heat the tomato sauce. Drain the cooked pasta and mix in the tomato sauce. Set aside.

Place the fish under the broiler for 30 seconds until lightly browned.

To serve, mound pasta mixture onto 6 plates and top each with a serving of fish.

Makes 6 servings.

Per serving:

calories: 322
fat: 5.5 g
protein: 27.9 g
carbohydrates: 40.2 g
sodium: 435 mg
fibre: 2.0 g
cholesterol: 59 mg

Vegetarian Dishes

Healthy Pizza

6-15 cm. (6")	whole wheat pita breads
2-170 ml (6 oz.) cans	tomato paste
60 ml (1/4 cup)	water
2 cloves	garlic, minced
5 ml (1 t.)	oregano
10 ml (2 t.)	basil
500 ml (2 cups)	sliced mushrooms
3	tomatoes, sliced
125 ml (1/2 cup)	onions
1	medium green or red pepper, cut into strips or rings
350 g (12 oz.)	shredded, part-skim mozzarella cheese

Place pita breads on non-stick baking sheets or ones sprayed with non-stick spray. Mix the tomato paste with the water, garlic, oregano and basil. Spread over each pita.

Arrange the vegetables on each crust and sprinkle with cheese. Bake at 180°C (350°F) for 10 to 12 minutes or until cheese bubbles.

Other delicious toppings include:

- pineapple cubes
- sun-dried tomatoes
- zucchini
- broccoli
- shrimp
- eggplant

Makes 6 servings (1 pita each portion).

Per serving:
(not counting variations)

calories: 428
fat: 11.4 g
protein: 25 g
carbohydrates: 58 g
sodium: 569 mg
fibre: 4.6 g
cholesterol: 34 mg

Healthy Scramble in a Pita

5 ml (1 t.)	olive or canola oil
60 ml (1/4 cup)	diced onions
125 ml (1/2 cup)	diced red or green peppers
125 ml (1/2 cup)	diced tomatoes
4-6	egg whites
60 g (2 oz.)	low-fat jarlsberg or Swiss cheese
15 ml (1 T.)	chopped fresh parsley
to taste	salt and pepper
2	small pita pockets

Heat oil in a non-stick pan or one sprayed with non-stick spray. Stir fry the onions. Add the peppers and stir-fry until tender. Add the tomatoes, egg whites and cheese, and cook until ready (approx. 2 to 3 minutes). Add salt and pepper to taste. Cut one-quarter of the way around the edge of the pita, and open up to form a pocket. Serve half the egg mixture in each pocket.

Makes 2 servings.

Per serving:

calories: 284
fat: 10 g
protein: 18.7 g
carbohydrates: 30.1 g
sodium:
fibre: 2.4 g
cholesterol: 24.5 mg

Healthy Vegetable Omelette

5 ml (1 t.)	olive or canola oil
60 ml (1/4 cup)	diced onions
60 ml (1/4 cup)	diced red or green peppers
80 ml (1/3 cup)	chopped mushrooms
60 ml (1/4 cup)	diced zucchini
8-10	egg whites or 4 whole eggs
to taste	salt and pepper
120 g (4 oz.)	shredded low-fat cheddar or low-fat jarlsberg cheese
80 ml (1/3 cup)	diced tomatoes

Heat oil in a non-stick pan or one sprayed with non-stick spray. Stir fry the onion and peppers until tender, then add the mushrooms and zucchini. If vegetables begin to stick, add a little water, 15 to 20 ml at a time. Stir-fry 1 more minute and put aside. Beat the egg whites or whole eggs in a bowl with salt and pepper to taste. In another non-stick skillet or one sprayed with non-stick spray, add the eggs. Cook over medium heat and as the eggs begin to set, gently pull the sides of the omelette up to let the uncooked part flow under the cooked egg. Add the shredded cheese, diced tomatoes and sauté vegetables on top of the eggs. Fold in half and cook until the cheese melts.

Makes 4 servings.

Per serving:

	Egg whites only	Whole eggs
calories:	111	156
fat:	3.0 g	8.0 g
protein:	14.4 g	14 g
carbohydrates:	7.2 g	7.2 g
sodium:	568 mg	528 mg
fibre:	1.0 g	1.0 g
cholesterol:	12 mg	215 mg

Light Grilled Cheese Sandwiches

4 slices	whole wheat bread
120 g (4 oz.)	part-skim or low-fat cheddar sliced
	tomato slices (optional)

Place 2 slices of bread in a non-stick skillet or one sprayed with non-stick spray. Place 56 g (2 oz.) of cheese on top of each slice (add tomato slices if desired). Top each with another slice of bread. Grill on both sides until cheese is melted.

Makes 2 sandwiches.

Per 1 sandwich serving:

calories: 291
fat: 13.1 g
protein: 20.9 g
carbohydrates: 24.9 g
sodium: 265 mg
fibre: 0
cholesterol: 2 mg

Stuffed Baked Potato with Broccoli

2	baking potatoes
80 ml (1/3 cup)	low-fat cottage cheese
30 ml (2 T.)	low-fat milk
45 ml (3 T.)	grated Parmesan cheese
15 ml (1 T.)	fresh chives, minced
10 ml (2 t.)	dijon mustard
to taste	salt and pepper
60 ml (1/4 cup)	part-skim mozzarella cheese, grated
300 ml (1-1/4 cups)	medium broccoli florets, steamed until just tender (garnish)

Cover potatoes with foil and bake 1 hour at 180°C (350°F) or until tender. Let cool. Halve potatoes lengthwise and scoop out, leaving 1-1/4 cm. (1/2") border. Mix scooped potato with cottage cheese, milk, Parmesan cheese, chives, mustard, salt and pepper in a food processor for about 5 to 10 seconds, or mash in a mixing bowl until smooth.

Refill potato skins. Divide mozzarella cheese and broccoli florets over each potato. In a covered baking dish, bake potatoes 10 minutes or until cheese melts and potatoes are hot.

Makes 4 servings.

Per serving:

calories: 131
fat: 3.0 g
protein: 10.1 g
carbohydrates: 17.1 g
sodium: 256 mg
fibre: 3.3 g
cholesterol: 8 mg

Zucchini Stuffed with Spinach and Cheese
(Served with Fresh Tomato Basil Sauce)

6	medium zucchinis
5 ml (1 t.)	garlic powder
to taste	black pepper
5 ml (1 t.)	thyme

Filling:

45 ml (3 T.)	vegetable stock
1	large shallot, minced
1 clove	garlic, minced
to taste	black pepper
120 g (4 oz)	spinach, chopped
4-5	sundried tomatoes, reconstituted in water, minced
15 ml (1 T.)	dried basil
250 ml (1 cup)	non-fat ricotta cheese, or tofu
45 ml (3 T.)	grated Parmesan cheese
500 ml (2 cups)	Piquant Tomato Sauce* (page 166) or commercial brand red pasta sauce

Halve zucchinis crosswise. With apple corer, scoop out pulp; leave 1/4" intact shells. Season inside shells with garlic powder, pepper and thyme.

In a skillet, soften shallot, garlic and pepper in stock. Cook until liquid is absorbed, then add spinach and cook until wilted. Transfer to a bowl. Stir in sundried tomatoes, basil, ricotta or tofu, Parmesan cheese and pepper. Chill mixture.

Spoon filling into each zucchini half. Spoon 80 ml (1/3 cup) tomato sauce on each zucchini and broil for 5 to 6 minutes

Makes 6 servings.

Per serving:

calories: 207
fat: 5.8 g
protein: 14.1 g
carbohydrates: 30.2 g
sodium 257 mg
fibre: 2.4 g
cholesterol: 15 mg

Breakfast Dishes

Buckwheat Pancakes

125 ml (1/2 cup)	buckwheat flour
125 ml (1/2 cup)	all-purpose flour
10 ml (2 t.)	baking powder
160 ml (2/3 cup)	skim milk
25 ml (1-1/2 T.)	maple syrup
1	egg

Combine flours and baking powder in a bowl. In a separate bowl combine milk, maple syrup and egg. Add the wet mixture to the flour mixture and stir until smooth.

Spoon 60 ml (1/4 cup) batter for each pancake onto a non-stick skillet or one sprayed with non-stick spray. Cook pancakes over medium heat. Turn when the tips are covered with bubbles and the edges appear cooked.

Makes 4 servings (2 pancakes each).

Per 2 pancake serving:

calories: 168
fat: 2.0 g
protein: 6.7 g
carbohydrates: 31.7 g
sodium: 171 mg
fibre: 0.5 g
cholesterol: 54 mg

Breakfast Sauces

for pancakes, waffles or French toast

Creamy Maple Topping

60 ml (1/4 cup)	vanilla low-fat yogurt
60 ml (1/4 cup)	low-fat ricotta cheese
45 ml (3 T.)	light maple syrup

Blend ingredients in a food processor or blender until smooth.

Makes 160 ml (2/3 cup).

Per 80 ml (1/3 cup) serving:
calories: 116
fat: 2.3 g
protein: 4.5 g
carbohydrates: 20 g
sodium: 56 mg
fibre: 0
cholesterol: 8 mg

Berry Topping

300 ml (1-1/4 cup)	sliced fresh or frozen and thawed strawberries or blueberries
25 ml (1-1/2 T.)	brown or white sugar
15 ml (1 T.)	water

Blend ingredients in a food processor or blender until smooth.

Makes 250 ml (1 cup).

Per 60 ml (1/4 cup) serving:	Strawberries	Blueberries
calories:	36	45
fat:	0.1 g	0.3 g
protein:	0.2 g	0.2 g
carbohydrates:	9.5 g	11.2 g
sodium:	1 mg	0 mg
fibre:	0.8 g	1.6 g
cholesterol:	0	0

Fruity Yogurt Dressing *(for fruit or pancakes)*

125 ml (1/2 cup)	low-fat plain yogurt
60 ml (1/4 cup)	all-fruit jam

Makes 180 ml (3/4 cup).

Per 60 ml (1/4 cup) serving:

calories: 26
fat: 0.06 g
protein: 2.2 g
carbohydrates: 4.2 g
sodium: 31 mg
fibre: 0.2 g
cholesterol: 0.8 mg

Cinnamon Whole Grain Pancakes

180 ml (3/4 cup)	all-purpose flour
180 ml (3/4 cup)	oatbran
2 ml (1/2 t.)	baking powder
1 ml (1/4 t.)	baking soda
10 ml (2 t.)	sugar
2 ml (1/2 t.)	ground cinnamon
2	egg whites
250 ml (1 cup)	buttermilk
60 ml (1/4 cup)	orange juice

Combine flour, oatbran, baking powder, baking soda, sugar and cinnamon. In a separate bowl beat the egg whites, buttermilk and orange juice with a fork. Add the egg mixture to the dry mixture and stir until combined.

Spoon 60 ml (1/4 cup) batter for each pancake onto non-stick skillet or one sprayed with non-stick spray. Cook pancakes over medium heat. Turn when tops are covered with bubbles and edges appear cooked.

Makes 4 servings (2 pancakes each).

Per 2 pancake serving:

calories: 180
fat: 2.1 g
protein: 9.5 g
carbohydrates: 37.3 g
sodium: 181 mg
fibre: 3.7 g
cholesterol: 2 mg

Easy Breakfast Shake

for breakfast on the run

125 ml (1/2 cup)	unsweetened fruit juice or orange juice
125 ml (1/2 cup)	skim milk
30 ml (2 T.)	skim milk powder
5 ml (1 t.)	honey
5 ml (1 t.)	vanilla extract
15 ml (1 T.)	oatbran

Blend all ingredients in a blender until smooth.

Makes 1 serving.

Per serving:

calories: 179
fat: 0.7 g
protein: 9.0 g
carbohydrates: 34.8 g
sodium: 112 mg
fibre: 1.3 g
cholesterol: 3 mg

Healthy Breakfast Danish

90 ml (1/3 cup)	low-fat cottage cheese
20 ml (4 t.)	all-fruit jam
15 ml (1 T.)	raisins
one-half	English muffin

Combine cottage cheese, all fruit jam and raisins. Spread on half an English muffin. Broil 3 to 4 minutes until heated.

Makes 1 serving.

Per serving:

calories: 249
fat: 0.6 g
protein: 18.8 g
carbohydrates: 43.1 g
sodium: 350 mg
fibre: 0.9 g
cholesterol: 0

Orange Cinnamon French Toast

6 to 8	egg whites
30 ml (2. T.)	skim milk
45 ml (3 T.)	frozen orange juice concentrate
5 ml (1 t.)	cinnamon
7 ml (1-1/2 t.)	vanilla extract
4 slices	whole wheat bread
60 ml (1/4 cup)	all-fruit jam

Beat egg whites with milk, orange juice concentrate, cinnamon and vanilla. Soak bread slices one at a time in mixture. Cook each in a non-stick skillet or one sprayed with non-stick spray. Cook until golden brown on each side.

Serve each slice with 15 ml (1 T.) all-fruit jam, Creamy Maple Topping* (page 230), Berry Topping* (page 230), or Fruity Yogurt Dressing* (page 231).

Makes 4 (1 slice) servings.

Per 1 slice serving:

calories: 125
fat: 0.8 g
protein: 8.3 g
carbohydrates: 21.7 g
sodium: 233 mg
fibre: 2.0 g
cholesterol: 0.98 mg

Desserts and Baked Goods

Angel Food Cake Delight

1	angel food cake
250 ml (1 cup)	Strawberry Sauce*
250 ml (1 cup)	sliced fresh strawberries
5	kiwis, peeled and sliced

Cut angel food cake into 8 slices. Top each slice with a few slices of strawberries and kiwis. Drizzle 30 ml (2 T.) Strawberry Sauce* (page 247) on top.

Makes 8 servings.

Per serving:

calories: 212
fat: 0.4 g
protein: 4.9 g
carbohydrates: 49.0 g
sodium: 170 mg
fibre: 2.5 g
cholesterol: 0

Apple Crisp

125 ml (1/2 cup)	sugar
45 ml (3 T.)	all-purpose flour
10 ml (2 t.)	grated lemon rind
15 ml (1 T.)	lemon juice
1-1/2 litres (6 cups)	sliced apples

Topping

125 ml (1/2 cup)	packed brown sugar
125 ml (1/2 cup)	rolled oats
60 ml (1/2 cup)	all-purpose flour
30 ml (2 T.)	melted margarine
5 ml (1 t.)	maple or vanilla extract
5 ml (1 t.)	cinnamon

Combine first 5 ingredients in a bowl and mix well. Spoon into a 22 cm (9") non-stick baking pan or one sprayed with non-stick spray.

Combine the topping ingredients. Mix well and sprinkle over filling.

Bake at 190°C (375°F) for 45 minutes until the topping is golden brown.

Makes 12 servings.

Per serving:

calories: 156
fat: 2.3 g
protein: 1.2 g
carbohydrates: 34.4 g
sodium: 27 mg
fibre: 1.9 g
cholesterol: 0

Baked Apples

6	apples
125 ml (1/2 cup)	packed brown sugar
5 ml (1 t.)	nutmeg
15 ml (1 T.)	cinnamon
125 ml (1/2 cup)	water

Core apples but do not go right through the bottom. Remove top 2.5 cm (1") of peel. Place apples in a baking dish lined with aluminium foil. Combine brown sugar and spices and spoon into centre of apples. Add water to bottom of baking dish. Bake at 190°C (375°F) for 25 minutes or until apples are tender when pierced with a fork.

Makes 6 servings.

Per serving:

calories: 157
fat: 0.7 g
protein: 0.3 g
carbohydrates: 40.7 g
sodium: 6 mg
fibre: 3.0 g
cholesterol: 0

Banana Nut Bread

3	large bananas
1	egg
30 ml (2 T.)	oil
80 ml (1/3 cup)	skim milk or buttermilk
125 ml (1/2 cup)	sugar
2 ml (1/2 t.)	baking powder
5 ml (1 t.)	baking soda
125 ml (1/2 cup)	chopped walnuts
180 ml (3/4 cup)	whole wheat flour
180 ml (3/4 cup)	all-purpose flour

Mash the bananas with a fork. Add the egg, oil, milk, sugar, baking powder and baking soda; beat well. Add the chopped walnuts and mix. Then add the flours, mixing gently until the flour is moistened. Do not overmix. Pour into a non-stick 10 cm x 20 cm (4" x 8") loaf pan or one sprayed with non-stick spray.

Bake at 180°C (350°F) for 45 minutes or until a cake tester comes out clean.

Let cool for 15 minutes. Remove from pan.

Makes 12 slices.

Per slice:

calories: 178
fat: 6.4 g
protein: 3.7 g
carbohydrates: 28.4 g
sodium: 171 mg
fibre: 2 g
cholesterol: 18 mg

Carrott Muffins

250 ml (1 cup)	whole wheat flour
125 ml (1/2 cup)	all-purpose flour
15 ml (1 T.)	cinnamon
5 ml (1 t.)	ground ginger
5 ml (1 t.)	baking powder
5 ml (1 t.)	baking soda
1 ml (1/4 t.)	salt
300 ml (1-1/2 cups)	raisins
1	egg
180 ml (3/4 cup)	skim milk
45 ml (3 T.)	oil
125 ml (1/2 cup)	packed brown sugar
10 ml (2 t.)	vanilla extract
180 ml (3/4 cup)	finely shredded carrot
15 ml (1 T.)	grated orange rind

Combine first 8 ingredients. Set aside. In another bowl, beat egg until fluffy, then stir in milk, oil, sugar, vanilla, carrots and orange rind. Add flour mixture and stir gently to combine until the dry ingredients are moistened. Do not overmix. Spoon into 12 muffin cups. Bake at 200°C (400°F) for 20 minutes or until springy to touch.

Makes 12 muffins.

Per muffin:

calories: 194
fat: 4.2 g
protein: 3.8 g
carbohydrates: 37.4 g
sodium: 167 mg
fibre: 3.1 g
cholesterol: 18 mg

Chocolate Angel Cake

1 pkg.	angel food cake mix
80 ml (1/3 cup)	cocoa, sifted
7 ml (1-1/2 t.)	powdered instant coffee

Follow directions on the angel food mix package, adding the sifted cocoa and instant coffee to the dry mix. Beat 1 to 2 minutes. Bake 45 minutes in an ungreased tube pan. Invert and cool.

Makes 12 servings.

Per serving:

calories: 148
fat: 0.4 g
protein: 3.2 g
carbohydrates: 33.9 g
sodium: 87 mg
fibre: 0.1 g
cholesterol: 0

Cornbread

250 ml (1 cup)	yellow cornmeal
330 ml (1-1/3 cup)	skim milk
45 ml (3 T.)	vegetable oil
1	egg
125 ml (1/2 cup)	all-purpose flour
125 ml (1/2 cup)	whole wheat flour
60 ml (1/4 cup)	sugar
15 ml (1 T.)	baking powder
2 ml (1/2 t.)	baking soda
2 ml (1/2 t.)	salt

In a bowl, mix together cornmeal, milk, oil and egg. In a separate bowl, mix the flours, sugar, baking powder, baking soda and salt. Mix the wet mixture into the dry mixture, stirring just until all the dry ingredients are moistened. Do not overmix.

Pour batter into a 20 cm (8") square non-stick baking pan or one sprayed with non-stick spray.

Bake at 200°C (400°F) for 20 to 25 minutes until golden and springy to the touch.

Makes 12 servings.

Per serving:

calories: 140
fat: 3.8 g
protein: 3.6 g
carbohydrates: 23.3 g
sodium: 173 mg
fibre: 1.5 g
cholesterol: 0

Fruit Compote

450 g (1 lb.)	mixed dried fruit (prunes, peaches, apricots, pears and apples)
500 ml (2 cups)	water
5 ml (1 t.)	lime juice
15 ml (1 T.)	lemon juice
60 ml (1/4 cup)	orange juice

Combine the dried fruit with the water in a bowl. Stir. Cover and refrigerate overnight. The next day, place the fruit and water mixture into a saucepan. Add the lime juice, lemon juice and orange juice and stir. Bring to a boil, then reduce heat, cover and simmer for 45 to 50 minutes until the fruit is tender. Chill prior to serving.

Makes 8 - 125 ml (1/2 cup) servings.

Per 125 ml (1/2 cup) serving:

calories: 171
fat: 0.4 g
protein: 1.8 g
carbohydrates: 45 g
sodium: 20 mg
fibre: 3.7 g
cholesterol: 0

Fruit Kabobs and Dip

12	melon chunks
12	fresh strawberries
12	pineapple chunks
12	thick banana slices
30 ml (2 T.)	lemon juice
5 ml (1 t.)	sugar

Dip:

180 ml (3/4 cup)	plain low-fat yogurt
45 ml (3 T.)	all-fruit jam (any flavour)

Place alternating chunks of fruit on kabob sticks. Mix lemon juice and sugar and drizzle on top of kabobs.

To make dip, blend together the yogurt and all-fruit jam well.

Makes 6 kabobs and 180 ml (3/4 cup) dip.

Per kabob and 30 ml (2 T.) dip:

calories: 77
fat: 0.46 g
protein: 2.5 g
carbohydrates: 17 g
sodium: 26 mg
fibre: 1.7 g
cholesterol: 0.59 mg

Light Berry Tarts

125 ml (1/2 cup)	red currant jelly
10 ml (2 t.)	cornstarch
10 ml (2 t.)	water
250 ml (1 cup)	blueberries
250 ml (1 cup)	sliced strawberries
250 ml (1 cup)	raspberries
15 ml (1 T.)	lemon juice
8	meringue shells or sponge cake shells

Heat red currant jelly in saucepan to a slow simmer. Make a paste of cornstarch and water and add to the saucepan. Add the fruits and lemon juice and stir gently while heating for 1 to 2 minutes.

Cool in refrigerator for 30 to 60 minutes. Just prior to serving, spoon 60 ml (1/4 cup) into each shell.

Makes 8 tarts.

Per tart:

calories: 140
fat: 1.3 g
protein: 1.9 g
carbohydrates: 31 g
sodium: 34 mg
fibre: 2.0 g
cholesterol: 46 mg

Light Lemon Poppy Seed Cake

300 ml (1-1/4 cups)	sugar
1	whole egg
2	egg whites
15 ml (1 T.)	lemon extract
25 ml (1-1/2 T.)	grated lemon peel
60 ml (1/4 cup)	softened margarine
500 ml (2 cups)	all-purpose flour
125 ml (1/2 cup)	skim milk
125 ml (1/2 cup)	low-fat plain yogurt
80 ml (1/3 cup)	poppy seeds
10 ml (2 t.)	baking powder
2 ml (1/2 t.)	salt

Preheat oven to 180°C (350°F). Place first 5 ingredients into mixing bowl and mix at high speed for 4 to 5 minutes. Reduce speed and add rest of ingredients, mixing until completely blended.

Pour batter into bundt cake pan sprayed with non-stick spray. Bake for 45 to 50 minutes or until cake tester comes out clean.

Cool cake for 15 minutes and remove from pan.

Makes 24 servings.

Per serving:

calories: 116
fat: 3.0 g
protein: 2.5 g
carbohydrates: 20.3 g
sodium: 93 mg
fibre: 0.4 g
cholesterol: 9 mg

Oatbran Raisin Muffins

125 ml (1/2 cup)	whole wheat flour
125 ml (1/2 cup)	all-purpose flour
250 ml (1 cup)	oatbran
10 ml (2 t.)	baking powder
80 ml (1/3 cup)	raisins
300 ml (1-1/4 cups)	skim milk
5 ml (1 t.)	vanilla extract
1	egg
15 ml (1 T.)	grated orange rind
60 ml (1/4 cup)	liquid honey
30 ml (2 T.)	vegetable oil

Combine first 5 ingredients in a large bowl. In a separate bowl, combine milk, vanilla, egg, orange rind, honey and oil. Stir well. Mix the wet mixture into the dry mixture, stirring just until the dry ingredients are moistened. Do not overmix.

Spoon batter into paper-lined muffin tins. Bake at 200°C (400°F) for 20 minutes or until springy to touch.

Makes 12 muffins.

Per muffin:

calories: 131
fat: 3.5 g
protein: 4.3 g
carbohydrates: 24.7 g
sodium: 64 mg
fibre: 2.5 g
cholesterol: 18 mg

Raspberry Corn Muffins

125 ml (1/2 cup)	whole wheat flour
125 ml (1/2 cup)	all-purpose flour
2 ml (1/2 t.)	salt
250 ml (1 cup)	yellow cornmeal
60 ml (1/4 cup)	sugar
15 ml (1 T.)	baking powder
250 ml (1 cup)	skim milk
1	egg
30 ml (2 T.)	oil
5 ml (1 t.)	vanilla extract
60 ml (1/4 cup)	all-fruit raspberry jam

Combine first 6 ingredients in a large mixing bowl. In a separate bowl, combine milk, egg, oil and vanilla. Add the wet mixture to the dry mixture stirring just until all the dry ingredients are moistened. Do not overmix. Fill 12 paper-lined muffins tins one-quarter full.

Place 5 ml (1 t.) all-fruit jam in the centre of each and top with the rest of the batter. Bake at 200°C (400°F) for 20 to 25 minutes or until muffin springs back when lightly touched.

Makes 12 muffins.

Per muffin:

calories: 152
fat: 3.1 g
protein: 3.6 g
carbohydrates: 27.8 g
sodium: 148 mg
fibre: 1.5 g
cholesterol: 18 mg

Strawberry or Raspberry Sauce

1 - 300 g (11 oz.)	box frozen, unsweetened strawberries or raspberries, thawed and strained
15 ml (1 T.)	granulated sugar
15 ml (1 T.)	fresh lemon juice

Place fruit, sugar and lemon juice in a blender and purée.

This sauce is delicious spooned over:

- fruit salad
- angel food cake
- yogurt
- cottage cheese
- frozen yogurt, sherbet or ice milk

Makes 625 ml (2-1/2 cups) = 10 - 60 ml (1/4 cup) servings.

Per 60 ml (1/4 cup) serving:

calories: 19
fat: 0.2 g
protein: 0.3 g
carbohydrates: 4.8 g
sodium: 0
fibre: 1.5 g
cholesterol: 0

Snacks

Healthy Popcorn

60 ml (1/4 cup) corn kernels

Air-pop the popcorn or try the following low-fat method:

Heat the 30 ml (2 T.) oil in the bottom of a saucepan. Add 60 ml (1/4 cup) of kernels and cover. When the popcorn just begins to pop, carefully drain off half of the oil but leave the kernels behind. Start to cook again, popping the kernels.

Season with any of:

- grated Parmesan cheese
- Italian seasoning
- powdered salad dressing mixes
- paprika and salt
- garlic powder or garlic salt
- onion powder or onion salt
- taco seasoning mix
- cinnamon sugar

To get the seasonings to stick to the popcorn (without butter) spray the popcorn with cooking spray (e.g., Pam), then sprinkle the seasonings on.

or

Place water or low sodium soy sauce in a spray bottle and mist the popcorn before adding the seasonings.

Makes 1-3/4 litres (7-8 cups) of popcorn.

Per 1 litre (4 cups) serving: (Analysis does not include seasonings)

	Air-popped	Oil-popped
calories:	148	206
fat:	1.93 g	8.4 g
protein:	4.9 g	4.9 g
carbohydrates:	29 g	29 g
sodium:	0	0
fibre:	3.1 g	3.1 g
cholesterol:00		

Tortilla Treats

1-15 cm (6")	tortilla (whole wheat, white or corn)
to taste	seasoning (choose from paprika, salt and pepper, garlic, salt, grated Parmesan cheese)

Cut tortilla in to 6-8 wedges. Place on baking sheet and sprinkle with seasonings. Bake at 200°C (400°F) for 5 to 10 minutes or until golden brown.

Makes 1 serving.

Per serving:

calories: 74
fat: 1.6 g
protein: 2.8 g
carbohydrates: 13.1 g
sodium: 38 mg
fibre: 0
cholesterol: 1 mg

Beverages

Healthy Soda

125 ml (1/2 cup)	unsweetened fruit juice
5 ml (1 t.)	lemon juice club soda or sparkling mineral water

Pour fruit juice and lemon juice into a measuring cup. Add enough club soda or mineral water to make 180 ml (3/4 cup). Stir and pour into a glass.

Makes 1 - 180 ml (3/4 cup) serving.

Per 180 ml (3/4 cup) serving:

calories: 58
fat: 0.1 g
protein: 0.9 g
carbohydrates: 14.2 g
sodium: 12 mg
fibre: 0.5 g
cholesterol: 0

Hot Cider

500 ml (2 cups)	unsweetened apple juice
one-half	orange, thinly sliced
one-half	lemon, thinly sliced
2	cinnamon sticks
500 ml (2 cups)	diet ginger ale

Combine all ingredients except ginger ale in a saucepan. Cover and simmer for 10 minutes. Add ginger ale and heat 2 to 3 minutes more. Remove cinnamon sticks and fruit slices and serve hot.

Makes 4 - 250 ml (1 cup) servings.

Per 250 ml (1 cup) serving:

calories: 78
fat: 0.3 g
protein: 0.4 g
carbohydrates: 20.3 g
sodium: 12 mg
fibre: 1.2 g
cholesterol: 0

Mock Milkshake

250 ml (1 cup)	skim milk
3-4	ice cubes
125 ml (1/2 cup)	fresh or frozen fruit
5 ml (1 t.)	vanilla flavour extract

Place all ingredients in a blender and mix at high speed for approximately 1 to 2 minutes.

Frozen strawberries or raspberries are delicious in this recipe.

Makes 1 serving.

Per serving:

calories: 132
fat: 0.6 g
protein: 9.1 g
carbohydrates: 21.1 g
sodium: 138 mg
fibre: 1.2 g
cholesterol: 4 mg

Recipe Index

Chicken and Turkey

Pasta

Vegetarian Dishes

Breakfast Dishes

Desserts and Baked Goods

Snacks

Beverages

Appendix

How Much Should I Weigh?

The Body Mass Index

The challenge of The Healthy Weigh approach is to promote greater acceptance of a variety of body shapes and sizes. Healthy Weight means shifting your focus from weight and the number on the scale to encouraging healthy eating habits, regular physical activity and personal well-being.

A recent concept, The Body Mass Index (BMI) is used to determine your personal range of healthy weights. You choose your most comfortable weight within this range. This index will show you whether your present weight puts you in low, moderate or high risk zone for developing health problems.

Please note: The BMI is designed for adults aged 20 to 65 years—those whose body size and composition are fairly stable. **It does not apply to babies, children, adolescents, pregnant or nursing women, senior citizens, very muscular people and endurance athletes such as runners.**

How to use the Body Mass Index chart at right:

1. Find your height along the bottom (inches/feet) or at the top (centimetres).

2. Find your weight on the left (pounds) or on the right (kilograms).

3. Follow both lines until they intersect. This is your BMI.

BMI less than 20	BMI 20 - 25	BMI 25 - 27	BMI greater than 27
A BMI of less than 20 may contribute to health problems in some people. Some of the health risks you face by being underweight are: • heart irregularities • depression and other emotional distress • anemia • diarrhea	This a good range for most people. If you fall within this zone and eat sensibly, your weight shouldn't cause any health problems.	This is a caution zone; watch your weight. While still in an acceptable range, a BMI of 25 - 27 could lead to health problems for some people.	The higher your BMI goes above 27, the more you risk developing these health problems: • high blood pressure • diabetes • heart disease • certain cancers • arthritis • poor mental health caused by low self-esteem

Body Mass Index (BMI)

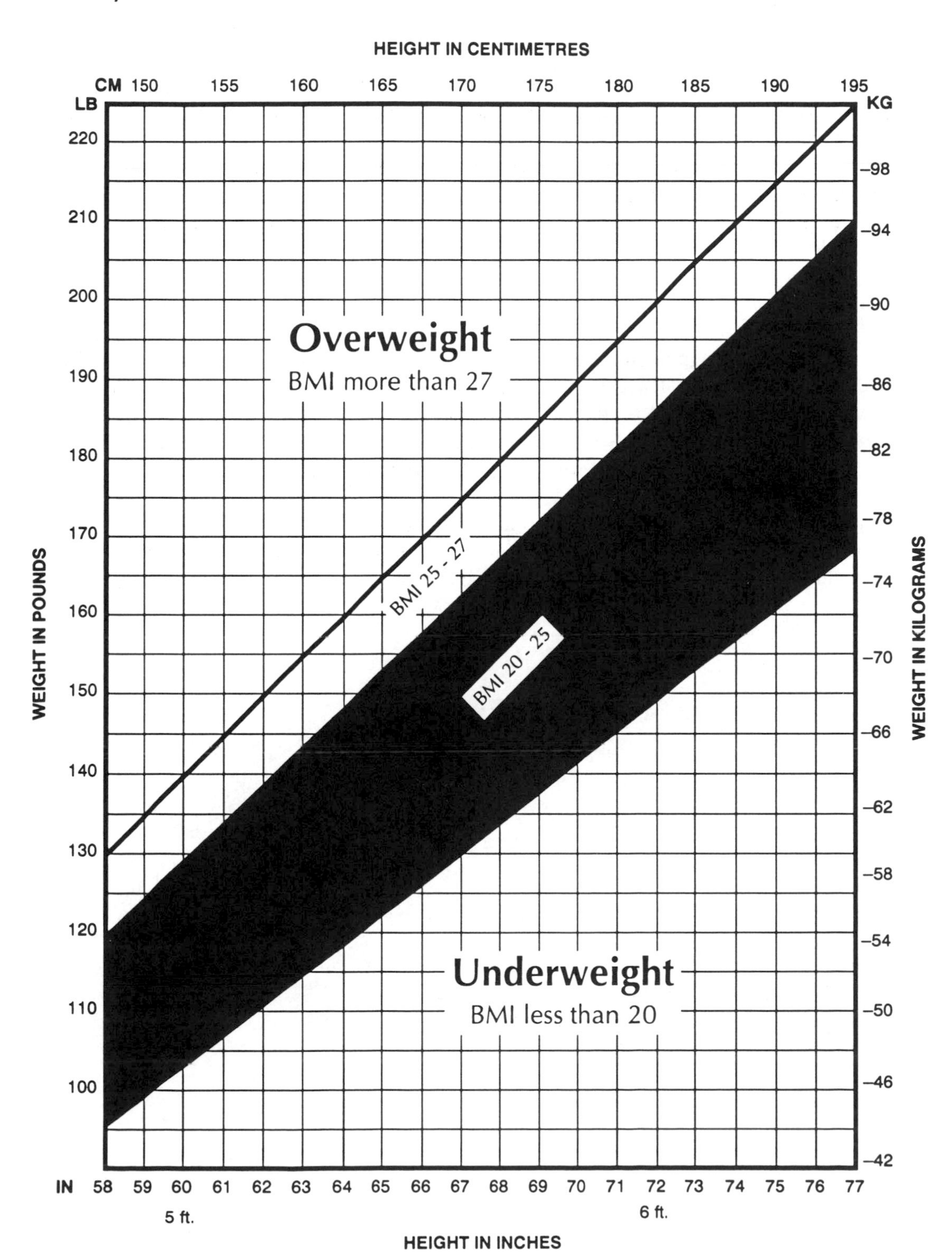

About the Authors

Claire Friefeld, B.Sc., P.Dt., co-author and mother, has over 40 years of experience in the field of dietetics and nutrition. She has worked as a consultant nutritionist for major food companies, including Australian Fruits, Cordon Bleu, Standard Brands and Hygrade Foods, where she tested and developed recipes, consulted for TV commercials and recruited dieticians across Canada. For the past 18 years, she has been in private practice in Canada as a Consulting Dietician-Nutritionist to a large number of clients with varied nutritional needs.

As Director of Operations and Corporate Dietician at Scott's Food Services, Franceen Friefeld, R.P.DT., P.H.Ec., co-author and daughter, specializes in menu planning, recipe and food product development for major companies, restaurants, airports and tourist sites. She also consults to clients on healthy restaurant choices, supermarket shopping and how to use food products in the preparation of healthy and tasteful meals.

Franceen frequently lectures and conducts workshops on the non-dieting approach to weight control, cardiovascular fitness, disease prevention and health promotion. She has set up numerous wellness programs in major business and industry establishments.